IN THE FRONT LINE

IN THE FRONT LINE

Martyn Pedrick

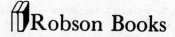Robson Books

The author and publishers would like to thank the following for their kind permission to reproduce photographs: ITN, Paul Carleton, Alan Downes, Mike Doyle, Chris Faulds, Keith Hatfield, Peter Read, Chris Squires, Nigel Thomson and Peter Wilkinson.

FIRST PUBLISHED IN GREAT BRITAIN IN 1983 BY ROBSON BOOKS LTD., BOLSOVER HOUSE, 5-6 CLIPSTONE STREET, LONDON W1P 7EB. COPYRIGHT © 1983 MARTYN PEDRICK

British Library Cataloguing in Publication Data

Pedrick, Martyn
In the front line
1. Independent Television News   2. Television broadcasting of news – Great Britain
I. Title
070.1'9'0924   PN4784.T4

ISBN 0-86051-224-X

Photosetting by Strewlight Ltd., London W1

Printed in Great Britain by Hazell Watson and Viney Limited Aylesbury Bucks

CONTENTS

FOREWORD

The relationship between a television reporter and the camera crew is a very special one, closer than any other, apart perhaps from marriage. When they go away, especially on a foreign assignment, the reporter, cameraman, and sound recordist spend virtually all their time together, for possibly weeks on end, working, eating and sometimes even sleeping together – although only in terms of sheer proximity, I hasten to add. I remember sharing a 'hooch' with Alan Downes and Mike Williams in Vietnam during the Tet offensive in 1968, although I may have been under the 'bed' which was a table, and they alongside it. There was a lot of noise that night, as the Americans and the North Vietnamese shot at one another with total disregard for the people who were trying to get some sleep. It was slightly less unnerving when you learned to distinguish between 'incoming' and 'outgoing' but only slightly. Luckily, there seemed to be much more 'outgoing' than the other way round.

As in all cheek-by-jowl relationships, you get on one another's nerves, and there are plenty of times when I am sure the crew wished the ground would open and swallow me up, and, dare I say it, the opposite thought occasionally crossed my mind, to be instantly rejected. It is a truism to say that to get the best results in television news reporting the whole team must work closely together. But few people outside the business can realize just how much each member of the team depends on the other, and how, at the end of the day, the success of the assignment will be decided by the degree of rapport between the members of the team. I remember once, early in my ITN career, trying to 'doorstep' Archbishop Makarios in Cyprus. There was a tremendous crush of fervent Greek-Cypriot admirers, police and hangers-on, and I found myself on the wrong side of his Beatitude, who was showing every sign of wishing to depart. As I tried to shoulder my way through the crowd, I realized that I would be too late. At that point, the sound recordist, the late Derek Scott-Lesley, an even more imposing figure than the Archbishop, simply interposed himself in front of Makarios, announcing smoothly that we wanted to obtain a brief interview, and keeping the great man pinned down until I was able to force my way through the crush. A small matter, you may say, but a vital one since without the Scott-Lesley's blocking move, we would have missed the richly opaque words the great man eventually vouchsafed and with them the story.

I am enormously glad Martyn Pedrick has undertaken such a worthwhile task with *In the Front Line* and honoured to contribute the Foreword because, by the very nature of things, too much of the glamour and the glory tends to go to the reporters and too little to the men who take the pictures and record the sound. Not only do I have vivid and happy memories of many successful and sometimes dangerous joint assignments which have enriched my life and career as a foreign correspondent, but I know what a debt of gratitude I owe to the crews who taught me the business in the early days and saw me through the quite alarming business of addressing the camera as if it were an old friend. It is now but it was not then! There are too many individuals and too many occasions to mention here, but I think one of the best moments for me, and for everyone at ITN, was the night in Johannesburg in November, 1978 when Michael Nicholson, Tom Phillips, and Mick Doyle stepped out of their executive jet after four hair-raising months, when they were missing in Angola.

I was very gratified that I should be the first to greet and film them, and particularly pleased that in the rush of getting to the airport, I had not forgotten to bring the champagne – Dom Perignon of course. After all, only the best for the brave.

Sandy Gall

INTRODUCTION

The idea was born during a Sunday lunchtime session in a pub in Epsom. I was in the company of a couple of itinerant news cameramen who were deeply engrossed in the newsman's favourite topic of conversation. They were 'talking shop', recalling a string of unlikely dramas and events which had overtaken either themselves or their colleagues:

> 'Who took that flight out of the Yemen with a bomb on board? ' . . . 'Remember the crew who had their bums searched for drugs in Saigon?' . . . 'Who paid a tenner for a toilet roll during the Jordan siege?' . . . 'Remember Cyprus, and the crew who were within seconds of being murdered by Turkish soldiers?' . . . 'and the blokes who walked 1,400 miles while lost in Angola for four months.'

It made compulsive listening and to discover that it was all true was a bonus! All assignments to overseas war zones are obviously a little bit hairy, and the danger level, I learned, is reflected on a scale from one to ten. This is known throughout the television news game as the BPF, or the Bum Pucker Factor. 'Eight and over means you're thinking about your insurance policies, and ten is when you actually shit yourself with fright,' one of the cameramen lucidly explained. 'Someone should write a book, I don't know why it's not been done before.'

Taking the hint, I received a promise of full co-operation from ITN and assiduously launched myself on a programme of research which has yielded enough material to fill three books. I have, therefore, taken 1967 – the year of the inception

of 'News at Ten' – as my point of reference, and tried to take
you behind the camera in the battle for television news. I have
also tried to illustrate the personalities and the characters of
news crews who have, for too long, been overlooked by a
public which is always so ready to make cult personalities out
of television reporters and newscasters.

Much of the crew's work is routine, and most of it is domestic. For the purposes of this book, I have concentrated on the
overseas assignments in the world's trouble-spots where
cameramen and sound recordists have had to live and survive
on their guts and their wits in a game where the stakes and the
risks are high, but the rewards are richly satisfying.

This is not an attempt to relate the history of the world's war
zones since 1967. Many, like Aden, Bangladesh, Indo-
Pakistan, and Iran have been omitted for a variety of reasons.
Others, notably the Falklands, have been already extensively
covered by newsmen who were there, and it was felt that space
would be better devoted to assignments which have been less
widely chronicled.

In compiling this dossier, I have received assistance from
many quarters and my debt of gratitude is great. Firstly to
David Nicholas, Editor and Chief Executive of ITN for his
permission to proceed, and to Bill Hodgson, ITN's Director of
Development, who first listened patiently to the idea and
helped greatly to get it off the ground. To Frank Duesbury and
Rosemary Kent in the Press Office, who have borne my
irregular arrivals with fortitude and understanding; for the
assistance of Ronnie Hubbard and his team on the assignment
desk; to the staff of the ITN News Information Library and the
Film Library; and to reporters Michael Nicholson, Peter
Sissons, Martyn Lewis, Tony Carthew, Desmond Hamill,
Keith Hatfield, and Jon Snow for access so willingly given to
their memory banks. Special thanks to Sue for her frenzied
bouts on the old Remington in The Barns, to my wife Elaine
for holding the pieces together and keeping me fed, and to
Annie Scott for keeping me watered.

But most of all I must record my deep appreciation to all the
cameramen and soundmen who so willingly gave me their
time, and allowed me to probe their personal, and sometimes
painful, recollections of operating in the front line.

THE MIDDLE EAST

&&&&&&&&&&&&&&&&&&&&&&&&&&&&&&&&&&&

Israel: the road to Sinai

They get beaten up, shot at and bombed. They have been imprisoned, interrogated, hijacked, and kidnapped. They suffer from food poisoning, dysentery, ulcers, and, occasionally, hangovers, and they call it the best job in the world. As members of television news teams, they can be sent anywhere from Kowloon to Kingston, from Nairobi to Nantwich, at a moment's notice and the rewards of their job vary from cocktails in Downing Street to a kick in the crutch in Belfast.

At any given time at least a dozen of them are dotted around the world filming wars, revolutions, and disasters, sometimes at great personal risk. That they return from these assignments relatively unscathed is a feat in itself; the fact that they succeed in filming and dispatching dramatic footage of front-line action under almost impossible circumstances is little short of miraculous.

To most ITN cameramen and sound recordists the adrenalin created by the challenge and the immediacy of the job is as necessary as the air they breathe, and they neither know, nor wish to sample, any other way of life. It is a job subjected to the pressures of deadlines, and the escalating demand for news with the advent of two additional independent channels.

For most senior crews, the big change came towards the late sixties, when 'the News' was injected with the magic of production, and became a programme, rather than a staccato bulletin. The summer of 1967 was memorable for the 'new look' which was introduced to Independent Television News.

Not only had the constituent companies of the Independent Television Authority passed a tremendous vote of confidence by extending the evening bulletin from twenty minutes to half an hour, but also the programme had been switched to the more readily identifiable peak-viewing spot of ten o'clock.

Alastair Burnet introduced the first edition of 'News at Ten' on Monday 3 July. The programme was launched on a wave of strong home stories: the threatened rail strike had been called off; Francis Chichester was warmly welcomed after his attempt to become the first man to sail singlehanded around the world; the Queen seemed to be enjoying her trip to Montreal for Expo '67 and, amazingly, an Englishman had even upset the form-book by reaching the semi-finals of the men's singles at Wimbledon. Throw in a 'natural' in the form of the giant oil tanker Torrey Canyon, lying crippled off the Cornish coast, and it can be seen that the inaugural edition of 'News at Ten' had the benefit of a fat domestic news day.

There was strong news from the Foreign Desk, too. Britain was involved in its own skirmish in Aden, and more misery was being generated by the troubles in Vietnam, Biafra, and Suez where fighting had again broken out following the Israeli victory in the Six-Day War the previous month.

Since the early sixties, Egypt had been involved in the Yemen where they were actively supporting rebel groups in their struggle to overthrow the Royalists, but now war with Israel was the new priority. Throughout the spring the two Nations had been engaged in a vicious snapping match and political observers predicted that it was only a matter of time before it erupted into a full-scale war. By early summer, most major news organizations had newsmen strategically placed around the Suez Canal and their prudence was justified. When war eventually broke out it came suddenly and normal routes into Egypt, Israel, and Sinai were closed, and for those not already occupying a seat, the doors were shut. By the time Tel Aviv airport re-opened a week later, the war was over.

Sensing the imminence of war, ITN had already dispatched reporter Alan Hart to Israel, accompanied by cameraman Alan Downes and sound recordist Hugh Thomson. Downes, now one of the world's top news cameramen, was still in his twenties in 1967 but had already covered action in Vietnam and was rapidly gaining a reputation as a specialist war cameraman. Thomson, on the other hand, was relatively inexperienced in front-line action, although he has subsequently earned a high reputation for his coverage in Biafra, Vietnam, and Israel. Hart was a by-word in war reporting during the sixties and both he and Downes had covered the escalation of the Nigerian civil war earlier in the year. Now they were paired together again with a brief to remain in Tel Aviv where they would play a waiting game and, at the same time, take the opportunity to film background material around the Israeli borders for 'Reporting '67', the series of weekly documentaries produced by ITN. Downes recalled the documentary assignments without relish; the crew were on edge waiting for the war to start and found it difficult to muster any enthusiasm for documentary pieces until the day they drove to Jerusalem. They had been filming only a few minutes when a small girl rushed out of her house, shouting excitedly in Hebrew. The ITN men turned questioningly to their interpreter who shrugged. 'The war has started,' he said sadly.

As they sped back to the Dan Hotel in Tel Aviv, they discussed their plans knowing that they would be the only ITN crew in Israel. True, they had the assistance of a stringer, but they would still be stretched to the absolute limit. The Americans, catering for the demands of a large Jewish population, had three or four crews assigned to Israel and even the BBC had two. Downes remembered the frustrations of being understaffed: 'We had been screaming for another crew,' he said, 'but once war had broken out, they found it impossible to get into Israel by the accepted route. We were, quite literally, on our own.'

They reached the Dan Hotel to discover that the management was evacuating all the upper floors as a safety precaution, and the ITN men asked if they could rent the penthouse suite. It was on the tenth floor and provided the best facility for filming action at sea, and a point of vantage from which to film air raids. Their request was granted, although it raised a few eyebrows and the observation that they must be suffering from a permanent mental disorder.

In retrospect, Downes feels that it was probably a naive

move, but at the time had little chance to debate the wisdom of
the decision. They had been there only a few minutes before
their attention was distracted by a warning siren and, grabbing
the camera and sound gear, they rushed up to the roof in
anticipation of an air raid. Instead, they heard a single Jordanian shell whistle over the hotel and explode in the centre of
the city. They felt that this marked the beginning of the end for
the Israeli capital, yet strangely the expected barrage never
came. 'It was weird,' recalled Downes. 'Just one solitary shell
was fired and nothing else. Perhaps it was a token gesture, or
perhaps the gun jammed – we never found out.'

Later that day – the first of the six – they discovered that they
were not alone in their view that Tel Aviv was about to be flat-
tened. Most traders and businessmen had been called up into
the Israeli Army and they learned that the women of Tel Aviv
were prepared to shoot themselves rather than succumb to
inevitable rape and humiliation by hordes of Egyptians,
Syrians, and Jordanians who, they feared, would soon be
overrunning their beloved city.

The crew had already covered the Israeli victory in Gaza – a
short sharp skirmish which resulted in Israel resuming its rule
over the Strip which, for the past ten years, had been adminis-
tered by Egypt. The defeated Palestinian unit, which had been
under the direction of an Egyptian commander, had changed
into civilian clothes and hidden with their arms in houses,
occasionally sniping at the thin Israeli force which had been
left to guard the town. It was not until later in the war, when
the Israelis had consolidated their overall position, that they
were able to strengthen their presence in Gaza and clear it of
Palestinian snipers and the lethal anti-personnel mines they
had planted. 'There were white tapes all over the streets warning people about the mines,' Thomson recalled. 'It was
bloody hairy — you had to look carefully before taking every
step and that's not much fun when you're trying to film
action.' Sadly, not everyone escaped these traps and an Israeli
cameraman working for CBS was killed by one. These dangers
were to be echoed in Cyprus seven years later when BBC sound
recordist Ted Stoddard died in the same tragic way.

The war had escalated since Gaza, and the ITN crew was
being stretched to the limit. Shortage of equipment and man-

power was not the only problem they faced; if they were to be competitive it was imperative that they received immediate and maximum co-operation from the Israeli authorities who were beginning to appear unnecessarily obstructive. Repeated requests for assistance were met with little or no response from the official government Press office whose main task is to facilitate the requirements of the international news force. Without either transport or an official military escort, Downes and the others were virtually helpless, and when the formidable Hart started to spit fire in the direction of the Press liaison officer, both Downes and Thomson were convinced that he was blowing their final chance of receiving any co-operation. Downes remembered the embarrassing incident clearly: 'We were getting nothing – no help at all. The air was very blue as Alan gave the officer a real bollocking, threatening that we would leave Israel if we could not get the required facilities.'

As they returned to the hotel, both Downes and Thomson were in sombre mood, knowing that on this occasion their colleague had overstepped the mark, and that his tactless outburst had almost certainly anchored them firmly at the foot of the assistance list. To Downes' astonishment, however, it had entirely the opposite effect. Shortly afterwards, they received a telephone call at the hotel from the Press office, asking if they would like to be the first television crew to reach the Suez Canal and offering to provide them with a military escort.

There were restrictions, however. The Press office insisted that the crew would have to find its own four-wheel-drive vehicle, fifty gallons of fuel and its own supplies of food and water. Only if these conditions were met would the military escort be provided. 'It's up to you – we've no spare vehicles,' was the apologetic signing-off line. Downes, Thomson, and Hart knew it was a chance that they could not pass up. After pooling their resources with a crew from CBS, the American network, they were able to purchase an old unsprung four-wheel-drive truck which had been captured from the Egyptians during the Suez crisis of 1956. The initial problem of obtaining fifty gallons of petrol was overcome by the payment of a gratuitous wad of Israeli currency, and water and food was arranged by the hotel. The prospect of being bounced towards the Canal in

an ailing old truck without springs held limited appeal.
Instead, they decided to travel as far as they could in their air-
conditioned Chevrolet Impala (hired from the Israeli tourist
board), and switch to the truck when necessity dictated the
adoption of four-wheel drive.

The Israelis agreed to the use of the car for the first part of
the journey but insisted that it should be suitably camouflaged,
and the three men spent much of the afternoon mixing mud,
water, and sand into a thick porridge which they poured over
the gleaming Chevrolet much to the chagrin of the driver from
the Israeli tourist board. The CBS crew, following the ITN lead,
enthusiastically applied a layer of clinging camouflage to their
own car. The unlikely convoy of two mud-encrusted
limousines, an antiquated and rusting Egyptian truck, and an
Israeli military escort, left Tel Aviv that night heading for the
Suez Canal and at last it seemed that Downes, Thomson and
Hart were about to get to grips with the latest in a long line of
Middle East conflicts. They drove through the night to lessen
the chance of attracting unwelcome attention, stopping for a
dawn breakfast. They ate well, but the bouncing, unsprung
truck had rendered the wine totally undrinkable, and they
were forced to commit it to the roadside dust before continuing their journey by the early morning light. Downes recalled
watching the peaceful sunrise and finding it difficult to accept
the fact that such natural splendour would merely be seen as
the signal to start round two of this brief, but bloody, war.

They had been driving for nearly two hours before they
spotted the outline of a convoy in the distance. As they
approached, they could see it was in obvious disarray, and
there were tell-tale wisps of smoke swirling silently above in
the morning breeze. They looked in horror at the almost
unrecognizable remains of a dozen Israeli armoured personnel carriers, now reduced to twisted steel hulks. Scattered
across the road were the bodies of slaughtered Israeli
troops. Some were unrecognizable, having taken the full blast
of an enemy shell. Others were headless or limbless bodies,
bloated by the heat of the morning sun, and through the
carnage ran the black scars of dried blood made by the tracks
of the tank which had crushed the final vestige of life out of
those who had somehow survived the initial attack.

They later established that the crew of an Egyptian tank, thought by the Israelis to have been abandoned, had crept back under cover of darkness to reclaim their chariot. They had started it and had no trouble in blasting their way through the lightly armoured Israeli unit (which had apparently stopped for the night) before heading back to the safety of the Egyptian lines.

The driver of the ITN Chevrolet screamed in horror at the sight and vomited. There was no way around the carnage and he refused to drive over the bodies of his fellow Israelis. Sobbing like a child, he let Downes move across into the driving seat and follow the military escort in front as it bounced unevenly over the bodies.

By now, there were regular signs of action and within five miles the road had become virtually impassable for a standard car. Leaving the rented Chevrolet at the roadside, the ITN men quietly and methodically checked their equipment and rations into the old truck, and climbed aboard. Thomson remembered that this controlled exercise was a sharp contrast with the CBS team who were operating with an American reporter and a German camera crew: 'The reporter was getting wildly excited, not wanting to waste a second,' he said. 'He was sceaming at his crew to hurry, hurry, hurry, and the poor blokes were in a flat spin. It's not the way to get the best out of a camera crew.'

Thomson's point was clearly proved barely half an hour later, as the old truck carrying both the ITN and CBS news teams continued their journey through Sinai towards the Suez Canal. They were still about fifteen minutes' drive from the Canal when a dozen armed Egyptians appeared from a slit trench and ran towards the truck. Thomson immediately assumed that they had been ambushed and hoped that a bullet through the guts would not hurt too much. He had instinctively closed his eyes as the soldiers appeared and opened them half a second later to find that they were standing around the truck with their hands in the air. It took a few seconds for it to sink in that a patrol of a dozen Egyptians with an officer, were surrendering to an ITN news team. With a whoop of delight, Downes and Thomson moved into action with their camera and sound gear, only to be distracted by a

howl of anguish from the German cameraman, followed by a
stream of Teutonic expletives. The CBS crew, almost certainly
as a result of being hustled by the American reporter, had left
their supply of 16mm colour stock in their car when they
transferred to the truck. British television was still two years
away from colour news programmes and, while the CBS men
gratefully accepted Downes' offer of a reel of 16mm monochrome, they later had an embarrassing time explaining to
their network chiefs why their first dramatic footage of the
Suez Canal was in black and white. Thomson, while feeling
sorry for his cameraman colleague, smiled in silent satisfaction, hoping that at least one hustling, loud-mouthed,
American reporter had learned a lesson.

The surrender of the Egyptians had provided a nice feature
piece, but the ITN men were impatient to push further south
towards the Canal and resented the precious time lost in
'holding' the prisoners until they could be handed over to
Israeli troops. Downes remembered that, even in war, there
was a sharp distinction between the Egyptian troops and their
officer, who disassociated himself from his men, and chose to
sit alone, twenty-five yards away while he contemplated the
shame of imminent defeat. The war was little more than three
days old, but Egypt was already foundering under successive
Israeli air strikes. They had barely a usable airstrip left, and the
endless lines of burnt-out vehicles which the crew later saw
still smouldering in Sinai had been sitting ducks for the penet-
rating Israeli rocket attacks.

It was two days later – the fifth day of the war – when Downes, Thomson, and Hart, pushing south towards Sinai, discovered that the bridge linking the Egyptian canal town of
Ismailia with Sinai had been blown, and the Israelis were concealed behind the sand-dunes with a powerful self-propelled
gun unit. In addition to possessing superior strength in the air,
Israel now effectively controlled the Suez Canal, and it was
destined to remain closed for the next eight years.

The commander of the gun unit seemed as affable as any
officer on the brink of a famous victory, and eagerly co-
operated with the crew's suggestion that they should be
allowed to film their reporter on the edge of the Suez Canal
with the Israeli troops, as they celebrated their victory. 'It

should be quite safe,' they were assured by the officer, 'There's meant to be a cease-fire.'

For the first two days of the war, the ITN men felt that they had been at a definite disadvantage operating with only one crew. Now, however, their spirits were high; they had a strong story in the can and Alan Hart's 'into camera' piece would prove to be one of the greatest exclusives in the history of television war coverage.

For Downes and Co. the priority was now to get the 'hot' film back to Tel Aviv for immediate transportation to London by whatever means possible. Their rush back to Tel Aviv was greatly assisted by the appearance of their driver in the Chevrolet who had managed to overcome the severe road damage and was heading towards the Canal zone. Knowing that the powerful car would save them hours in their charge back to the Israeli capital, they murmured heartfelt thanks and collapsed into the back of the limousine where they slept for hours.

The film was dispatched to London within an hour of reaching Tel Aviv and the joint ITN/CBS pictures chalked up a world exclusive beating other networks to the news by more than a full day. It was screened at peak viewing time on the Sunday night, and Independent Television News was even granted a ten-minute extension to accommodate the full dramatic bulletin.

Yemen: the flying bomb

Chris Faulds spent much of the summer of 1967 commuting across the Mediterranean to trouble spots in the Middle East. He had covered the aftermath of the Six-Day War and barely had time to return to London to see the birth of 'News at Ten' before he was off again to cover the latest developments in the Yemen civil war, which had been simmering for five years.

The Yemen throne had fallen and the Royalists were falling back before the rebels who, in their efforts to establish a republic, were being actively supported by Egypt. The Egyptians, however, had not found it easy to wage war in the barren, open land of the Yemen and, earlier in the year, had their attentions diverted by the brief, but furious, skirmish with Israel. Consequently, the Yemen's internal squabble lasted longer than anyone thought possible, although the Royalists were reduced to living in caves and fighting very much a guerilla rearguard action. It was beginning to become one of those interminable irritations in the Middle East and the media tended to keep a watching brief with one half closed eye, waiting for 'something to happen'.

It was mid-August when rumours filtered through that Egypt had escalated the war by the unprincipled use of poison gas on Yemen villages. This was breaking the rules, and raised world wide disapproval; foreign editors howled for proof and assignments managers picked up their telephones.

At TV House in Kingsway, London, the home of ITN before they moved to Wells Street, a crew was briefed for a six-week stint in the Yemen. They were to fly to Saudi Arabia where they would be met by Yemeni officials and guides who would take them across the border where they would live among the Royalist sympathizers. Faulds' soundman was Barry Martin and the reporter was Richard Lindley (now with the BBC).

The crew flew from Heathrow by scheduled BOAC flight to Jidda on the edge of the Red Sea, transferred to one of the battered old DC-3s which were legion in that part of the world during the sixties, and flew to Najran, near the Yemeni border. Here they were met by trucks which bounced them through rocky terrain and, eventually, across the border to Omara.

For weeks, they lived among the Royalists like fugitives, making two major excursions in their search for proof that Egypt had adopted a policy of using gas. The first was an expedition to an old fortress at Sad'aa, one of the few remaining Royalist strongholds. By Yemeni standards, this was local – a mere three days' walk – but there was little action and, although the crew filmed more documentary footage, they were unable to obtain proof of the rumoured gas attacks.

This was followed by an eight-day trek to San'aa, capital of the Yemen which was now in Egyptian hands. There are few negotiable roads to the north of the Yemen, and the accepted mode of travel is by foot, with camels to carry the luggage. Faulds was armed with a 16mm Auricon Cinevoice, a notoriously heavy piece of equipment which was then standard among TV newsmen. This, together with Martin's sound equipment and a large supply of canned food, was loaded onto one of the two camels, and the crew made steady progress across the hot, hard sands, covering up to fifteen miles a day.

They obtained valuable footage of Egyptian troop movements and attacks on villages, but were again unable to confirm the use of outlawed poison gas. Faulds, while disappointed, viewed it philosophically: 'We had no doubt that they were using it, but they selected their targets carefully,' he said. 'By the time we heard about it, the attacks were over, and it could have taken us up to three days to reach the destruction.' By the time this sojourn in the Yemen was over, however, they had filmed and recorded an in-depth report of the Royalists' plight and the escalation of the Egyptian action, to take back to London.

The Royalist officials took them to the airstrip at Najran where they checked in their baggage and equipment, bought their tickets to Jidda and climbed the rickety old steel ladder into the cabin of the DC-3. As he relaxed in his seat, Faulds reflected on the frustrations of the trip: they had produced a very thorough job in difficult circumstances but although Faulds had been in the business long enough to know that fate does not smile on you all the time, he felt that fortune could have blessed them with perhaps a little more drama.

He looked out of the window and saw the baggage being wheeled across the tarmac towards the aircraft where it would be loaded at the rear of the cabin, behind the passenger seats. At that moment he had no way of knowing that he was barely twenty minutes away from a terrifying drama and that he, Lindley and Martin would be the central characters. The American pilot made a brief appearance to mutter a standard welcome and perform the mandatory headcount. Faulds remembers that there were eighteen passengers, the pilot, and a Saudi Arabian who passed as a steward. The luggage was safely aboard, the cabin door was closed and the pilot drawled his intention to kick the old Dakota into life and head for

Jidda. The aircraft taxied slowly down the runway, and turned into the light breeze. Then, with its engines revving and vibrating every spar and rivet, it moved forward down the tarmac strip, steadily gathering momentum until it lifted into the clear blue skies above the vast expanse of arid wasteland which forms the major part of Saudi Arabia.

For ten minutes, the aircraft climbed steadily before levelling out at 10,000 feet, and Faulds wondered whether this reliable old aerial ferry had been equipped with the facility to serve refreshments. A coffee, he told himself, would go down quite well. But when the Saudi steward appeared at his side two minutes later, it was not to ask what he wanted to drink, and it was without the friendly 'fly me' smile that has become an accepted part of twentieth-century air travel. Instead, he looked worried and asked Faulds what he had in his luggage, justifying the enquiry with the punch line, 'it's making a noise'.

Understandably bewildered, Faulds allowed himself to be led to the back of the aircraft, where the steward pointed to the box which contained spares for the camera and sound equipment. It was indeed making a noise and Faulds quickly established that it was also hot. His brain raced through the contents of the box as he fought to find a logical solution, then he nodded confidently to himself. The box contained spare batteries for the camera and, somehow, one of them must have short-circuited and he unlocked the lid of the box to prove his theory. As he lifted the lid and the wisps of smoke cleared, he knew that his diagnosis had been miles wide of the mark. Lying on top of the spare batteries and film magazines, were six sticks of dynamite with slow-burning fuses. Three of them had burnt down to the detonator and should have already exploded, blasting the Dakota, and everyone on board, to a premature grave. They had been faulty and had emitted a sharp, distinctive crack instead of exploding. The fuses on the other three were still smouldering and Faulds set little store on the hope that they too might be duff. That, he felt, would be pushing his luck a little too far.

If the steward had appeared worried at the thought of faulty batteries, the sight of six sticks of smouldering dynamite transmogrified his swarthy Arabian complexion to a whiter shade of pale. Faulds told Lindley and Martin, but nobody else, before insisting on 'somewhat urgent' discussions with the pilot. He explained the situation in detail, adding that the logical solution would be to open the cabin door at the rear, and simply jettison the box with all its contents somewhere over southern Saudi Arabia, where it could do no harm at all.

There seems to be something of the maverick instinct deep within every freelance American pilot which makes him want to do things the hard way. Perhaps it is the opportunity to play a John Wayne hero just once in his life, or maybe it is just the need to break away from the routine ferry jobs to get the adrenalin pumping. Whatever the motivation, the captain of the daily DC-3 run from Najran to Jidda was no exception. 'No,' he said, adamantly. 'Leave it where it is and don't touch it.' Faulds could hardly believe his ears. He tried again, explaining that the dynamite was still smouldering and, although three of the sticks had failed to explode, he felt that they were already somewhat overdrawn on their luck. 'Why not just throw it out instead of risking everybody's life longer than necessary?' he argued.

Milking every ounce of drama out of his role, 'John Wayne' was unflinching. 'It stays where it is,' he drawled, 'until we find somewhere to land.' To Faulds, it seemed sheer lunacy, and he felt it was a major concession when the pilot radioed to Jidda that he was at the controls of a 'flying bomb', and received clearance for an emergency landing at the nearest available airstrip.

To the ITN crew, the next hour seemed interminable. Knowing that the aircraft could explode at any moment, they sat in silence with their fingers crossed, while the other passengers chatted amongst themselves, oblivious of the danger until shortly before the landing.

Eventually, a slight bump told them that they were again on terra firma and the aircraft seemed to screech to a standstill in a remarkably short distance. Faulds and Co. were then treated to the unexpected sight of 'John Wayne' appearing from the flight deck and scurrying down the gangway to ensure that he was first off the aircraft. Whether he was tired of the role, or if pilots tend to become more rational at ground level, Faulds

neither knew nor cared. At least they were down and, for the
first time in an hour, the odds of surviving seemed to be
lengthening.

As the passengers were ushered off the plane, gathering
somewhat foolishly beneath a wing of the Dakota, Faulds
looked questioningly at the pilot who, an hour ago, had
seemed to be in sole authority. Now, the mask dropped.
'Don't ask me, Mac' he shrugged. 'It's your bomb – you get it
off.' Realizing that the responsibility, like the bomb, had been
thrust upon them, the three newsmen carefully edged the hot
box towards the doorway and gently lowered it. It was still
smouldering and another sharp 'crack!' reminded them that it
was still a major threat to their lives as they carried it slowly,
with the solemnity of a coffin, to a remote corner of the airfield. Breathing a sigh of relief and, in rather colourful terms,
expressing gratitude that the experience was over, they
returned to their seats on the aircraft and conducted an
inquest as they resumed their flight to Jidda.

The explosives had obviously been placed in their spare
boxes by a loader at Najran. They determined that he was
probably a Yemeni sympathizer acting under the orders of
rebel leaders who wanted to stop the ITN stories at all costs. It
had been so easy – he had simply taped together six sticks of
dynamite, dropped them in the equipment box, and lit a slow-
burning fuse with his cigarette, knowing that in twenty
minutes the aircraft, the passengers and the all-important
film, would be gone for ever.

To Faulds, the motive if not the deed was understandable
but he felt it was a classic overkill situation. 'Why they didn't
jump us at the airport and simply take the film is baffling,' he
said. 'They seemed to go to ridiculous extremes to stop it
reaching London.' Of the other two imponderables, the
failure of the dynamite to explode was dismissed purely as a
mixture of fate, justice, and 'a bloody great slice of luck', but
Faulds has never been able to come to terms with 'John
Wayne's' decision to subject all the passengers to the danger of
the flying bomb for an hour, rather than jettison the
explosives immediately. 'I've thought about it for over fifteen
years, and I'm still convinced it was the most lunatic and irres-
ponsible decision,' he said.

Although they admit that they could well have done without it, the incident provided the crew with the drama that they had lacked in the Yemen, and they were not slow to grab the chance of committing the experience to film with a graphic 'into camera' piece at Jidda Airport, providing the Foreign Desk with an unexpected bonus.

The tailpiece to the drama was played out the following morning in the airport lounge, where Faulds and Co. were queuing for a BOAC flight to London. As the queue moved slowly toward the airline desk, Faulds realized that the smiling family of tourists immediately in front of them was the American pilot with his wife and two daughters. His casual greeting and nod of recognition was met with a look of undisguised horror and within seconds 'John Wayne' had ushered his family and baggage away to find an alternative flight.

Jordan: a wet day in Ealing

For Paul Carleton, Thursday 10 September 1970 started in a fairly routine way with a watching brief on a current news story at Ealing. By the time he returned home he had been diverted to Cyprus and Beirut before becoming enmeshed in a civil war in Jordan, where he was beseiged in his hotel for seven days on starvation rations, narrowly escaping death at the hands of the Palestinian Arab guerillas.

He remembers the name Leila Khaled, not so much for her notoriety, but rather for the assignment which provided a sequel to her infamous exploits and triggered off a crazy chain of events which almost claimed his life. Khaled, who had adopted Lebanese nationality, first came to the attention of the world's Press in August 1969 when she was involved in the hijacking of a TWA Boeing 707, which was 'persuaded' to land at Damascus, and was eventually blown up at the third attempt.

Her second target, a little over a year later, was a London-bound aircraft operated by El Al, the Israeli airline, but this

time she overestimated her ability to terrify. Her Palestinian
colleague was shot and, after a scuffle, she was overpowered.
She was taken to Hillingdon hospital to be treated for the cuts
and bruises and the episode ended somewhat ignominiously
in a cell in Ealing police station.

Khaled's detention in a London suburb did not please her
comrades in the Palestinian terrorist trade, and they quickly
retaliated by hijacking three more international airliners and
diverting them to Dawson's Field, a remote landing strip in
the desert fifty miles north of Amman. They had hijacked a
BOAC VC 10, a TWA Boeing, and a Swissair DC-8 and, in return for
the safety of the passengers, were demanding not only the
return of Khaled but also other terrorists held in West
Germany, Switzerland and Israel. The deadline was set for
12 September and, although the passengers were eventually
freed, the terrorists blew up the three aircraft in a conflagra-
tion which was estimated at £12 million, and could be seen
fifty miles away.

Britain was under pressure to release Khaled (although they
later used the word 'deported') and Carleton, together with his
soundman and reporter Keith Hatfield, was dispatched to
Ealing with a 'wait-and-see-what-happens-next' brief. Traditionally, doorstepping in Downing Street rates as the worst
assignment in the book for newsmen, but in Carleton's view,
standing outside Ealing nick in the rain, hoping for a glimpse
of a failed hijacker, runs it a fairly close second.

By early afternoon, they felt that the chances of an
appearance by Khaled and her escort were remote. Besides,
they had been waiting for over two hours, and were uncomfortably wet. Carleton decided to contact the assignments desk
and went back to the two-way radio which is standard equipment on all ITN crew cars. He found that the red light was
showing, indicating that the office had beaten him to the draw
and that he should return their call urgently. Within seconds,
he was being asked to forget rain-lashed Ealing and stand by at
Heathrow airport ready to catch a flight to Cyprus where, it
was rumoured, Khaled had been taken that day, presumably
to be handed back to the Palestinian terrorists.

They stayed at Heathrow overnight, catching the first available flight the following morning, united in the view that

although it was unlikely that they would find Khaled in Cyprus, a few days in the Mediterranean sun was rather more attractive than a soaking in Ealing High Street. They arrived to find Nicosia particularly hot and humid. A cooling dip in the pool at the Ledra Palace Hotel was high on their priority list but any hopes of half an hour's relaxation after their flight were dispelled by an urgent telex message from ITN in London, telling them to drop the Khaled story. Instead, they were to charter a private aircraft if necessary and proceed with all haste to Jordan. There it seemed that civil war was about to break out, despite the peace treaty signed between the Jordan government and the Palestinian Arabs in June, and the aggressive activities at Dawson's Field had done little to calm the position.

The Dawson's Field drama had escalated considerably, culminating in the last-minute release of the passengers and the blowing-up of the three airliners. ITN had dispatched reporters Gerald Seymour and Michael Nicholson to cover the drama with a UPITN crew and, while waiting for their flight from Nicosia, Carleton and Co. met producer David Phillips who was flying back to London with the world exclusive film of the Dawson's Field incident in his briefcase. Although Amman airport had been closed, he had managed to persuade the authorities to allow him to charter a Caravelle airliner to Cyprus and was waiting to catch a flight to London to ensure that the story would be screened in Britain that night.

The worsening situation had stopped all air traffic between Cyprus and Jordan, but the crew was eventually able to fly into Beirut from Nicosia, catching what proved to be the last scheduled flight before all air traffic to the Lebanon and Jordan was suspended. The ITN men were then able to catch a flight from Beirut to Amman and it seemed that their arrival in the capital had been planned to coincide precisely with the outbreak of war; they could barely hear each other's warning shouts as the Palestinian rebels clashed with King Hussein's government troops, located in and around the Intercontinental Hotel.

As the Royalist activity became more intense, strengthened by the arrival of more tanks and mortars, it became obvious that the centre of activity would be the immediate area around the Intercontinental where Carleton, Hatfield, and the rest of the world's news army was housed.

Carleton was on the sixth floor which, under normal circumstances, would have provided him with a pleasant view of the city. The current situation, however, was far from normal and he was discouraged from making full use of his vantage point by a Royalist major who politely and rather apologetically told the news contingent that anyone seen on the balconies of the hotel would be shot on sight. The law of averages decrees that there is normally a minority of one who, motivated by alcohol, bravado, or a death wish, insists on putting a threat to the test. This time it was a Swedish television newsman who ignored the warning and waved at a tank crew in the hope of getting a personal response for his camera. Instead he received a personal and painful reminder of the major's warning as a fusillade of machine gun bullets tore through his legs. Later, a Soviet correspondent, falsely believing himself to be out of sight and impregnable on the top floor balcony was killed with a single shot through the head.

The ITN crew, understandably reluctant to offer their lives so cheaply, was able to film surreptitiously through a chink in the curtain, shooting footage of both Hussein's Royalist troops and the Palestinians battling around the beseiged hotel. They were soon to discover that this practice had only short-term prospects; the rebels had succeeded in occupying a large block of flats opposite, and the slightest movement would be met with a broadside from their Soviet-supplied automatic rifles. More than once, Carleton and Co. had to dive for their lives as bullets crashed through the windows of the hotel and, on one occasion, shattered the glass doors and windows of Carleton's room.

By the second day, the hotel was under total seige without either water or electricity, and what little food was available was eked out among the fifty or so newsmen trapped in the hotel with the Indian Ambassador and his wife, and a handful of Jordanian businessmen who had been caught by the sudden outbreak of war. Carleton remembered the starvation rations without enthusiasm:

'We had half a cup of foul tea and some rice at about 5 am, and then nothing more until late afternoon. Then it was only half a cream cake and another cup of disgusting liquid which passed for tea.'

As the siege continued supplies and tempers became shorter. The crew was tired, hungry, and dirty, and their frustrations at not being able to get film out of the hotel only compounded their misery. Carleton had been an ITN cameraman for barely two years and this was the first time that he had been thrust into the heart of a war, but he remembers being motivated by a mixture of danger, and the immediacy of the challenge. 'It was really bloody dangerous,' he said later. 'The Palestinians were firing indiscriminately through the hotel windows and, in retrospect, I don't know how we escaped injury.'

The more experienced correspondents, sensing that water shortages were likely, had taken the opportunity to fill their baths while supplies were still available. Most of them shared the water among their immediate colleagues but Carleton vividly recalls his horror at the disgusting behaviour of the French who, having no water of their own, defecated in the dwindling supplies of their rivals. The Army eventually arrived at the hotel with supplies of clean drinking water but, again, the French abused the facility by washing their hands in it and were almost lynched by inflamed British and American newsmen. This taught Carleton an unforgettable lesson and now he never travels to a war zone without a water purifier and a supply of glucose tablets and emergency food rations.

By the third day, there was little food left, water had been rationed to one cup per person and sanitary facilities were virtually non-existent. Inevitably these shortages fertilized the black market and Carleton found it a painful experience parting with the equivalent of ten pounds for two small candles and a toilet roll. Normally the standards of cleanliness in Jordan are not the most salubrious in the world and, in the almost intolerable conditions dictated by civil war, it became a breeding ground for germs and disease, and the attendant internal ailments. Hatfield was among the worst sufferers, contracting an acutely uncomfortable dose of dysentery which saw him lying helpless on the floor of the hotel corridor for long periods, while the Indian Ambassador's wife assumed the role of a latter-day Florence Nightingale to administer succour.

While Carleton had every sympathy with Hatfield who was now in a very bad way, he suddenly had to contend with an even more worrying problem. His sound recordist who, by necessity, had been diverted from a watching brief in the streets of Ealing to cover a civil war in Jordan, was beginning to show signs of strain. Carleton's fears were confirmed when in a sudden outburst his young colleague announced his plans for sprinting from the hotel, grabbing the nearest available jeep and driving to freedom across the desert toward Aqaba on the Red Sea. 'We were all under great pressure, but he was taking it very badly,' said Carleton. 'You can't blame him. Most hardened newsmen are able to defend themselves mentally but even some of the more experienced correspondents were starting to fray around the edges.'

After five days, war was still raging and although the firing began to show signs of subsiding in the immediate vicinity, it would have been certain suicide to venture outside the hotel. Food was desperately short but there was a brief respite when newsmen discovered a small confectionary kiosk in the hotel and, smashing it open, looted the entire supply of sweets and chocolate which they distributed liberally among their colleagues. Carleton, one of the last to hear about the discovery of the Aladdin's Cave, was ferreting disconsolately among the debris when he found what was probably the last remaining Mars Bar in Jordan. 'It was unbelievable,' he said. 'It was absolute manna to a starving man.' Glancing around furtively to ensure that nobody had seen him chance upon his prize, he thrust it into his pocket and scurried to his room, intent on breaking the unwritten law that all goodies should be shared. In an uncharacteristic moment of greed, he sat on his bed and, frenziedly tearing away the paper wrapping, stuffed the bar into his mouth. He was still chewing it, with tell-tale channels of melted chocolate dribbling down his chin, when the door opened and in walked Michael Nicholson who had moved into Amman following the conclusion of the Dawson's Field incident. The memory of being caught red-handed, rather like a naughty schoolboy, haunts him to this day. 'I was consumed by pangs of guilt at not playing the white man,' he said. 'I suddenly felt very ashamed by the fact that I had betrayed my own principles. Michael just looked at me, delivered his message and left without saying a thing. I felt that I should have been taken away to be shot.' This display of selfishness was still preying heavily on his mind the following day when the black marketeers among the hotel's skeleton staff magically produced a few bottles of beer which they distributed on a 'first come, first served' basis at grossly inflated prices. This time, Carleton was among the front runners and was about to lift the bottle to his lips when a dishevelled Royalist soldier lurched into the hotel lobby. His dejected, battle-weary features seemed to epitomize the mood as Hussein's troops battled desperately against the rebels who were now strengthened by the support of Syrian tanks. The intervention of the Syrians had triggered off fears of broader outside involvement with both the United States and the Israelis announcing that they were prepared to intervene to prevent a Royalist defeat.

Carleton looked at the soldier and remembers thinking that the King's troops must be suffering a hard time. He was covered in grime and sand, his shirt was torn to shreds, and he looked in urgent need of refreshment. Perhaps seeking atonement for his sins of the previous day, Carleton extended the bottle in a gesture of friendship. The soldier's face seemed to twitch visibly and his eyes glazed at the sight of the beer. Swiftly reversing the rifle, he drove the butt savagely into Carleton's fist, smashing the bottle into a dozen pieces. Then, cocking his rifle, he started screaming Arabic abuse and seemed rather keen to blow the cameraman's head off. Carleton beat a strategic retreat and, when he was told five minutes later that the Royalist soldier was still prowling the corridors looking for him, he headed for the safety of his room. Again feeling like a schoolboy seeking refuge from retribution, he locked the door and hid under his bed, reflecting on the second lesson he had learned from the assignment: Bedouins don't drink.

By the sixth day of the siege, the Red Cross had started to evacuate the seriously wounded, and any room left on the aircraft was available for civilians. The pressmen drew straws and both Carleton and Nicholson won seats to Beirut while, ironically, both Hatfield and the sound recordist, who had suffered most, were unlucky.

The airport was in total disarray, and the arrival of the Red Cross convoy and assorted evacuees merely added to the confusion. Eventually, the injured were aboard and a party of women and children were making their way across the tarmac towards the aircraft when the Palestinian rebels commenced a mortar attack with shells exploding dangerously close to the plane. The rebels had already shown their complete disregard for the widely accepted assurance of 'safe passage' for the Red Cross by attacking the convoy en route to the airport; now it seemed that they were prepared to sacrifice women and children in their indiscriminate shelling of the airport during evacuation. Clearly, any attempt to fly out of Amman in such circumstances would have been madness, and the party had no alternative but to rally back at the hotel for a re-think, and hope that the Royalists would soon flush out the rebel threat and restore both sanity and safety to the airport.

By now, Carleton and Nicholson had decided that their seats on the aircraft would be better used by Hatfield and the sound recordist, who had become quite depressed at the prospect of being left in Amman, albeit only for a few days, without his cameraman. There was also a professional motive behind Carleton's and Nicholson's decision to stay in Amman; successful strikes by Hussein's Air Force against the Syrian tanks had seen a remarkable shift of fortune in favour of the Royalists, and it now seemed likely that the King would agree to an interview for British television.

At the airport, they had spotted a Land Rover belonging to the King's personal guard, and persuaded the driver to give them a lift back to the Intercontinental Hotel. They felt that, by acquiring the services of a sympathetic servant of Hussein, they would be in a strong position to put one over the BBC by making a pitch for an exclusive interview with the King. As they sat in the Land Rover, waiting for the driver to whisk them back to their hotel, they congratulated themselves on their vision and good fortune. The sudden appearance of an old friend in the form of Alan Hart suggested, however, that their mutual back-slapping may have been a little premature. Hart, a by-word in television reporting during the sixties had recently left ITN to join the BBC and was covering the Jordan war with cameraman Bernard Hesketh. As soon as they spotted Carleton and Nicholson, Hart insisted that they too should benefit from the Royal taxi service. Carleton knew from experience that when Hart insisted on something he inevitably got his way.

The drive back to the hotel was a hedging game, with both the ITN and BBC men tossing casual but loaded questions at each other, hoping to establish what they already had in the can and glean some hint about their future plans. It was apparent that Hart and Hesketh were also chasing the chance of an interview with Hussein, but the ITN men had already set wheels in motion and were quietly confident of pulling off what would prove to be the hottest 'exclusive' of the war.

They continued to liaise with the palace through official, and less official, channels and when news filtered back, two days later, that His Majesty King Hussein was prepared to grant one interview to British television, they felt justifiably pleased that their delicate ground work appeared to have paid off. When, at the appointed hour, the Royal Land Rover arrived to transport them to the palace, they knew that they were within minutes of crowning some excellent and dramatic war coverage with the ultimate exclusive interview. They grabbed their gear and hurried down to the hotel foyer just in time to see Hart and the BBC crew hurl their equipment into the Land Rover and disappear in the traditional cloud of dust, waving sympathetically. It was the classic, eleventh hour 'heist'.

After screaming a stream of colourful expletives at their rivals, the ITN men stared blankly at each other, realizing that, in confidence tricksters' parlance, they had been well and truly 'taken', and the BBC won the prized interview with Hussein. 'It was sheer professionalism,' Carleton reflected later. 'We were playing for very high stakes and, given the chance, we'd have probably done exactly the same to them.'

While this sort of 'one-upmanship' is accepted among rival newsmen in their bid to outflank each other, deliberate sabotage operations are not tolerated. Carleton recalls having his exposed film removed from its magazine by a reporter from a rival news service while covering a bomb scare on the

QE-2. 'A cameraman would never have done it,' he said. 'It's an unforgivable breach of our professional code to tamper with someone else's equipment. I've never forgiven the bastard.'

They may have missed the royal interview for which they had so strenuously striven, but the material sent back to London with the sound recordist was widely praised. Carleton was in Jordan for a total of ten days, although at times it seemed considerably longer. When he eventually returned to London, he was wearing the same clothes which had started their service outside Ealing police station. Colleagues who met him at Heathrow presented him with a bottle of champagne as a welcome home present, and then quickly whisked him off to ITN House in Wells Street to appear on 'News at Ten'.

Leila Khaled subsequently wrote two books on her hijacking activities, and the sound recordist found himself a safer job in television.

BIAFRA

୧୨୧୨୧୨୧୨୧୨୧୨୧୨୧୨୧୨୧୨୧୨୧୨୧୨୧୨୧୨୧୨

Page and a pram

Cyril Page joined ITN in August 1955, just a few weeks before
commercial television was introduced to offer alternative
viewing to what was then BBC's monopoly. He was lured to the
Company in the capacity of chief cameraman, after several
years with the Beeb's epoch-making 'Television Newsreel',
(prior to this, they took the standard Movietone News, which
was updated halfway through the week). In more than thirty
years as the top news cameraman, he has travelled half a
million miles, covering everything from weddings to wars,
from coronations to crusades, and from debutantes to disasters (although, he claimed, these two are virtually the
same).

To look at him, tall, grey-haired, and distinguished, few
would believe that he has been bombed, beaten up, and
imprisoned, and has looked death in the face a dozen times.
He has done everything expected of a man who is Britain's
most experienced television news cameraman. He has seen
and filmed every human emotion; his camera never wavered
as he watched a man being torn apart in thirty seconds during
the Congo war yet, like other tough newsmen, he shed many
tears while covering the disaster which befell the small mining
village of Aberfan in South Wales in 1966.

But there is one haunting memory that is more vivid than
the others – a memory of the day he watched a friend die next
to him, and helped to save the life of a badly shot colleague,
while believing that he himself was only seconds away from the

newsman's Valhalla. It is the memory of Biafra in the autumn of 1968.

Throughout the year, the Nigerian civil war had escalated as Federal and Biafran troops became locked in see-saw battles for strategic strongholds. In the West, emotions were running high as the media shelled out its daily dose of film and photographs of pot-bellied, starving Biafran children, often supplied by the Swiss PR agency retained by the Biafrans to whip up world sympathy. For Fleet Street, radio and television, it was an African tragedy which troubled the Western conscience. It was a third-world nation in the grip of civil war; food was scarce and children were starving. Several crews had already been to Nigeria as ITN, together with the rest of the world media, focused its attention on this war-torn corner of West Africa. Page had already been behind the Biafran lines twice and had sent back the sort of highly emotive stories which helped create images of starvation and deprivation every time the word 'Biafra' was mentioned in the late 1960s.

His first assignment had been the previous year when he had entered Biafra through the Cameroons with reporter Sandy Gall and soundman Mike Doyle. They had taken a taxi to the Nigerian border, but the driver had refused to take them any further. Fortunately, they were able to purchase a ride on a makeshift ambulance used for ferrying personnel equipment to and from the Cameroons border. It was a painfully slow ride through the jungle, and the crew virtually lived in the van for four days. At least twice a day, they were stopped at gunpoint by villagers, but had little difficulty in buying their freedom for a couple of tubes of Polos or some cheap jewellery from Woolworth's bought specifically for the purpose. In fact the guns were not much of a threat; according to Page, they were either First World War rejects, or rough hand-made affairs which would probably have inflicted a greater injury on the assailant than the target, but the lethal panga knives held at their throats were a different matter.

By his second assignment, early in 1968, access to Biafra was relatively easy. Dozens of freelance pilots were being rewarded handsomely for flying money, arms, and supplies to the rebels in their beaten-up old Constellations and DC-45's and normally a lift was simply a matter of negotiation. Much of this support was coming out of Lisbon via São Tome, a tiny island to the south of Nigeria, off the Guinea coast, and Page had bought a ride for the customary fistful of dollars. He had the choice of 'seats' – either a box of rifles or a chestful of money. He chose the money. 'The whole flight was a bit of risk,' he said. 'I thought if anything happens, I might as well try to take a few bob with me.'

Now it was September 1968 and his turn had come again, although this brief was different. Together with his soundman Archie Howell, he was to link up with the Federal government troops as they battled to quell the rebellion by the Biafrans, and Page could see immediate improvements. Instead of risking their lives at the hands of a mercenary pilot in an obsolete Constellation, there would be the comfort of a BOAC VC10 all the way to Lagos, where they were booked into the plush Federal Palace Hotel. This time, however, there would be no Sandy Gall. Instead, the Foreign Desk was sending reporter Peter Sissons who, although only twenty-six years old, had already impressed with his coverage of the aftermath of the Six-Day War, the previous year.

The ITN team arrived in Lagos on 24 September, and spent the next few days trying to arrange official transport to Port Harcourt, Nigeria's southernmost town on the Niger Delta, and the nearest operational airstrip to the battle zone, sixty miles away.

The crew was friendly with Walter Partington of the *Daily Express* who was on first-name terms with the Nigerian President. Partington had previously been behind the Biafran lines and had taken some slides which the President was anxious to see. Accompanied by Sissons, they spent an amiable few hours in the presidential palace where senior government officials took great delight in spotting Biafran 'Colonels' and 'Majors' who had been mere corporals or less in the Federal army before the rebellion. By the end of the evening, they had emerged with presidential permission to fly to Port Harcourt on the next available military aircraft.

Unfortunately, however, the President's favours cut little ice with one junior officer, and on arriving at the military base, they were bluntly told that they were regarded as 'non-essential personnel', and refused admittance to the airfield. For the next four days, they applied and re-applied for military assistance to get them to Port Harcourt, to no avail. Then, on the fifth day, the window started to open when they met a mercenary pilot who had been contracted to fly a consignment of mortars and coffins to the front. 'It was a very economic way of operating,' Sissons observed. 'They would fill the coffins with mortar bombs on the way out, and replace them with dead Federal troops on the way back.'

After the customary exchange of currency, the ITN crew clambered aboard the ailing old DC-4 and the high-risk factor became immediately apparent. The plane wouldn't start and, to make matters worse, one engine was leaking a steady pool of oil over the tarmac. By his own admission, the American pilot was not an aircraft engineer, but seemed to have confidence in his assertion that 'it was probably the plugs'. Ten minutes later, the plugs had been scraped clean with sandpaper, and the four engines reluctantly creaked into life. After a shuddering charge down the runway, the DC-4 lifted itself grudgingly into the air and headed south towards Port Harcourt with its macabre cargo of bombs, coffins, and newsmen. They could still see the black stream of oil trickling from one engine and did not need to be reminded that the previous day a similar aircraft had crashed on its approach to Port Harcourt, killing the pilot and forty Nigerian troops on board. The sight of the wreckage from the air did litle to inspire confidence, and the last few minutes of the flight gave the crew some anxious moments.

Once safely on terra firma, they made contact with the 'Black Scorpion', the commander of the Nigerian forces in Port Harcourt. He was Colonel Benjamin Adekunli, a formidable figure with a reputation for bullying and even shooting his subordinates for the slightest offence. To foreign newsmen, however, he was mostly helpful, and willingly provided a large covered Land Rover with a military escort to take the ITN team together with an American crew from ABC , a handful of journalists, and a *Time-Life* photographer Prier Ramrakha, to the front line at Owerri, sixty miles away.

Ramrakha was a tall Kenyan Asian with a squint and an international reputation as a first-rate photographer. His presence in Port Harcourt was an unexpected bonus for Page: the two men had been friends for years, covering many international assignments together, and the journey gave them a chance to compare notes and reminisce.

Owerri had been a hotbed for weeks, regularly changing hands as first the Nigerian troops, then the Biafrans, gained control of the small town. The Nigerians had retaken it within the last twenty-four hours and, although the Biafrans were putting up a spirited resistance, they were slowly being squeezed out. It was a situation which seemed certain to provide the newsmen with some dramatic action.

The Land Rover stopped just outside Owerri. The retreating Biafrans had dug a wide trench across the road to hold up military traffic and the crews walked the last mile to the battle zone. Sissons took the opportunity to record a 'wild' narrative (not synchronized with film), as they advanced towards the front line, but found that he was falling behind the main party and decided to abandon it until the return journey. He rejoined the other newsmen as the party came across a small clearing where there were obvious signs that the rebels had been camping before they retreated.

There was an old high-sided pram, a rusty bicycle and, in the centre of the encampment holding pride of place among the empty cans, papers, and other debris, was an old wind-up gramophone with a pile of Vera Lynn records. As Page jumped on the bicycle and started to sell imaginary Wall's ices, Sissons was struck by the incongruity of the situation: 'It was a bizarre contrast to the stench of war,' he said. 'It was probably the only pram for hundreds of miles, and the thought of Biafran rebels playing British records in the middle of the jungle was almost incomprehensible. He made a mental note to do an 'into camera' piece, accompanied by the strains of 'We'll Meet Again', on the return journey.

They continued walking towards the sound of war in the distance when they were alerted by the crack of rifle fire a couple of hundred yards away. They took cover and, after their Commando escort had returned a few desultory rounds in the general direction of the snipers, it was considered safe for them to proceed. They were approaching the action, and Page instinctively held his camera at the ready. Howell, who would be recording the action 'wild', also had his finger on the button as the party headed warily towards the hill ahead.

About two hundred yards in front of them, a figure darted out of the bush and squatted on one knee. He fired the first shot and, suddenly, all hell broke loose. They had walked into an ambush. 'I've never seen foreign correspondents scatter so fast,' said Page. 'Fortunately, there was cover on both sides of the road. I went for a tree on the right, while Peter and Archie dived into a ditch on the left.' Ramrakha and the ABC sound-man also bolted to the right, and huddled with Page in the cover of the large tree, as bullets cracked all around them. 'I remember thinking that we looked like the three wise monkeys,' he said later. Sissons, however, remembers it rather differently.

> 'I could see Cyril standing rather nonchalantly behind this tree, with his camera at the ready. It was rather like a scene from *High Noon*, as he waited to shoot the bad guys. Both Cyril and Archie were extremely cool, as you'd expect from veterans of several campaigns. I was more scared than anyone – I just hoped that it didn't show.'

Howell had switched on his tape recorder the moment he landed in the ditch. His recording was subsequently used as a Scotland Yard training film to help recruits recognize weapons by their distinctive sounds. Sixteen different types of firearm were identified on Howell's tape.

After a few minutes' continuous firing, Page felt a piece of bark hit him on the head. It told him that the rebels were moving in from the flanks, and the three men would soon be easy targets. Signalling their intention to their colleagues, they made a life-or-death dash across the road and dived into the ditch as the bullets sprayed around them. Soon, the firing was coming from three directions and the Commandos, heavily outnumbered, could offer only token resistance.

For half an hour, the barrage continued, as the newsmen crouched together in the ditch, unable to move and hardly daring to breathe. Then, almost as suddenly as it had started, the shooting stopped. For nearly thirty seconds nobody moved, then Prier Ramrakha picked up his camera. Page, crouching next to him in the ditch, shook his head, partly in warning, and partly in disbelief. Surely, he was not going to try for a picture, he thought. Suddenly, Ramrakha was on his feet with his eye on the view-finder. He had not time to push the shutter button before a single shot rang out, hitting him in the back. He fell forwards into the road.

The memory of seeing his friend fall, still haunts Page. 'I thought he was messing about at first. Then I saw the back of his shirt turn red, and I knew it was the end.' The ABC sound-man still had his tape recorder running. The crack of the rifle, and the sound of Ramrakha falling served as a macabre record of how one of the world's most respected war photographers fell in action. 'My God – he's been hit,' someone said, and the tape faithfully recorded the verbal shock waves which swept through the tiny, cramped ditch.

Sissons, at one end, looked around for alternative cover and, lying flat on his stomach, eased himself out of the ditch into the bush, about twelve feet away. The heavy firing resumed, hampering the efforts of Page and the Federal Commandos to drag Ramrakha to safety. Eventually, they hauled him out of the road and, carrying him by the arms and legs, scurried back past the deserted encampment to their Land Rover. One by one, the journalists and camera crews followed, making the most of the cover at the roadside.

They eased Ramrakha into the Land Rover and climbed in, providing as much comfort as possible for the injured photographer who was now bleeding profusely. It was Page who noticed first, after a quick head count, that someone was missing. 'Where's Peter?' he asked, and Howell remembered that he was last seen edging towards the bush.

Sissons, now under cover, had kept his head down and was unaware that the rest of the party had pulled out with the injured Ramrakha. Any noise they might have made had been nullified by the continuous firing which was now easing off. Sissons looked back towards the ditch and realized he was now on his own. Still under cover, he lifted his head to try to locate his colleagues and, again, a fusillade of bullets crashed around him. Sissons had been spotted by a Biafran barely twenty yards away, and he realized that if he remained where he was he would be a sitting duck.

The firing stopped briefly as the marksman changed his magazine. Sissons realized that it was the only chance he would get, and he threw himself towards the deepest hole he could find. He was, quite literally, in mid-air as the firing started again, and he felt a kick just below his pelvis, and the unmistakable experience of his flesh being torn. He crashed to the ground, numbed, and watched in horror as his lightweight beige trousers rapidly turned to crimson.

He had no idea how many times he had been hit, but the extent of the mess suggested that perhaps three or four bullets had smashed into him. Were his legs still there? He could not feel them. He felt little pain, but was still very conscious and could think clearly. Then he was struck by a chillling thought – perhaps one of the bullets had severed his femoral artery. His brother was a doctor and he had gleaned enough medical knowledge to know that this would give him about two minutes to live. Suddenly, he felt very angry; if it was the end, this was not exactly the ideal place to snuff it, he told himself. Then, he began to count the seconds.

He was still conscious three minutes later, and started to yell for help. 'I'm a British journalist. I've been hit. Get me out.' The cry was heard by the Major commanding the Federal Commando troops. They were a hundred yards away and had provided covering fire as the television crews and newsmen carried Ramrakha back to the safety of the Land Rover. Together with four men, the Major charged back towards Sissons, firing from the hip and taking advantage of what cover they could. They kept up a barrage of covering fire as Page pulled Sissons from the bush and used Howell's shirt to tie a tourniquet around the reporter's legs. The men then picked him up by the legs and shoulders and started back towards the jeep.

Suddenly Page had an inspiration. He dashed into the encampment, emerging seconds later pushing the old pram with a board on it and headed for the Commando party who were struggling to get Sissons to safety.

The firing had' started again, and Sissons and the rescue party were the prime targets. Page's arrival allowed the four Commandos to provide some cover as he helped lay the stricken reporter in the pram. Then, with bullets kicking up small clouds of dust around his feet, Page ran 'like buggery' up the road towards the Land Rover.

A mile outside Owerri was a tiny school house which had been converted into a makeshift first aid post. Page remembered it being pathetically inadequate: 'It didn't consist of much more than a bottle of Friars Balsam and a pair of rusty scissors,' he said. 'They weren't geared to saving lives. The only other thing in the room was a pile of coffins which didn't inspire much confidence.'

By now, Ramrakha was dead and Sissons, who was laid next to him on the table, was not expected to live. He was slipping in and out of consciousness, while Page tried to avert his attention from the dead man by his side. Apart from cleaning the wound and putting a First World War paraffin and bismuth field dressing into the gaping hole in Sissons' leg, there was little they could do. He had been hit by one bullet which had tumbled as it passed through one leg and smashed through the second leg, leaving four wounds. He was still losing blood and it was obvious to the ITN men that the only chance of saving their colleague's life was to get him out of Owerri. With a mixture of threats and bribery, Page virtually hijacked the station's Bedford ambulance to drive them to the old Shell hospital at Port Harcourt, sixty miles away.

They eased Sissons into the old converted van and returned for Ramrakha's body. 'We can't leave him here – he's a mate of mine,' said Page, still unable to digest the fact that the *Time-Life* man had covered his last job. Selecting a coffin, they put Ramrakha inside, but had to bend his knees because it was several inches too small. The photographer was six inches taller than the average Nigerian.

Sissons barely remembers the journey to Port Harcourt. He felt little pain and his bouts of unconsciousness were becoming longer, and more frequent. By the time they reached the old-fashioned Shell hospital, he seemed barely alive to Page and Howells, and their fears seemed to be confirmed as they saw Sissons being unceremoniously laid out on the white tiled floor. Excessive loss of blood leads to dehydration and Sissons was conscious enough to beg for water, with little effect. Eventually they capitulated, and the reporter was violently sick. 'I felt terribly ashamed,' he said later. 'Then I remember nothing until I awoke the following morning, heavily sedated.'

For Page, the main problem was getting to Lagos. The planes were few and they might have to wait a week, or even more. He phoned *Time-Life* to break the news of Prier Ramrakha's death. He had lost one friend and seemed in danger of losing another, and he, too, had come closer to death than ever before.

Sissons was hardly well enough to travel, but the choice was simple – fly to Lagos, or die. The following day saw Page and Howell at Port Harcourt airstrip with Sissons on a stretcher and Ramrakha's body in the coffin. All they could do was shelter from the sun beneath the wing of a parked aircraft, and pray that one of the fleet of maverick cargo planes would appear that day. After what seemed an interminable wait, they heard a familiar, uneasy drone in the sky overhead and recognized it immediately as a four-engined Constellation. They watched it bounce unevenly down the runway, and Page was at the pilot's side seconds after he emerged from the flight deck.

After a brief explanation and the customary transfer of Nigerian currency, the flight was on. Two hours later, the stretcher bearing Sissons was being eased up a ladder into the cabin of the aircraft, and Ramrakha's coffin, which once carried a cargo of mortar bombs to the front line, was lifted on board for its return journey. To these pilots, flying bombs and bodies was all part of the day's work.

They were met in Lagos by representatives from the British Embassy who had arranged to fly Ramrakha's body home. Page said a silent farewell to his friend before climbing aboard the ambulance which was standing by to rush Sissons to the University Hospital. Page contacted ITN in London and plans were immediately set in motion to fly a top orthopaedic surgeon to Lagos to supervise any operation which might be necessary.

Conditions in Lagos, while an improvement on the Shell hospital at Port Harcourt, were still fairly spartan. Sissons remained there for a week where, under the watchful eye of Mr Ken Hesketh, consultant orthopaedic surgeon at Winchester Hospital, he had his wounds cleaned and his legs were saved.

He has little doubt that it was Hesketh's presence which saved his life: 'If I'd been a Nigerian, they would certainly have amputated my legs – in fact, one of them wanted to do it anyway,' he said. 'In Lagos you don't stand much chance of recovering from an operation like that.'

By now, the pain was excruciating, and Sissons had to be heavily sedated until it was decided to fly him to London for intensive care, a week later. He was driven to Lagos airport where a BOAC VC-10 provided the best visual tonic he could hope for: 'It was a beautiful sight,' he said. 'The gold, silver, and blue livery, and the sight of those crisply laundered stewardesses gave me tremendous confidence.'

The airline was particularly helpful. Six first-class seats were removed to accommodate the large cot in which Sissons was to travel, but access to the aircraft posed a problem. He was eventually hoisted aboard by a fork-lift truck. With Kenneth Hesketh still in attendance, and the attentive stewardesses on hand to provide any assistance necessary, the six-hour flight passed comfortably for Sissons, although his bed bottle presented a minor problem. It was too large to be rinsed out in the aircraft's tiny basin, and Sissons probably has the unique distinction of being the only patient to have his bottle washed out with champagne at 30,000 feet! Coincidentally, the chief stewardess on the flight was the daughter of Mr David Turner, the surgeon who was to play a major role in his recovery at the Royal National Orthopaedic Hospital in Great Portland Street.

He remained in intensive care for a month during which he almost died from the spreading infection which had gripped his legs. Only the strongest antibiotic available reversed this deterioration in his condition. He was confined to the hospital for ten weeks – or should have been. Towards the end of his stay, ITN were moving office from Kingsway to Wells Street, just a few hundred yards away, and a couple of colleagues decided that he should be included in the celebrations.

In a carefully planned escape, Sissons was marched out of the hospital, wearing a borrowed raincoat over his pyjamas, and supported on each side by his mates. It bore a close resemblance to a true life escape story: 'I felt like the dummy in the film *Albert RN*,' he was to recall. Five minutes later, he was sitting in the Green Man at the top of Great Portland Street. The first pint went straight to his head and, after ten minutes he admits, he was smashed out of his mind. The route back to his hospital bed was not quite so easy. He had been barely capable of walking *before* the drink, and now it was virtually impossible. To make matters worse, he had been missed, the alarm had been raised and he became the victim of a heavy bout of matronly wrath.

Twelve months later, Sissons was again in action, reporting on the troubles in Northern Ireland. He had undergone several painful skin grafts, still wore a steel caliper on one leg and remembered 'hopping around to dodge the bricks'. He later had a second operation and, although his leg still troubles him, he is quite philosophical about it: 'I owe my life to Cyril and Archie,' he said. 'If I'd been with a lesser crew, it could have been a different story. I know it affected them both, deeply.'

Both Page and Howells have many prizes and souvenirs from their worldwide assignments. Few hold as many emotional memories as the pairs of gold cufflinks presented to them by Peter Sissons. Sissons has his own souvenir of Biafra, which he keeps in his office drawer. It is the remains of the bullet which smashed through both thighs and was later found to have missed his femoral artery by less than half a centimetre.

Biafran Christmas

Most of the ITN crews had a spell with either the Federal or Biafran troops in Nigeria during the late 1960s, sometimes sending back haunting tales of starving children and, on other occasions, capturing dramatic – and often horrific – scenes of front-line action.

Alan Downes had a total of five Nigerian assignments: four via Lagos to cover the Federal side of the action, and one behind the Biafran lines. His first sortie came a few days after returning from the Six-Day War and its aftermath in 1967. He

returned to London for a well-deserved rest, but was soon
winging his way to Nigeria with a brief to cover the Federal
troops in their battle against the rebels. For Downes, the mission was memorable largely because it was his first experience
of the Nigerian war, but it is his single assignment to Biafra a
year later, which holds more vivid recollections. It was late
November. Page and Howell had followed the injured Sissons
home a few weeks beforehand and tales of escalating action,
deprivation and starvation behind the Biafran lines, were
reaching the Foreign Desk. Downes, together with soundman
Mike Doyle, were given their brief: cover the action generally,
but concentrate on the 'Biafran Christmas' angle. Their reporter was to be a young man covering his first overseas assignment. His name was Michael Nicholson.

The accepted route into Biafra was from Lisbon to São
Tome, the small Portuguese island in the Gulf of Guinea, and
then ride shotgun on one of the Dakotas or Constellations
which were ferrying food and arms to the rebel troops. It was
the Biafrans' only lifeline, and they had widened a stretch of
road to form a makeshift runway at Uli, where freelance pilots
risked life, limb, and aircraft to deliver the fruits of the
worldwide Biafran Aid programme.

A small parliamentary delegation, headed by Labour MP
Fenner Brockway, took the same flight to São Tome as the ITN
crew. They were on a fact-finding mission to Biafra to check
whether the truth actually coincided with world opinion.

Meanwhile, British newsmen had fallen out of favour with
the Biafrans after several World Service news bulletins had
broadcast claims that the Federal troops had gained control of
certain vallages, when, in fact, the opposite was true. Biafran
troops were sitting in captured towns, listening to the normally reliable overseas broadcasts telling them something
which had been invented by the Federal propaganda
machine. Because the ITN crew were assumed to be a part of
'British Broadcasting', they felt the backlash and should have
been refused permission to enter Biafra. However, the Biafran
representatives in São Tome wrongly presumed them to be a
part of Fenner Brockway's political missionary team, and they
were escorted aboard the most comfortable old Dakota and
flown to Uli. The airstrip was primitive, to say the least, and

most flights into Uli were undertaken at night to avoid the
Federal fighters. As many as a dozen aircraft would be circling
overhead without lights, and the inadequate system which
passed for air traffic control would call them in one at a time,
flicking on the airstrip lights for a few brief seconds as the
pilots made their approach. Mid-air collisons were a constant
probability, and even aircraft which landed safely were in
danger of being hit by another plane coming in behind them.
Significantly, there was a small cemetery at the end of the runway where many of these bucanneering pilots were buried.

As they headed towards Biafra, Doyle and Downes chatted
to the pilot. He was a friendly Scot, aged about fifty who had
commenced his career in the Berlin airlift after the war. He
had grabbed this chance to make some money, he told them,
as he felt his flying days were almost over. They were hideously
prophetic words. He was killed forty-eight hours later, when
his Dakota crashed in flames a hundred yards short of Uli
runway.

The first signs that the crew was not welcome in Biafra came
within minutes of landing. While the Fenner Brockway party
was ushered away to be cosseted by their hosts, the three ITN
men were immediately apprehended by a Biafran major, who
escorted them to a caravan surrounded by an armed guard.
After an hour's interrogation, they were whisked away by car
to Government House, a building considerably less grand
than its title suggests, and paraded before the Minister of
Information.

'You are here without authority,' the Minister told them.
'You must go back to São Tome and come in again.' To
Downes, this was like a game of human Monopoly, and his
blood started to boil: 'If we go out, we stay out,' he snapped.
'We're not going through all this again just for the sake of a bit
of bureaucratic lunacy.' A compromise was reached, and they
were put in the hands of Father John Ryan, a Catholic priest
who ran the local mission. They would remain there under
technical house arrest, until official permission was obtained
for them to remain in Biafra.

The crew's first impression of Biafra was one of surprise.
'We expected to see people lying on the ground, literally dying
of starvation,' said Downes. 'It simply wasn't true. Adults can

live for weeks on minimal food intake – the tragedy was the lack of food for growing children.' He remembered, too, the scale of the black-market operation. 'Most aid programmes are like a long tube full of holes,' he said. 'Only a fraction of what you put in comes out at the end. I couldn't count how many times we saw bags of food being dropped off at the wrong destination "by special arrangement".'

With the prevalent shortages in Biafra, the crew had come well victualled. Doyle and Downes had proved their gastronomic 'je ne sais quoi' by visiting a supermarket and scooping dozens of tins of spam, peas, carrots, and sweet corn into a large equipment box, and although their diet was somewhat repetitive, they ate well and regularly. They also produced a couple of bottles of whisky which seemed to provide the answer to at least one of Father Ryan's many prayers.

With the priest's co-operation, they were able to film the tragic, but now familiar, scenes of starving Biafran children with their pathetically thin limbs and their swollen stomachs, with barely the strength to climb steps. Often the men wanted to give them food, but were advised against it by Father Ryan; a glut of food after months of starvation might do irreparable harm and, anyway the Mission was helping to feed the children with regular, if pitifully inadequate, rations. The crew were reminded of the story told by cameraman John Collings, after returning from Biafra the previous year. He had given one child a sweet, and watched amazed as it was broken into seven pieces, and distributed among the group.

Despite repeated requests, there seemed little chance of obtaining even short-term parole to film Biafran action, and the crew were beginning to despair when new hope arrived in the form of Frederick Forsyth, formerly a journalist with the *Daily Express* and BBC, and now working freelance.

Forsyth was slightly infamous at this stage, and had thrown in his hand on the side of the Biafrans. It would be another two years before his first book *Day of the Jackal* pitched him headlong into literary stardom and the attendant rewards. 'He sauntered into the Mission House, wearing full combat gear, with a .45 revolver protruding from a holster strapped to his leg,' remembered Downes. 'We asked him if he could help, and he said he would do what he could. A couple of days later our freedom was extended slightly, but there was still no chance of filming any action. British radio and television were still regarded as untrustworthy by the Biafrans and the co-operation we were getting was absolutely nil.'

To make matters worse, the ITN men had caught an occasional glimpse of a French TV crew who were wandering about, filming at will. While rivalry is always there, it is usual for crews to at least acknowledge each other socially – particularly in war zones. The French, however, kept their distance and seemed to give the ITN crew a wide berth. This puzzled Downes and Co., particularly as they thought they recognized the reporter. They could not remember his name, but they were sure they had seen him somewhere.

Two nights later, Downes awoke with the realization that the 'French reporter' was, in fact, Olivier Todd, a member of the BBC Panorama team, who had succeeded in gaining the co-operation of the Biafrans by masquerading as a foreign TV journalist. The dear old Beeb, who had inadvertently triggered off the situation by upsetting the Biafrans when they broadcast a report they believed to be true, had pulled a fast one, and finished up with some first-class exclusive material for Panorama.

The following day, the crew were prepared to call it quits and return to London. They had missed out on the action shots, but still had their highly emotive footage of children for their 'Biafran Christmas' feature. They were having a snack lunch at the Mission, discussing the merits of having another attempt at twisting the arm of the Biafran authorities, when their conversation was punctuated by the scream of a jet overhead. Seconds later, the Biafran anti-aircraft battery boomed into action as three more fighters came into range.

Downes' first reaction was to dive for cover, but Nicholson charged towards the door, screaming 'Come on – this is it!' Grabbing the gear, Doyle and Downes followed him onto the balcony which gave them a grandstand view as the four Russian-built MiGs began their rocket attack on the nearby railyard. Suddenly, the frustrations of the past twelve days were behind them, and the news crew moved smoothly into action.

Nicholson was standing on top of the balcony in the shade, describing the scene as Downes' camera followed the MiGs, swooping to attack in the bright sunshine. The effect was a dramatic contrast, with the bonus of some unexpected close-ups of the fighters flying straight and low towards the Mission balcony, as they prepared for their second attack.

Doyle, crouching behind a huge plant holder, was picking up everything on sound – the piercing scream of the jets as they roared overhead, the thump-thump of the hopelessly inadequate anti-aircraft fire, and the screams and explosions from the railyard. And all the time, Nicholson was describing the action as pandemonium broke out all around the tiny village, alternating between 'wild' narrative, and 'into camera' pieces. 'We didn't realize, until afterwards, that he described the fighters as MiGs 15s, 17s and 19s – all in the same story,' said Downes, 'but it didn't seem to matter. It finished as an excellent team effort, with both the camera shots and the sound complementing the report.'

With the long-awaited footage of military action now in the can, the crew decided to pull out and get back to London with all haste. Believing that they had scored a victory over the ITN crew by witholding permission to film front-line action, the Ministry of Information arranged transport to Uli airstrip the following night. Since their arrival, it had been the target for regular Federal bombing raids – usually hit-and-miss affairs which consisted of a couple of Nigerian soldiers throwing twenty-five-pound shells out of the open door of a DC-3. The uneven repairs added to the already considerable dangers in landing and taking off, and the skeletal remains of another two burnt-out Constellations suggested that the grave-diggers had been kept busy at the far end of the airstrip.

They boarded an old Dakota, returning empty to São Tome after disgorging its cargo of grain and arms to the waiting Biafran troops. Apart from the flight deck, there were only two makeshift seats at the rear of the plane. The smell of sacking and grain reminded Doyle of a huge flying barn. Nicholson took the seat beside the pilot, with Doyle and Downes crouched at the rear of the aircraft. The only company they had was a heavy twenty-foot plank, used for lowering supplies from the cabin doors to the tarmac.

As the old engines coughed into life, the two men breathed a sigh of relief. They were on their way home at last, they had filmed first-class material in spite of their limited opportunities, and they were both due to have Christmas off. They didn't realize that the next hour would be among the most frightening of their lives.

The Dakota had struggled off the ground and was heading out towards the Gulf of Guinea and São Tome. Doyle, normally a non-smoker, accepted a cigarette from Downes, when a brilliant flash seemed to toss the tired old aircraft two hundred feet in the air. For the next hour, the Dakota was at the mercy of the worst electric storm that either man had ever seen. They sat in frozen immobility, glued to their seats as every few seconds the plane would either be lifted higher towards the stars, or plummeted a hundred feet or more towards the ground. Between them they had flown half a million miles, but never had they experienced anything like this. To make matters worse, the heavy plank was being tossed about like a matchstick inside the cabin, frequently bouncing off a bulkhead or the frail-looking ribs of the fuselage. 'I was convinced it was going to tear a gaping hole in the side,' said Doyle. 'That would have finished us completely. It made me realize what the phrase "shit scared" really meant!' For Downes, too, it seemed like certain death. 'We were going up and down like a yo-yo,' he said. 'We were too terrified to move; we couldn't speak and the flight seemd to last for ever.'

Eventually, after the longest hour of their lives, they saw the lights of São Tome in the distance. Twenty minutes later, the old Dakota bounced triumphantly down the runway and two ashen-faced film crew emerged, still holding their unlit cigarettes. Nicholson agreed the flight had been a bit uncomfortable, but had no knowledge of the unsecured, bouncing plank which almost sent the three ITN men to an unknown grave, somewhere in the Gulf of Guinea.

It took them another four days to get home. They managed to hitch a lift on a French Red Cross transporter to the nearby island of Fernando Po, and then it was a two-day spell in the Cameroons before flying to London, via Lisbon.

By the time they reached ITN's new headquarters in Wells Street, they had been away for three weeks, and not a word had been heard from them. If Editor Nigel Ryan was glad to see them, he was even more delighted by the news coverage they had brought back with them. A month later, delight blossomed into pride when Downes' film of *Christmas in Biafra*, with the dramatic scenes of the raid by MiG fighters, won a coveted American news coverage award.

The Black Scorpion

By the end of 1969, it was the turn of cameraman Chris Faulds to do a stint in Nigeria, this time covering the movements of the Federal troops as Cyril Page had done during his ill-fated mission with Peter Sissons, just twelve months beforehand. It was Faulds' only assignment to cover the Biafran war, but it was an experience which left an indelible mark on his memory and, he later admitted, his conscience, too. It was also one of the briefest assignments of the war but, by the time his crew left at the behest of the Nigerians, they had witnessed and filmed an act of atrocity which had the world howling in anger.

Faulds flew in to Lagos on a scheduled BOAC flight from Heathrow, accompanied by sound recordist Hugh Thomson. Again, the reporter was Michael Nicholson. For the first couple of days, their visit was an exact carbon copy of the frustrations experienced by Page and Co., as they waited in vain for accreditation and a flight to Port Harcourt, still the nearest airstrip to the main theatre of rebel action.

Eventually they were offered crouching room on a Hercules carrying Federal troops to the battle zone, and Faulds remembered spending that night in 'the worst hotel in the world' – a broken-down hovel, with no lights, no food, and an abundance of mosquitoes.

The following day, the ITN crew, together with other TV and pressmen, were driven towards the Federal front lines. By now, the Nigerians were gaining the upper hand and were anxious to show their successes to the world through the window so willingly provided by the mass media.

On the return journey later in the afternoon, they were approaching the Federal front line – about an hour's drive outside Port Harcourt – when the convoy stopped at a small village. Under the direction of a Federal officer, a dozen armed troops leapt out and started checking the apparently deserted huts. Faulds remembered it vividly: 'The officer in charge of the party was a real cowboy. He would kick open the doors of the huts and spray them with indiscriminate machine gun fire. It was as though he'd seen one war film too many.'

The village seemed deserted. Newsmen, who had taken up their positions in the hope of capturing some action, climbed disappointedly back into their jeeps. Then, somebody yelled: 'They've got a prisoner.' A young Biafran in his late teens, appeared from behind one of the huts with his hands in the air. At gunpoint, he was prodded to the side of the road where the over-zealous Federal officer started to interrogate him.

For the newsmen, this was prize action indeed. While Thomson recorded the heated threats on tape, Faulds and the other newsreel cameramen filmed the rare confrontation as the Federal captain launched a verbal salvo at the terrified young Biafran. Suddenly, the Federal officer was silent and held up his hand to signal the end of the interrogation. He seemed satisfied to take the youngster prisoner and two soldiers leapt forward to tie the boy's hands behind his back.

One or two of the newsmen began to wander back to their jeeps, when they were halted in their tracks by a cry of horror. They turned to see the youth kneeling at the roadside with the Federal officer holding an automatic rifle at his head. 'Christ!' whispered somebody. 'The bastard's going to shoot him.' Instinctively, Faulds and the other cameramen put their eyes to the view-finders as the Nigerian flicked off his safety catch and squeezed the trigger. The crack of the bullets echoed around the tiny village momentarily, then there was silence as the Biafran pitched forward into the sparse grass and dust which formed the roadway through the village.

The newsmen looked at each other in stunned silence, hardly able to believe what they had seen. Slowly it dawned on them that the murder had probably been staged exclusively for their benefit, and by filming it they had played right into the hands of the power-crazed, publicity conscious Federal officer. Faulds summed up their feelings later when he said: 'I'm sorry I filmed it. My immediate reaction should have been to switch off the camera, but you can't suddenly sever your news instincts – it was happening and it had to be filmed, otherwise nobody would have believed it. The moment haunted me for years afterwards, and I know now what I should have done.'

As they headed back to Port Harcourt, the mood was sombre. Even hardened newsmen, educated in the death and destruction of war, were sickened by the needless murder. Much as they would deliberate over whether it could have been stopped, the cruel fact was that it had happened, and it was now the priority of the ITN crew to get the filmed evidence back to London with all haste.

Nicholson succeeded in hitching a lift in a supply plane to Lagos, where he despatched the film to London, while Faulds and Thomson, unable to face another night in the 'Mosquito Palace' made alternative arrangements, and stayed in a hostel for Nigerian officers.

Unknown to the Press contingent, one journalist had persuaded a Nigerian minister to accompany him to the UK where, after seeing the ITN film transmitted, he publicly exonerated the Nigerian Government from all blame.

Shock waves following world reaction to the incident were felt back at Port Harcourt, where Benjamin Adekunli, the infamous Federal officer known as the 'Black Scorpion' was known to be angered by the whole affair. He ordered the immediate arrest of his murdering officer, and the expulsion of British newsmen, including the ITN crew whose film, he claimed, was largely responsible for the mounting anti-Nigerian feeling. The Black Scorpion's word was law. If you were told to leave the country, you started to pack straight away; there would be no second bidding. Other British journalists had also been shown the door and there was to be a mass exodus of the media from Lagos.

The day before the departure, however, the ITN crew was approached by a young Nigerian officer, who asked them if they would like to delay their departure for forty-eight hours, and fly back to Port Harcourt. Any thoughts that the Black Scorpion might have relented were only fleeting. He had decided that the offending officer would face the firing squad, and the ITN crew, together with other camera teams, were being invited to film the execution. 'Perhaps he felt it was the best way to even the score,' said Faulds. 'We declined the invitation and flew straight back to London. The whole thing was becoming tragic theatre.' This time there was no doubt that the killing was staged purely for the benefit of the media. The execution was delayed for ten minutes while one TV crew replaced a battery in their camera.

VIETNAM

Three majors and a tin hat

To most British television viewers, the Vietnam War was a distant, all-American problem somewhere in the Far East. This view was perhaps strengthened by the rather anonymous footage piped in from all-American networks with a studio 'voice-over' replacing the dramatic, staccato tones of an all-American TV war correspondent. Viewers frequently felt rather detached, and it was only when bulletins were dispatched from British television reporters who were actually there, that the horrors and suffering in this tiny corner of South-East Asia seemed real.

For any British news team to maintain a permanent presence in Vietnam would have been uneconomical. With both BBC and ITN having exchange agreements with US networks, most of the day-to-day action was filtering through to the Foreign Desks, and it was only for in-depth reports or major developments in the war that it was considered necessary to dispatch a crew to Saigon.

Between 1967 and 1972, Alan Downes was given four assignments in Vietnam but it was not until his second mission for the massive Tet offensive in 1968 that he experienced the full drama of the war with all its attendant misery. His first trip in 1967 had been part of a thirteen week tour of the Far East with Sandy Gall during which they decided to test the temperature of the escalating war in Vietnam. For Downes the excursion was memorable for learning the lesson that one never, under any circumstances, fills a water bottle with gin and tonic. 'The midday sun took its effect and anyone who was ever subjected to lukewarm gin and tonic knows that it's the last thing to quench your thirst,' he recalled.

It was during the first sortie that he covered a 'Defoliation Mission' with the US Air Force in a C-123 Provider Aircraft spraying Agent Orange over the jungle. Camera crews filmed through the open tail of the plane and Downes still remembers vividly the feeling of insecurity perched in the airframe over a yawning space. At the time, the media believed the Americans' assertion that the chemical was 'just like weedkiller, but stronger', and it was not until much later that it became linked with deformed babies and cancer.

Three months later his attentions were diverted by the Six-Day War in Israel, but it was only a matter of months before he and Gall were again heading east en route for Tan Son Nhut airport in Saigon, with sound recordist Mike Williams. It was January 1968, and ITN had eventually succumbed to Gall's plea that they should send a crew to Vietnam to cover any Viet-Cong offensive which might be planned to coincide with the oriental New Year celebrations at the end of January. They arrived in Bangkok on schedule, and after refuelling continued their flight to Phnom Penh in Cambodia and on to Saigon.

As both Gall and Downes had been to Vietnam before, they were able to brief Williams on the life-style he could expect while a 'guest' of the US Army in Saigon. The Americans seem to regard the Press as a valuable part of their war effort and foreign news teams are normally afforded the same degree of co-operation as the US media. Williams learned that the three men would have to equip themselves with US combat gear from the black market in Saigon where, it was claimed, one could buy *anything*. The US military would issue them with 'C' ration, provide escorts where possible, and give them the honorary status of Major for the duration of their stay, enabling them to pull rank over bona fide junior officers for transport and other requirements. By the time they touched down at Phnom Penh, Williams felt he knew Saigon as well as his colleagues and there was an unmistakable air of confidence among the men as they took the opportunity to stretch their legs before the final hop to Saigon, 350 miles away.

Seconds later, their bubble of optimism was cruelly burst. Gall had been right about the communist offensive, but even he had not anticipated that it would be aimed at the heart of the American operation in Saigon. It had started at dawn that day, 30 January 1968, and Tan Son Nhut airport had come under attack and had been closed several hours earlier, leaving the ITN crew marooned in Cambodia, where the horrific effects of the war were still some years away. They cursed their luck vehemently. Despite their cajoling and meticulous planning, they had arrived just one day too late, and although Saigon was barely an hour away, it was completely inaccessible, and might as well have been on the other side of the globe.

They later learned that the BBC news team was also locked out, but Julian Pettifer of 'Panorama' and a freelance cameraman had already arrived in Saigon, winning for themselves exclusive coverage of the attack on the presidential palace.

The attack on Saigon was a joint offensive by the North Vietnamese Army and the Viet Cong, which, translated, simply means Vietnamese Communist. Generally the NVA were more active to the north, around Da Nang and Hue, while the Viet Cong sapper-squads would utilize their local knowledge to great effect on prominent targets in Saigon.

Consumed with frustration, the ITN crew decided to fly to Hong Kong, but still had difficulty in finding an alternative route into South Vietnam. Eventually, after five of the longest and most tantalizing days that any of them recall, they decided to try their luck in Bangkok and, although Tan Son Nhut was still closed to civil aircraft, they were able to hitch a ride with other pressmen on a US supply aircraft heading for Saigon. It was early evening when they arrived and although most of the Viet Cong had now been squeezed out of the centre of Saigon, they were still active in pockets on the outskirts of the city. The airport came under attack as they landed, and the crew had to sprint the few hundred yards to the airport terminal building as mortars and machine guns opened up from the perimeter of the airstrip. Already, a rocket had blown a gaping hole in the roof of the airport lounge.

To leave the airport was impossible, and the crew, together with the other news teams which had flown in from Bangkok, resigned themselves to spending the night in the airport lounge, instead of the anticipated comfort of the Caravelle Hotel. Although it did not seem too funny at the time, Downes now looks back fondly on the memory of the cabaret provided by a television crew from Texas who had been dispatched to Vietnam for the sole purpose of conducting into-camera 'Hello Mom' pieces with local conscripts. The reporter was under five feet tall despite wearing the standard Texan high-heeled cowboy boots and a one-piece jumpsuit which he fondly described as his 'hand-made correspondent's outfit'. He wore a peaked jockey cap; the caricature was completed with the addition of an enormous cigar. Now, however, he had lost the touch of bravado which had been his main prop when the crew first met him in Bangkok, and was more than a little alarmed to find himself caught up in the hostilities. He spent most of the night buttonholing anyone who looked remotely official and bewailing the fact that he was in Vietnam to cover 'human interest stories – not this combat crap'. 'He looked like Norman Wisdom,' Downes remembered. 'When we saw him again, two weeks later, he was still doing his head-and-shoulders "local boy" stories, completely ignoring the biggest offensive in the Vietnam War.'

All normal services had ceased to operate in Saigon but the following morning they succeeded in reaching the Caravelle Hotel and registered with the Army Press Office for official accreditation. All newsmen, whether staff or freelance, were required to produce written evidence of financial backing to cover any medical expenses to avoid being a financial burden on either the US government or the Republic of Vietnam. It was also necessary to obtain accreditation from the Vietnam Ministry of Information, together with their press visa before the US authorities (Military Assistance Command, Vietnam) would issue the all-important MACV press card. Once armed with this, they were able to lock themselves into the official Press system with all its advantages, and head immediately for Cholon, the Chinese quarter of Saigon where the Americans, together with the Southern Vietnamese Army and police were still trying to flush out the last of the Viet Cong. The urgency of getting their first story back to London was magnified by the six-day delay in reaching Saigon and the chance of filming troops rounding up the last of the Viet Cong raiders suggested that fate was perhaps trying to atone for the crew's previous bad fortune.

A few months before, Williams had been in Aden and found that the 'softly, softly' approach adopted by British troops there under Colonel 'Mad Mitch' Mitchell contrasted sharply with the American strategy in Saigon. The difference was clearly illustrated in Cholon where the crew found that US and South Vietnamese troops had surrounded a residential block thought to be the refuge of the Viet Cong, and were all firing into the middle. Consequently most of the bullets humming over their heads were being fired by their allies, creating a completely distorted picture of the strength of the enemy.

Most of the regular Vietnamese troops had been given New Year's leave. They were replaced by raw recruits who did not seem to have much idea of what was happening, and the situation was reduced to the level of a Mack Sennet comedy with the arrival of two black American GIs carrying a bazooka. Downes recalled that one of them had 'The Destroyer' etched on the back of his combat jacket, and that subsequent conversations revealed that they were army cooks who had never fired a rocket before, but seemed desperately keen to break their duck! It seemed that they had been surplus to requirements in the cookhouse and dispatched to Cholon as reinforcements.

The arrival of the bazooka and the seige of the block were proved unnecessary a few moments later when a burst of machine gun fire behind them signified that the Viet Cong had been located. They had started a fire in a house to create a diversion, and had successfully escaped to another two hundred yards away before being spotted by a sharp-eyed police patrol. Six Viet Cong rebels, armed with rifles and a machine gun had been holed up in a house outside which Downes and Co. had stopped for a smoke, just ten minutes beforehand.

Keen to get among the heavier action to the north of Saigon, the crew applied to fly to Da Nang and, as 'Majors', were able to pull their Press rank and were ushered, much to their astonishment, past men more vital to the war effort. 'We were amazed,' said Downes. 'In effect, we were being treated like military VIPs.' The Press centre at Da Nang was a striking old building with a large courtyard, in the centre of town but on the river-bank overlooking the huge harbour. The pressmen who used it remember it as a building of considerable grace, although few were aware that, before its transformation by the US Marines, it had been a French military brothel. At the outbreak of the Tet offensive a Viet Cong suicide squad was shot down only a hundred yards from the gates; an event most of the Press corps missed as they were engrossed in watching a war film on the centre's open-air screen. Any bangs other than the film sound track were assumed to be New Year Celebration fire crackers, as the Viet Cong had intended.

Like most aspects of the Marines, the Press centre tried to be a model of efficiency. The ITN crew was given a room containing four beds and bath facilities, and then fully briefed on the importance of wearing US combat gear – the standard green uniforms which would readily identify them as 'friendly' military personnel. Helicopter Medivac rescue troops were ordered to deal only with injured personnel in green, and anyone refusing to comply with the edict did so entirely at the risk of being left to the mercies of 'Charlie' – the slang term for the Viet Cong inspired by the initial letters 'Victor Charlie'. The suggestion was ignored only by one pressman – an Italian photographer who, clad in light-weight crutch-hugging trousers, a perfectly tailored sports shirt and trendy basket-work shoes, seemed better equipped for a fashion session in a Rome studio than a bloody war in South-East Asia. Even he was forced to change his view after jumping from a jeep into two feet of clinging red mud.

From Da Nang, the ITN men wanted to push further north towards Hue, the old Imperial city still occupied by the North Vietnamese Regular Army and under constant attack from American and South Vietnamese troops. There was no official transport, so the men hitched a lift on a truck, through the teeming cold rain which mixed eagerly with the red mud to form something resembling a thick tomato soup, until they reached the Perfume River, an infamous waterway which arcs around the southern perimeter of Hue. The bridge had been blown and the only way across was by a small fleet of landing craft which were ferrying troops, ammunition, and supplies across to the north bank. As they passed the lines of American and South Vietnamese troops waiting to cross the river, Downes was startled to see a pair of yellow pigtails protruding from beneath a standard issue Marine helmet. It was his first sight of Cathy Leroy, the celebrated war photographer who, although petitely French, was obviously very much at home in a man's world and had adopted the 'American' tongue with such success that she was banned from a US Marine operational region for using bad language!

For Downes, Williams, and Gall, the trip across the river was a nightmare. Everything erupted at once, with aircraft strafing the North Vietnamese positions around the Imperial Palace and artillery and machine gun fire pounding the opposite bank and the citadel. By the time they reached mid-stream, columns of water were appearing all around them as the North Vietnamese opened fire with mortars and 75mm recoilless rifles. It was Williams' idea that they should do an 'into-camera' report 'while they were still alive' and, in full combat gear, the unflappable Gall recorded an immediate 'mood' piece as they bobbed through the North Vietnamese shelling towards Hue. In London, the Foreign Desk was delighted with the piece, but felt that Gall's Marine helmet was perhaps 'overdoing it a bit'. 'Sandy had a capacity for British understatement,' recalled Downes. 'While Alan Hart would have milked every ounce of drama from the situation, Sandy made it sound as casual as boating on the Serpentine. Believe me, he would only wear a helmet when it was absolutely necessary.'

Gall's coolness was all the more remarkable since the three men were seated on ammunition boxes and one stray round could have blown them all to pieces. Fortunately the NVA mortar positions were taken out by American air strikes before they inflicted much damage on the tiny flotilla, and the ITN men were able to scramble ashore, inching their way forward to where the Marines had engaged the enemy in furious house-to-house fighting. The progress of the US troops was hampered as civilians of all ages, loaded with personal possessions, headed out of the town towards the river, jamming the narrow streets. Amid the confusion, the ITN men dodged from house to house, searching for a suitable 'front-line' position.

It was early evening by the time they reached the temporary Company HQ – a medium-sized house which was once the

home of a middle-class Vietnamese family. It was apparent
that the occupants had left in a hurry to avoid the North
Vietnamese slaughter of intellectuals and government sympathizers. Behind them, they had left ample evidence of a
normal domestic life-style suddenly disrupted by the horrors
of war. There was food, furniture, beds, books, and toys, even
unfinished maths homework on a table, all details which, to
Downes, made the whole scene much closer to home.

By now, the light was failing and, since it would have been
impractical to move location, they decided to stay there overnight. Here, Downes, Williams and Gall listened to the
increasing cacophony of sound as action intensified around
the centre of Hue. They knew that the US Marines were taking a
battering and watched appalled as the wounded were brought
back to the Company HQ for cursory medical attention with
the limited facilities available. To Downes, one of the heroes of
the Vietnam war was the leathery Marine 'Gunny'-Sergeant –
the equivalent of an RSM – who stood over the injured and
broken young men as they were brought back from the assault
line on Hue. A veteran of the Second World War, he was able
to reach them with a smile and a few words of encouragement
which seemed to give them added strength and the will to survive. From a hardened professional soldier in one of the
toughest of all units, it was a strange mixture of authority and
compassion which left an indelible mark on everyone who
came into contact with him.

It was from the 'Gunny' that they first learned of the simple
Marine philosophy 'never leave a body behind'. It was good
for morale, he explained, if young soldiers knew their bodies
would always be brought home. To Downes and the others it
seemed a crazy policy to risk the group for the sake of a dead
individual and, predictably, Marines suffered further heavy
casualties while trying to retrieve bodies. Later they were to
witness first-hand the true meaning of the Marines'
'promise'.

For Downes and Williams, the night was both uncomfortable and restless. They lay on an old double bedframe,
without a mattress, listening as the mayhem of the battle for
Hue continued through the night. After a while, they slipped
into an uneasy sleep but even this brief respite was interrupted

by the nocturnal meanderings of a pig which, until it grunted, had both men convinced that they were about to be killed by NVA marauders who were known to crawl stealthily through sewers at night to come up behind their adversary.

The following morning they left the horror of Hue to the few civilians who had been unable to escape: they will not forget the woman sitting in the middle of the road screaming and beating her head as she cradled her dead child in an armful of straw. From the military, there were the endless demands for morphine for the injured and 'body-bags' for the dead, and there was the young Marine who was dying in the back of a truck with his head cradled in a padre's lap. It was his twenty-first birthday.

When they finally reached the rear area helicopter base, they saw for the first time the stark truth of the 'Gunny's' claim that 'they never left a body behind . . .' Before them were hundreds of olive-green body-bags in piles; some bodies were barely identifiable while others, in contrast, appeared to be at peace after sudden death at the hands of the North Vietnamese bullets. A few, which had not been reclaimed until after the later stages of rigor mortis, protruded from the sacks at hideously grotesque angles, like pieces of distasteful modern sculpture waiting to be unveiled. For all of them, the Marines' promise meant just one more flight to their final destination – home.

Any hopes they had of filming the aftermath of the nights' battle dissolved with Downes' discovery that the cumbersome batteries then in use with his 16mm Auricon camera were flat, and they now had little option but to return to Da Nang and dispatch the previous day's footage to London. With his camera out of action, Downes seized the chance to take some 'stills' with his Pentax, only to find that the constant vibration and movement had dislodged and broken the return mirror, and it was left to Williams to clinch game, set and match with the discovery that his sound-recording head in the Auricon had developed a crack.

Back at Da Nang, the crew made arrangements for the dispatch of their film and recorded material to ITN and were able to re-charge their batteries. The sound-head, however, presented a problem and, for the next few days, they were forced

to operate with a 16mm Arriflex silent camera and a tape
recorder without synchronization. For Gall's 'into-camera'
pieces they would have to rely on the old clapper-board
method, clapping their hands with both camera and recorder
running to ensure that, for play-back purposes, both sound
and vision were 'in sync'.

Anxious to compile more in-depth reports which would
help ITN viewers see the Vietnam War in a broader context, the
crew applied to the US authorities for facilities to reach Khe
Sanh, a notoriously 'hot' marine combat base to the north,
which was under siege by the NVA with the action escalating
day by day. Originally, the base had been established on
North Vietnamese supply routes, but the NVA had simply
changed their system and although the Khe Sanh base now
lacked any strategic purpose, the Marines could not withdraw
without loss of face. The North Vietnamese wanted it as a
supply base, and mounted a strong attack; the Marines,
strengthened by reinforcements, countered furiously, and
losses were heavy on both sides. Eventually, the base was surrounded and the story of the siege of Khe Sanh became the
immediate target of the ITN men. This time, however,
immediate assistance was not forthcoming. Transport to Khe
Sanh was at a premium and, like everyone else, the three
'Majors' would just have to wait their turn. Gall's politely pointed question 'How long?' was met with the observation that,
since it would probably be a week at the earliest, they would be
well advised to do something else in the meantime.

The advice matched their plans ideally; they had hoped to
put together a story around a heavy artillery base at Camp
Carrol, located some fifteen miles from Khe Sanh, and the
seven day wait for a flight to the besieged Marines provided
them with the ideal opportunity. The camp was impressive,
with a number of 175mm long-range guns ranged around the
central area of the encampment. With a range of around
twenty miles on full charge they posed a very real threat to the
NVA who would mount daily counterstrikes, normally around
mid-day, in the hope of hitting a packed cookhouse, which
they knew would achieve high casualties. The bombardment
of the US base would comprise either mortarfire or Soviet
122mm rockets, which were portable and launched from a

light-weight frame. By the time that the US units had determined the range to counter attack with battery fire, the
aggressors had packed up and moved on.

It was late morning and the feature piece was progressing
well, but there was an unmistakable feeling of tension in the
air towards mid-day, and gun crews were making excuses to
disappear for a few minutes for a variety of pressing personal
reasons. Then, on the stroke of noon, the ITN men fully
understood the reason for their uneasiness as a 122mm rocket
exploded in the compound less than sixty yards away and
everyone dived for the safety of the deep underground bunker
which offered the only protection. As they scrambled down
the steep make-shift steps they heard a cry of anguish from the
latrine block on their left as a door was savagely kicked open
and a Marine sprinted out like a greyhound from its starting
gate. The rocket had clearly interrupted his solitude and, clad
only in his tin hat, he dashed toward the bunker trailing his
trousers in the air and covering his vitals with his flac-jacket.
The incident inspired one of the loudest cheers of the war.

Inside the bunker, they could hear rockets crashing all
around them and Downes recalled tales he had heard about
the London Blitz, thinking it must have been something like
this. Then Williams dropped a bombshell of his own by
announcing in the rush to dive into the bunker, he had left his
'reserve' tape-recorder on the sandbagged parapet at the
entrance. Just one rocket thirty yards away could blow it to
pieces and bring a premature end to their activities – at least
until the replacement sound-head arrived for his original
Auricon gear. The crew was impressed by the calm attitude of
the base Colonel who offered to retrieve the equipment despite the fact that the base was still undergoing a particularly
heavy bombardment. Williams expressed his gratitude later
that night by beating the US officer at American scrabble –
complete with American spellings and with Webster's
dictionary as the ultimate work of reference.

Within a week, they found themselves at the top of the list
for a flight into Khe Sanh, but by now the NVA had tightened
the noose and the 6,000 US Marines and support units were
outnumbered eight to one. The Americans were under
tremendous pressure and had already been forced to

abandon the use of the giant C-130 transporters in favour of the
C-123, a lighter and more manoeuverable aircraft. Continued
bombardments of the landing zone had taken a heavy toll and
the twisted, skeletal remains of assorted burnt-out aircraft littered the edge of the airstrip. As the NVA shelling intensified,
even the C-123s were finding it virtually impossible to land, and
would simply touch down and taxi along the runway allowing
troops only a few seconds to leap from the moving aircraft and
dive for the scant refuge offered by the foxholes at the edge of
the airstrip, before giving full boost to its engines and taking
off again. As though they were not under enough pressure,
the Americans also had to contend with adverse weather
conditions; the monsoon season still had six weeks to run, and
the low cloud ceiling severely hampered air support sorties.

By now, it had become such a dangerous and uncomfortable scene that many international news desks felt it was unfair
to ask newsmen to face the dangers of Khe Sanh. To the ITN
men, however, it was a challenge. They had already been kept
waiting a week and were anxious to get in and out as quickly as
possible before the area was overrun completely by the North
Vietnamese and the Viet Cong, closing all doors to Western
news teams.

Understandably, their Press priority counted for little as
helicopters were turned around with maximum speed, sending in ammunition, supplies, and replacement troops to help
relieve the besieged base. Content to accept the promise that
they would be on a helicopter as soon as possible, Downes,
Williams and Gall camped in a flimsy hut by Dong Ha airstrip.
By day, they watched as fresh-faced young conscripts were
flown out to replace the dead and injured troops; by night they
lay in their bunks wondering what horrors Khe Sanh would
have in store for them.

The following day, they had their first serious doubts
whether they would ever reach Khe Sanh after seeing replacement troops take off from Dong Ha and return an hour later
without landing. Helicopters, too, were finding it impossible
to land and were forced to carry supplies and ammunition in
reinforced cradles slung beneath the fuselage which they
would drop at vantage points. Now, even these were returning
without dropping their cargo and eventually the Marines were

forced to adopt the rather haphazard method of dropping supplies by parachute from 1,500 feet.

Nobody reached Khe Sanh that day, and although frustrated, they had no alternative but to accept the US press officer's promise that they would try again the following day. The casualty rate in Khe Sanh was alarmingly high at one in three, and the ITN men knew that the odds of all of them escaping death or injury, were stacked against them. Such morbid thoughts were soon diverted, however, with the news that Hue was about to be recaptured and, in retrospect, it seemed to Downes and Co. that it may have been their guardian angel taking a hand.

Again, the crew found complete co-operation from the US Press centre and they were whisked by road to the Perfume River where a helicopter was waiting to transport them across to the centre of Hue. North Vietnamese troops were still active on the fringe of the city and there was a very real danger of stopping a sniper's bullet. After watching the Americans stand aside and allow the South Vietnamese to reclaim their city, Gall recorded a graphic report in his easy, conversational style. It delighted the Foreign Desk in London, but the men were somewhat deflated to read the tag line of the congratulatory message: 'Please *don't* wear tin hat while recording "into-camera" reports – it tends to over-dramatize the situation.'

Downes found himself back in Vietnam a year later when the American presence was at its peak. This time, however, he had no opportunity to repeat the triumphant scenes shot in Hue a year ago for, despite their strength in numbers, the US casualty list was growing at an alarming rate, and supplies of penicillin, dressings, and morphine were given the same priority as arms, ammunition, and men. This time, his soundman was Hugh Thomson, who had made one previous sortie to Vietnam and although reporter Michael Nicholson was new to the Asian war, Downes had previously worked with him in Biafra and knew his strengths.

The trip got off to a bad start when Nicholson dropped their only bottle of duty-free Glenfiddich on the tarmac at

Singapore. Later, they joined a US patrol which came under
fire from another US patrol, and twenty-four hours later, both
Thomson and Nicholson were laid out with an attack of the
Saigon trots, an acutely uncomfortable and often embarrassing stomach complaint. They were attended by a Chinese doctor who pumped some oriental potion into them, and,
although weakened by the experience, both men were able to
operate in and around Saigon.

Essentially, television news coverage is a team operation
with the reporter responsible for carrying the spares for the
cameraman and soundman who need both hands free to
operate their equipment. Nicholson had made his overseas
debut in Biafra and was keen to capitalize on his success, but
in the early days of the assignment his keenness proved more
of a hindrance than a help. 'He would break all the rules by
rushing ahead of us,' said Downes. 'If we had to film some
sudden activity it meant that he would be in the frame. We
eventually cured him by weighing down his rucksack with so
many unnecessary spares that he could hardly move, and so he
had to stay with us.'

The rapid rise of US casualty figures suggested that a feature
on Medivac – the evacuation of injured troops by helicopter to
field hospital units – would be both topical and informative
and with the full co-operation of the Saigon Press Office, they
were flown to join the unit at Cu Chi, some forty miles to the
south. Thomson later compared it to the set of the TV comedy
'Mash'. 'It was exactly the same – medics were sitting around
laconically, smoking and drinking. It was so quiet that it
seemed totally unreal,' he said. They accepted the suggestion
that they should 'sit down and wait until something happens'
and, by the early hours of the morning, were seriously
wondering whether this particular Medivac unit was operating
in the war, or simply sitting on the sidelines. They could not
have been more wide of the mark.

Suddenly they received a call that a unit was under attack
and taking heavy casualties and, as though by magic, the entire
place erupted into life. 'It was as though someone had thrown
a switch,' remembered Thomson. 'People appeared from
everywhere and seemed to know exactly what they were
doing.'

The first helicopter came out of the night sky heavily overladen with priority cases and others who had not survived the flight. Orderlies rushed around carrying the casualties to trestle tables where they were inspected to establish the extent of their injuries. Most were already full of morphine and oblivious of their gaping wounds or missing limbs. Downes had already checked the lighting in the theatre and knew it was barely sufficient for monochrome film. With colour, it would have been hopeless, but he knew that with forced processing, he could probably just get by.

Most of the injuries were horrendous, but none of them will forget the sight of one particular young conscript which still brings them out in a cold sweat and gives them the odd sleepless night: 'When a young man shot full of morphine with half his arse blown away and his genitals gone, asks you if he's going to be OK you just hope you lie convincingly,' said Downes.

They remained with the Medivac unit for three days, making several sorties to 'hot L. Zees' which, with their growing feeling for US military jargon, the crew correctly interpreted as 'landing zones under attack'. On these trips Thomson was able to plug his recording gear into the two-way radio system taping the conversation between the pilot and the ground base. This recording was laid over a section of the film with dramatic effect and was a vital contribution to the final award-winning Medivac feature.

For the three ITN men, the field hospital operation brought home more than ever before the harshness and suffering of war. But perhaps, more than this, they will remember the compassion of the American helicopter pilot who flew from a Medivac unit with the same dedicated urgency to lift a young Vietnamese who had slipped and fallen beneath the wheels of his father's ox cart. The boy's premature death in the helicopter provided a harsh reminder of the sorrow of human tragedy, even without the catalyst of war.

The little girl they remember

The picture of a nine-year-old Vietnamese girl running naked and screaming along a road with her back skinless after a napalm attack is, for millions of people, one of the haunting horrors of Vietnam.

It was 1972 and Downes was on his fourth and final assignment of the war. Shortly after his last sortie with Thomson in 1969, the United States had announced a policy of 'Vietnamization', with the South Vietnamese taking a major share of the responsibility. Consequently, American involvement was gradually scaled down. It was later learned that delicate negotiations had been held during this two-and-a-half year withdrawal period, designed to bring peace to South-East Asia.

These talks culminated in President Nixon's eight-point peace plan being presented in 1972, which included the immediate withdawal of all us troops and the release of all Viet-Cong prisoners. It was rejected by the North Vietnamese who, as if to emphasize their repudiation of the terms, launched a major offensive which took them deeply and permanently into South Vietnamese territory. The South Vietnamese, under mounting pressure, were forced to adopt desperate measures to counteract the guerilla tactics which were having increasing success in the Viet-Cong offensive.

Downes' sound recordist was Tom Phillips, a Geordie who had joined ITN in 1970 after ten years with Tyne-Tees Television. He had been a member of the team which had interiewed Idi Amin, the Ugandan dictator, in 1971 but Vietnam was his first taste of front-line action, and it was to provide him with more terrifying and emotional experiences in six weeks than he had had in a decade of regional television.

Together with reporter Christopher Wain, who later left to join the BBC, Downes and Phillips had arrived in Saigon to find that the excellent Press liaison service which had been so invaluable on previous visits, had virtually collapsed and pressmen and camera crews were wandering over South Vietnam virtually at will, sometimes finding themselves ahead of the action. Even local taxi drivers, once happy to risk anything in exchange for a wad of notes, were very wary, often refusing to take newsmen to their destination and dropping them at what they considered to be a safe distance from the danger zone. Often, their judgement was wrong, as one driver found when taking the ITN men to AnLoc, a town some seventy miles to the north of Saigon, which was under heavy seige from the Viet Cong. 'It was a very hairy drive,' said Downes. 'We were shot at several times and even mortared. We could understand why Vietnamese drivers charged astronomical rates – there was no liaison and reaching the combat zone was largely guesswork.'

Without the official Press centre, pressmen had to rely on rumours or reports from other news teams and, consequently, the Caravelle Hotel became an unofficial news exchange, with rivals bartering pieces of information in their effort to piece together the unpredictable jigsaw of guerilla warfare. 'It's not American-style warfare any more,' a Marine officer told Phillips. 'The British could handle it in Malaya, but we can't.' Morale was at an all-time low among many junior conscripts who were wondering why they were stopping bullets when so many South Vietnamese of their own age were speeding around Saigon on motorcylces making a comfortable living as pimps. Like their American counterparts, young men of a rich and influential background had the contacts to help them avoid combat duty.

For Downes and Phillips, the early part of this assignment was very unsatisfactory; instead of the six to seven minute reports which Downes had filmed on previous occasions, the direction of the war now limited them to short, sharp bulletins of between ninety seonds and two minutes each day. They would join a South Vietnamese patrol hoping for the chance to film some action but, more often than not, would have to be satisfied with nothing more than a slight skirmish. It was a hot June morning, little different from any other, when they heard that the Viet Cong were in possession of a village to the north of Saigon. They joined a South Vietnamese patrol intent on flushing them out, tacking themselves onto the rear of the column as it moved across dried paddy fields towards the village church which almost certainly housed Charlie's forward positions. They were right; the lead was soon flying,

forcing the Vietnamese patrol to withdraw and call up air support as the Viet Cong launched a savage counter-attack.
Within minutes, two A1 Skyraiders were screaming down
through the skies towards the village, identifying the Viet
Cong strongpoint and accurately depositing their cargo of
napalm on their enemy. Within seconds, the area was choking
with the thick, black burning smoke which had become the
familiar sign of one of the most controversial weapons of the
Vietnam War.

As the smoke cleared, the crew could see South Vietnamese
villagers running for the safety of the open fields as another
aircraft screamed down, preparing to attack the Viet-Cong
position. Then they watched in horror as the pilot, possibly
mistaking the villagers for escaping Viet Cong, dropped his
napalm bombs into their midst. Again, the tell-tale black
smoke ballooned into the air as panicking, burning villagers
ran screaming in every direction. An old lady hobbled along
the road towards the patrol carrying a young baby who
appeared to be draped in very fine muslin. As she came closer,
they could see it was the child's skin hanging limply from the
limbs. Then a young girl, aged nine, ran blindly towards them,
screaming as though the shrill cries of pain and terror would
somehow ease the torture of her grotesquely burned back,
skinless as a result of the misguided napalm attack. It was
Wain who reacted first, grabbing the stricken girl and pouring
the valuable contents of his water bottle over her to reduce the
body temperature. Then, grabbing Downes' and Phillips' can-
teens, he repeated the operation, providing the terrified child
with temporary relief from her agony. The incident was to
immortalize the young girl as the subject of one of the most
widely published photographs of the Vietnam War, and,
although severely scarred on her back, she survived her
injuries after treatment in a us burns unit.

Downes had filmed the scene, providing Wain with the
opportunity to record a compassionate report on the appalling
results of an erroneous attack which resulted in the suffering
of young children. Instead, he chose to dwell at length on the
chemical composition of napalm and its effects – a decision
which inflamed Downes at the time and one which he still
finds difficult to forget: 'It was a dreadful story which should

have been told with compassion,' he said. 'Most of it had to be scrapped by the scriptwriter in London as it was so insensitive.'

A week later, the crew was in Da Nang waiting for transport to Hue. Their attention had been diverted temporarily when a Cathay Pacific airliner crashed en route from Honolulu to Hong Kong, coinciding with the British tragedy when the BEA Trident Papa-India crashed shortly after take-off at Heathrow. Now, however, they were back on war duty and anxious to cover the hostilities just north of Hue, on the My Chan River.

The once-efficient Press centre in Da Nang was no better than Saigon, and it was left to the ITN men to reach Hue under their own steam. It seemed that they had little option but to chance a perilous seventy mile drive and they set about locating a reliable four-wheel-drive jeep among the dozens of ex-army vehicle dealers who had mushroomed around the city. By now, Richard Lindley (who later joined the BBC) had replaced Wain and was particularly keen to get among the action around Hue, but like Downes and Phillips, fully understood the importance of first locating a vehicle relatively free of mechanical defects. After a couple of false starts, they settled on a pea-green jeep which would have looked more at home in Disneyland than the battle grounds of Vietnam, but at least it appeared reliable. Plans for a dawn departure were disrupted that night by an emergency telephone call from Marvin Farkas, a UPI freelance working out of of Hong Kong. He had been contracted to ITN and had already reached Hue but had been rendered helpless by the sudden desertion of his sound recordist, an itinerant Dutchman who felt that he wanted to move on and had walked out at a moment's notice. Without the cover of a freelance crew, ITN were at a definite disadvantage, and Downes realized that the task of reaching Hue had assumed a new urgency.

A mixture of slick talking and begging managed to secure space on a US helicopter heading north and, although it seemed to answer the prayers of the ITN crew, the offer posed additional problems. There were only two seats available on the helicopter, and there was a definite 'no luggage' restriction. The freelance had all the necessary equipment and it was

decided that Downes and Lindley should take the helicopter
while Phillips, on his first mission to Vietnam, should try to
make his way to Hue in the jeep with all the ITN gear. It
would be easy, he was assured. There was a US military convoy
departing the following morning which would provide protection in the event of attack and Downes and Lindley flew
north satisfied that their colleage would arrive safely some
time the following day.

It was barely an hour later when Phillips encountered his
first problem. 'Holy shit - what's that?' squawked an American
major at the sight of the pea-green jeep, making it abundantly
clear that Phillips would not be welcome within ten miles of
the precious convoy. 'We're camouflaged. You'll stand out like
a luminous prick.' Bowing to authority has never been one of
Phillips' strong points, and, angered by the officer's attitude
and the apparent disregard for his safety, he responded with a
verbal V-sign. 'If that's your bloody attitude,' he said, 'I'll go
on my own.'

Downes and Lindley had found themselves in the fighting
almost as soon as they arrived in Hue. They had moved up
towards My Chan to cover the intensive attack by the North
Vietnamese who had now adopted the use of wire-guided missiles. In one of the most exciting actions Downes has covered
in his career, the South Vietnamese scored a remarkable victory, completely overcoming and annihilating an NVA ground
attack. 'They were popping out of trenches twenty-five yards
ahead of us and running away,' said Downes. 'We just couldn't
believe it. It's the closest most of us had ever been to the Viet
Cong and it made a dramatic piece of film.'

Their elation at their successful coverage was heightened
further when they returned to the dismal slum of a building
which passed for their hotel in Hue, on the edge of the
Perfume River. They were greeted by the familiar Geordie
tones of Phillips who was clearly the toast of the Press contingent after a remarkable five-hour drive from Da Nang.
When he reached Hue, his once pea-green jeep was covered in
mud, he had three flat tyres, and had narrowly escaped an
encounter with a mortar shell. He had also attracted the
unwelcome attention of a would-be twentieth-century high-
wayman who was caught trying to steal the crew's sound

equipment when Phillips stopped at the roadside for a drink. The soundman apprehended and admonished him in the time-honoured Geordie fashion: 'He's probably still got half a Coca-Cola bottle buried in his head,' said Phillips. 'He annoyed me.'

For both Downes and Phillips, the stay in Hue was memorably unpleasant. The bed linen had not been washed for weeks, and the filthy mattresses were a sanctuary to a variety of bugs. Downes developed an ugly open ulcer on his leg, while Phillips contracted a skin complaint after being bitten, which necessitated his being completely painted in a thick yellow ointment. American newsmen, normally enthusiastic about anything, were also beginning to show signs of discontent and frustration, seeking any diversion to relieve their boredom. A popular sport was to throw beer cans at the rats which scampered around the pelmets above the window. A young Vietnamese boy would even earn a few cents by covering them in petrol and setting fire to them, and the news contingent would sit back to see if their own particular 'choice' could outlast the others. Leaving the stench and vermin of Hue was an eagerly-awaited event for both men.

Lindley had flown to Saigon a few days earlier to dispatch some reports but the evacuation of Da Nang was beginning to start in earnest, and Downes and Phillips found difficulty in obtaining seats on the Air Vietnam flight. They looked American and, as far as the Vietnamese airline official was concerned, the USA was reneging on its undertaking to support Vietnam, and was at the bottom of the priority list. However, when Downes took a chance on his French, explaining that they were 'Television Anglais' it worked a charm, and two disappointed passengers had their tickets revoked while the two ITN men took their seats on board the Air Vietnam Caravelle for Saigon.

The cabin was full of middle-class Vietnamese women in national dress who had never flown before, and saw the flight to Saigon as a trip to safety. Downes recalled that many of them were violently sick on the aircraft: 'We were seated at the front, and the door on a Caravelle is at the back,' he remembered with distaste. 'We had to skate through a sea of vomit to disembark.'

During the six weeks, both Downes and Phillips experienced moments of high drama, deep emotions, and acute discomfort but these are regarded as par for the course when
covering war. It is the 'bon mot' or the tale of unscheduled
woe outside the arena of war which their colleagues wait to
hear when they return. Phillips was able to fulfill his obligation
by recalling the day early in the assignment when he was inadvertently given a VD jab instead of a cholera injection. The
apologetic vindication of the medic's error still rings in his
ears: 'Never mind, son–it won't stop you getting it, but it won't
hurt so much if we have to cure it.'

Last out of Saigon

The curtain was finally brought down on the Vietnam tragedy
in the spring of 1974, after a bitter guerilla war which had
raged for more than eight years. American troops had already
withdrawn leaving the South Vietnamese to fight a hopeless
rearguard action. Predictably perhaps, even the com-
paratively simple task of the final evacuation of Press and
Embassy officials was fraught with tragedy.

Both the fall of Cambodia and the ultimate surrender of
Saigon had been apparent several weeks beforehand and ITN
had decided to send a news team in to cover the last days of the
war, with the brief to remain until it was over. Soundman
Hugh Thomson again drew the short straw to chalk up his
third Vietnam assignment, and the team was completed by
Sandy Gall and cameraman Peter Wilkinson who was making
his first trip to the battleground of South-East Asia.

When the crew arrived in Saigon, the Vietnamese were battling to stem the Viet Cong's southwards advance and the
main theatre of action was a hundred miles to the north of the
city. Cambodia fell within days and four weeks later, encoun-
tering little but token resistance, the Viet Cong had swept
south to Newport Bridge, just three miles outside Saigon. It
was from here that Michael Nicholson – already in Vietnam
with a French-based UPITN crew – dispatched his award-

winning report signalling victory for the Viet Cong, and the start of an era of even deeper misery for the persecuted South Vietnamese.

Meanwhile, Wilkinson, Thomson, and Gall had been feeding back a string of reports on the plight of refugees, homing in strongly on homeless, injured, and starving children. The Vietnamese had picked up a little of the American flair for Press liaison but, although they seemed willing to help, they had few resources and, apart from nodding their official permission for crews to cover front-line action, they could offer little practical help. Only once did they launch a major PR exercise, when they organized a visit to a village several miles to the north where they claimed to have scored a major victory over the Viet Cong.

Wilkinson has covered wars and disasters in every corner of the globe, but has rarely seen a more sickening sight. Littered over the village compound were over a hundred bodies, each with a rope around its neck by which it had been dragged after being shot. Steeling himself against the grotesque sight, Wilkinson lifted the view-finder to his right eye and switched on his camera, forcing himself to concentrate on the professional coverage, rather than on the emotional impact, of the massacre. His maxim is simple: 'There's little time for emotion,' he said. 'As a professional cameraman, you must remain detached. I can escape from the reality of many of the horrors I see by simply closing my left eye and looking through a view-finder. It's rather like watching television.'

Although the Vietnamese had clearly gone to a great deal of trouble to lay on evidence of their victory, the exercise proved nothing. The bodies were unclothed and the more cynical among the Press contingent quietly suggested that the reverse was probably closer to the truth and they were more likely to be the victims of a Viet-Cong ambush, stripped of their identity and 'paraded' by the Vietnamese as evidence of a fictitious victory.

While waiting for the inevitable fall of Saigon, the crew took the opportunity to up-date the Medivac situation with the field hospital units now operated by Vietnamese. Wilkinson remembers an emergency dash by helicopter to pick up a colonel who was reported to be still alive after being shot through the head. They filmed the man being carried aboard and the efforts of the medical officers to insert a plasma drip into his arm, which were being hampered as the dying man was trying to grab Wilkinson's hand for comfort. They eventually bound the feed tube to his arm with the aid of camera tape, but he died before reaching the hospital base.

During the last few days of the war, the final vestiges of discipline and authority seemed to drain away from the beaten Vietnamese troops. The Press liaison centre had virtually ceased to function and the crews were able to move where they liked at their own risk, providing that they could coax a taxi to take them. Normally, the offer to pay a grossly inflated charge swayed even the most reluctant driver. The sight of groups of Vietnamese deserters scrambling back to the relative safety of Saigon became commonplace, although one party objected to being filmed and demanded at gunpoint that the crew should hand over the film. Another party of renegades poked rifle barrels through the car windows to emphasize their displeasure at having their desertion recorded on film until the taxi driver explained that, as it was for exclusive transmission in the UK, there could be no local reprisals. This explanation not only pacified them, but appeared positively to delight them and, assuming that they would be seen as heroes on British television, they went happily on their way.

By now it was clear that Saigon would fall within days, perhaps a week at the most, and aware of the need for concise and clear plans for evacuating the city, the US Embassy held a press conference. All newsmen, together with high-ranking Vietnamese officials and Embassy staff were briefed to assemble at various points where they would be collected by a convoy of buses and taken immediately to Tan Son Nhut airport. A special signal, explained the consulate official, would be broadcast on the US forces network within the next couple of days. Then, drawing himself up to his full height and milking every ounce of wartime drama from the situation, he delivered his punch-line: 'That signal,' he said, 'will be Bing Crosby singing "White Christmas".' For the next three days, every pressman in South-East Asia found himself either singing or humming the opening bars of the world's bestselling record.

When the familiar, if unseasonal, tones of the old Groaner crackled over the US forces airwaves on the morning of 27 April Wilkinson and Thomson had already packed their equipment, batteries, and film. Adhering strictly to the order 'no excess baggage', they were forced to leave their clothes and other 'luxuries' behind.

By now, they had been joined by Nicholson who was due to return to London while Gall would remain in Saigon with the French crew from UPITN. Although there was a definite feeling of hatred toward all 'round eyes' in the city, the French were receiving more co-operation. Many Vietnamese felt badly let down by the Americans and, since they could not differentiate between a London or Los Angeles accent, British pressmen were also finding favours in short supply.

Impressed by the briefing at the press conference three days earlier, the ITN men assumed that departure from Saigon would be an orderly operation supervised by the few hundred Marines who had been specially flown in from the US aircraft carriers which were still anchored in the South China Sea. Instead, they arrived at their assembly point to find total chaos. 'It was like the first day of the Sales,' said Wilkinson. 'There were people fighting and clawing to get on the bus – even some normally civilized pressmen were behaving like animals.'

The ITN men were elbowed, pushed, and punched out of the way in the scramble to get on the first bus, and when the second arrived, Wilkinson was swept on board while still trying to stay close to Thomson and Nicholson who were being pushed further and further away. Realizing the folly of being separated from the rest of the crew Wilkinson climbed out of the driver's window – an action caught by several photographers and wrongly interpreted by many picture editors as an underhand method of getting into, rather than out of, the bus. By the time the third bus arrived, the ITN men knew the score and forced themselves aboard, gaining a prime position at the front near the driver's cab, enabling them to film through windows if necessary. When finally it was impossible to squeeze another body on board, the armed plain clothed US Marine 'conductor' forced the hydraulic doors together and shouted the monosyllabic order 'Go!'. Slowly, with its engine over-revving fiercely, the bus edged forward.

The driver was a consulate official in his mid-fifties who had never driven a bus before. Suddenly, he had been forced into service as a guardian angel for pressmen and his attitude suggested that he was not altogether happy in his job. Every time the bus stopped at a crossroad, it would be surrounded by Vietnamese begging to be allowed inside. For one woman who succeeded in forcing open the hydraulic doors a few inches, a smash in the face with the butt of the Marine's pump-action shotgun was the reward and she fell back in agony with blood trickling from her eye. Wilkinson, realizing the delicacy of the situation, hesitated before picking up his camera to film similar incidents, and soon realized that it was a mistake. The bus screeched to a standstill almost squeezing the breath out of the passengers at the front, and, spitting venom, the driver grabbed Wilkinson by the lapels: 'You bastard,' he screamed. 'We're trying to get you out. Stop trying to drop us in the shit!' Surprisingly, the situation was calmed by the over-zealous Marine, who made it clear that he did not give a tinker's toss whether he was filmed or not; he had a job to do and if it meant smashing a rifle butt in some Goddam yellow face, he was gonna do it.

They arrived at Tan Son Nhut to find more panic. The airport had been shelled and was out of action, and the situation was aggravated by the endless cacophany of indiscriminate gunfire. A Marine sergeant greeted the driver with the news that his new orders were to drive to the dock, where helicopters would fly them out to the waiting carriers. After an agonizing three hour crawl through the city, during which Wilkinson swallowed a handful of pills 'to stop myself going ga-ga', they arrived at the dock to find total pandemonium. Panic was the by-word of the day, with Vietnamese clambering on to frail, overloaded boats and, just for good measure, a drunken lunatic with a loaded pistol who was holding up people at random.

There was not a helicopter in sight. The dock area had been regarded as completely unsuitable for the airlift, and the bus was re-directed back to the US Embassy in the centre of Saigon. By now, the atmosphere in the bus was unbearably humid and tempers were fraying. The crawl through the city was again agonizingly slow, with desperate Vietnamese clawing at the bus, almost as though they hoped to tear a hole in the steel with their bare hands, and scramble aboard to safety. Again a woman tried desperately to force open the hydraulic door, seeing the bus as the last chance of escape for herself and the tiny baby she held in her arms. This time, the door gave way a little and she was able to force her leg inside but fell backwards, dropping the baby as the bus lurched forward crushing the tiny infant beneath the back wheels.

Eventually, they reached the US Embassy and again the driver showed himself to be chronically inexperienced. He had already scraped along a fence, picking up several yards of tangled barbed wire which trailed from the back bumper, enmeshing screaming victims like flies in a web. Now, as he drove through the gates into the Embassy car park, he knocked down both pillars so the gates could not be closed, which heightened the already considerable security problem.

Eventually, one by one, they were helped over the wall into the Embassy grounds. Wilkinson has a vivid recollection of being grabbed by a young Vietnamese girl, pleading with him to take her baby with him. To the ITN men it was sobering to know that a young mother was prepared to give up her child for ever, in exchange for its freedom. He was still being held by the girl as, suddenly, he was yanked over the wall. When he landed, he found a thick tuft of hair and skin from her scalp which had wound around the button of his jacket, but the girl had not whimpered as she offered the baby hopefully towards him, as he disappeared from sight. Wilkinson's first reaction was to start filming the scene as 'official' evacuees were helped over the wall by Marines, but the Vietnamese were either pushed or kicked back. He was able to film Thomson and Nicholson being helped into the compound before he was frozen by the menacing tones of a US Marine levelling an automatic rifle at him: 'Put that camera down, or I'll blow your fucking head off,' was the warning, and Wilkinson had no doubt that he meant it.

There were two bodies floating in the Embassy swimming pool but after the experiences of the past few hours this seemed perfectly natural to the Press contingent, and nobody took much notice. Thomson, Wilkinson, and Nicholson

waited patiently as three or four helicopters took off with their
human cargo, and were finally ushered aboard themselves.
There was more drama to come, however. As the helicopter
rose, the rotor blades started to vibrate violently, and the men
had the strange sensation of flying backwards towards some
trees before the pilot succeeded in grounding the troubled
machine. By the time the fault was rectified, security at the
Embassy had virtually collapsed and dozens of desperate Vietnamese had found their way into the compound. Several of
them clung like leeches to the outside of the helicopter, prepared to risk their lives for a chance of safety, but the additional
weight merely prevented the machine from taking off and they
were savagely pushed away by the Marines. As the helicopter
lifted them above the roof of the Embassy, the newsmen
looked back for a final glimpse of the stricken city which had
featured so prominently in the world headlines for the past
eight years. The hundreds of fires dotted across the landscape
were being fanned by the breeze and soon Saigon would
appear to be a mass of smoke and flames. As they swept across
the coastline, they could see below them dozens of pathetically
frail and overloaded boats as the defeated, broken, and dis-
illusioned people of South Vietnam made a desperate bid for
freedom. They did not seem to know where they were going,
nor did they seem to care. Anywhere would do, as long as it
took them away from the threat of the tyrannical communist
rule which would soon grip their country. Some even set fire
to their boats in the forlorn hope that they would be 'rescued'
by the US Navy.

The helicopter landed on the deck of a US aircraft carrier just
long enough to allow the newsmen to scramble out, before it
took off again to collect its next consignment of evacuees. If
the men were expecting a warm greeting from the US Navy,
they were to be disappointed. Instead, they were treated more
like prisoners, as a brawny Marine sergeant snapped the order
to: 'Stand over there, and face the wall.' Meekly, they obeyed,
but were even more bewildered by the next order. 'Now drop
your trousers,' yelled the sergeant, 'and put your hands on
your knees.'

Wilkinson, Thomson and Nicholson were astonished by the
incongruity of the situation. Barely an hour ago, they were

battling furiously to assure their escape from Saigon. Now they were the 'guests' of the US Navy on a carrier, eight miles out to sea with their hands on their knees and their trousers round their ankles. It reminded Wilkinson of every naval joke he had ever heard.

Their fears were confirmed when the Marine put a condom on the forefinger of his right hand, dunked it in a jar of vaseline, and walked menacingly towards them. 'Bend forwards,' was the sharp order, and the three men braced themselves for the rare, degrading, and rather painful experience of having their rear orifices searched for drugs and explosives. Nicholson was first, and, between winces, discreetly enquired whether the sergeant was a trained medic. He was not, but tackled the task with the enthusiasm of a keen amateur before satisfying himself that both Nicholson and Wilkinson were 'clean'. Thomson bit his lip, fighting the temptation to tell the sergeant to pull his finger out, and turning to him a few seconds later smiled sweetly: 'That was nice, love – can I go around again?' he asked, to the amusement of everyone except the Marine sergeant.

By the time an officer had arrived to apologize for the mistake – 'you were in the wrong queue' – it was all over, and one of the legendary tales of the ITN Club Bar had been born.

UGANDA

&&&&&&&&&&&&&&&&&&&&&&&&&&&&&&&&&&&&&

The 'black Hitler'

In the early 1970s, Uganda was hardly ever out of the world headlines. A revolution, led by Idi Amin, a former corporal in the King's African rifles, had deposed President Milton Obote in 1971 and the new regime was making the world shudder by expelling Asians and other 'undesirables' at a few hours' notice

The coarse brutality with which Amin's troops readily carried out his outrageous demands made him one of the most despised – and dangerous – world figureheads, and his name soon became synonymous with degradation, destruction, and indiscriminate killings. His megalomania made him a natural subject for ridicule by satirists and cartoonists, and when he later promoted himself from General to Field Marshal, they were not slow to capitalize on the situation. The mockery and laughter, however, could not hide the deep-rooted mixture of outrage, disgust and fear generated by the actions of the bullying dictator.

In December 1972, Foreign Secretary Sir Alec Douglas Home described Amin's actions in Uganda as 'outrageous by any standards of civilized behaviour' after the takeover of many British and other foreign-owned businesses. Amin denounced this criticism, claiming the move had been necessary 'to transfer the economy to the Ugandan people'.

Chances of getting an ITN crew into Uganda seemed remote, and although the likelihood of getting newsworthy material dispatched back to London was even more distant, it was considered to be worth a try. It was felt that one man would be less conspicuous than three, and it was decided that reporter Keith Hatfield should fly to Entebbe alone, and clear the lines for the camera crew. If he was successful, he would contact London where cameraman Derek Seymour and sound recordist Tom Phillips were standing by and they would immediately fly out to join him.

Hatfield took an East African Airways flight to Uganda, arriving approximately ten hours later at Entebbe airport where the main runway actually disappears into the placid waters of Lake Victoria. A taxi took him the twenty miles to the Grand Hotel in Kampala, via Entebbe Road, the long, straight and now infamous scene of the many mass murders committed by Amin's troops, and the popular dumping ground for bodies killed elsewhere.

For more than twenty years the Grand Hotel had been the town's last true link with the days of colonialism. Its three storeys made it appear small by modern standards but, although its wallpaper was fading and the thick pile carpets were wearing thin, it held an atmosphere which provided an indestructible link with the past. If, in the 1950s and 60s, there was a demand for coffee mornings or tea dances in Kampala, there is no doubt that they would have been held at the Grand.

Now, Amin was in power and things had changed. Not only was Hatfield the only white man staying in the hotel, but he was treated with open contempt by the hotel staff, and kept under house arrest for long periods. Eventually he made contact with a man called Imajong at the Ministry of Information, and made an official request for an ITN news team to interview President Amin. Although Hatfields's visit had been expected by Imajong, the Ugandan was remarkably unforthcoming. 'Stay in your hotel,' he said dispassionately, 'you'll be contacted.'

Hatfield was contacted later that day, but not quite in the way he had anticipated. He stepped out of his room during the afternoon to find a Ugandan guard sitting on a radiator outside his door, with an AK-47 automatic rifle slung casually around his neck. The man did not speak, but his gestures were sufficiently menacing for Hatfield to get the general message, and he diplomatically withdrew into his room.

In spite of the frustrations of 'room arrest', Hatfield was fairly optimistic about getting the interview with Amin, and telephoned ITN in London. The two-man crew would leave for Entebbe the next morning but Hatfield, sensing that all might not be as smooth as it appeared, warned them about 'reception parties'. If they felt they were in any danger at all, ITN had insisted, they were to get back on the plane and fly down to Nairobi.

Strengthened by the thought that he would soon have Seymour and Phillips with him, Hatfield decided to have another go at leaving his room. Again, the Ugandan guard waved his AK-47 menacingly, but with the use of basic sign language, Hatfield made him understand that he was going downstairs for a drink. Walking into the bar of the Grand Hotel with the armed guard a mere pace behind him, was an experience Hatfield will never forget: 'It was packed, but as I walked through the door everybody stopped talking. It was dimly lit, and very eerie. All I could see were eyes and teeth, but I could sense the strong feeling of hostility.'

Thrown by this unreal silence, Hatfield walked slowly to the bar, and asked for a beer. The Ugandan barman ignored him. He asked again. Still nothing. 'Suddenly, I felt very frightened, but also very angry,' he said. 'Somehow, my spirits rebelled. I walked back to the door and, after every pace, I turned and scowled at them. Still nobody moved, and nobody spoke. It was a very peculiar sensation – almost as though they had been warned not to speak to me.' He returned to his room to seek comfort in his well-thumbed copy of *Punch* which he now knew by heart, and made a mental note to contact both the British High Commission and Imajong the following morning. He awoke from an uneasy sleep to find that his telephone had been cut off.

Seymour and Phillips were enjoying the flight. They had wined and dined well, and the British Caledonian stewardesses, with their pleated tartan skirts and neat white blouses, had been most attentive. Life could be worse, commented Phillips, before Seymour offered the sobering thought that, where they were heading, life would *definitely* be worse. With the co-operation of the British Caledonian captain, they adopted a contingency plan, in case things proved too hot when they landed at Entebbe. They would disembark and go through customs and immigration, hoping to avoid both arrest and interrogation. If, however, they sensed trouble, one of them would wave frantically towards the flight deck of the Boeing. This was a signal to the British Caledonian captain to delay take-off until the camera crew was safely back on board.

When they landed in Entebbe, the temperature was high and the air was humid, just as it had been when Hatfield arrived four days earlier. Confident that they would be able to join their colleague in Kampala with the minimum of hassle , Seymour and Phillips thanked the crew and, with the reminder 'if we wave, don't take off without us', walked across the tarmac towards the small immigration hall.

Their passports were snatched by a surly looking immigration official who inspected them intently before disappearing to a nearby office. When he returned a few minutes later, without the documents, Seymour's heart sank; he knew, instinctively, that the road to Kampala would be beset with problems. The pair were ushered into a corner of the hall, where a third Ugandan official joined them. 'Who were they? Where were they going? Why were they in Uganda? What was so interesting about Kampala?' they wanted to know. Seymour explained that they were ITN newsmen, but his assertion that they had permission to fly into Uganda cut little ice with the officials. They were told that their passports had been impounded and that they would be taken away for further interrogation. Suddenly, Hatfield's warning about the danger of reception parties seemed particularly pertinent. They argued that they were not prepared to be taken anywhere – they simply wanted to hire a taxi into Kampala to join their colleague who had already been given permission to interview the President. The surly official, however, was adamant: 'Not possible,' he said. 'You will come with us.'

Out of the corner of his eye, Seymour had seen a Ugandan baggage porter deposit their cases and camera gear outside the immigration hall. Under the pretext of checking that it had all been unloaded safely, he was allowed to walk outside for a few seconds. 'I waved frantically towards the Boeing, and just prayed that they could see me,' said Seymour. Then, after a perfunctory check of the baggage and other gear for the sake of appearance, he returned to support Phillips whose angry Geordie tones were getting louder and coarser as he insisted on the return of his passport.

Again, the camera crew asked to be allowed to continue to their destination in Kampala. Again, they were refused and were told that another car trip was being planned for them. For another fifteen minutes, Seymour and Phillips argued with the Ugandan officials before they were eventually handed their passports. Only then could they be seen to change their minds. 'All right,' said Seymour, 'if you don't want us here, we won't bloody well stay,' and, followed by Phillips, he marched out of the hall. The British Caledonian flight had already delayed its departure by twenty minutes as the ITN men humped their baggage and camera gear back across the tarmac towards the Boeing.

Ten minutes later, the aircraft was heading for the safety of Nairobi, and Phillips and Seymour were enjoying the miniature bottles of medicinal spirit provided by the airline to help them calm their shattered nerves and frustrations.

The stewardesses seemed even more attentive than before and, as they crossed the equator, the men drank a toast to the girls.

Hatfield was fuming. The withdrawal of telephone facilities in his room was the last straw, and he stormed past the armed guard into the Ministry of Information to demand an explanation, and to check on progress for his interview with Amin. He could hardly believe his ears when Imajong blandly told him that there was no question of an interview with the President, and that he should leave the country immediately.

Unaware that his crew had tried, unsuccessfully, to enter Uganda, Hatfield went immediately to the British High Commission where he contacted London. He was told that Seymour and Phillips had flown on to Nairobi, and he should join them there if it was getting too hot in Kampala. Realizing that he could trust nobody outside the British High Commission building, Hatfield made arrangements to catch the next flight to Nairobi, and insisted on an escort to the airport at Entebbe.

Late that afternoon, he sank back into his seat on board a VC10 bound for the cosmopolitan city of Nairobi, and reflected on the happenings of the past few days. His relief at leaving Uganda was tainted by his anger at the way he had been treated and his professional frustration at not being allowed to do his job. Soon, however, he would be able to relax at the New Stanley Hotel and reconsider the approach to Amin with Seymour and Phillips. They were good friends, and they would probably be waiting for him at the airport with a jeroboam of champagne to celebrate his freedom.

His disappointment at not being met at the airport was diluted by the certain knowledge that they would be waiting to greet him in the bar of the New Stanley Hotel, and that the bubbly was probably already on ice. Anticipation of the reunion inspired almost boundless generosity in Hatfield, and he paid his taxi driver double the normal fare before running through the reception area of the hotel into the bar. It was empty.

He eventually tracked them down at a steak house half a mile away, where they had been joined by the entire crew of the British Caledonian flight. Hatfield heard them several seconds before he actually saw them through the gloom of the dimly lit restaurant. 'They were sitting like emperors revelling in a bacchanalian orgy,' he said. 'The girls were strikingly pretty, and were hanging on to every word they said. As professional rakes and raconteurs, Seymour and Phillips were obviously very much at home.'

Seymour thrust a glass towards Hatfield and, with the explicit order 'Sit down and shut up', continued with his fisherman's tales. Totally deflated, Hatfield perched at the end of the table and watched bemused as Phillips and Seymour entertained the party with the more repeatable tales of their experiences as a front-line camera crew. 'Eventually, Seymour extended his hand toward me not in a gesture of friendship, but clutching an almost empty bottle of wine. It was obviously my job to finish it, replenish it, and pay for it,' he said.

Two days later, ITN sent a Telex message direct to Amin in Kampala seeking permission for an interview, and Hatfield had also cleared the lines with Imajong, who was now proving more flexible at the Ministry of Information. Within hours, the crew were on their way back to Entebbe, and this time their passage through immigration control was unimpeded.

Before heading to Kampala, and the uncertainty of the reception at the Grand Hotel, Hatfield decided to telephone the State House at Entebbe, the official home of the Ugandan President. Explaining he was from ITN and that the President had promised an interview, he found it remarkably easy to get through the ministerial red tape, and within seconds found he was talking to Amin himself. The dictator welcomed Hatfield and the others to his country, and confirmed that he would grant them an interview 'within a few days'. Meanwhile, he said, they should remain in Kampala and do nothing until they were contacted.

For Hatfield, checking into the Grand Hotel brought back harsh memories of hatred and house arrest, but in the company of his camera crew, there was little likelihood of a repeat performance, particularly since the visit had now been given the blessing of Amin.

In spite of the warning to keep a low profile and film nothing, the crew decided to do a fairly harmless general story of the state of the Ugandan economy, illustrated by the closing and subsequent take-over of many foreign-owned businesses. This story would also provide a suitable curtain-raiser to the Amin interview in a few days' time and they decided that the British American Tobacco Company – one of the largest and most successful businesses in Uganda – would provide a suitable location for the story. They had been shooting for only a few minutes, when they found themselves surrounded by four armed guards who had leapt, Chicago-style, from a gleaming white Peugeot, the standard transport for Amin's ill-trained personal 'heavies'.

They were told to stop filming and it was made abundantly clear that this would be their first and last warning. Back at the hotel, Seymour and Phillips discussed the problem with Hatfield. London had arranged the interview with Amin and would obviously expect co-operation in gathering other stories. The Foreign Desk would find it hard to swallow the fact that Amin's hoods had prevented them filming anything else.

In spite of the warning, the three men decided to have another try, this time using a government building as a backdrop, while Hatfield did a brief and furtive 'into-camera' piece on the situation in Kampala and the general state of the Ugandan economy. He had hardly finished the first sentence when the relative calm was again shattered by the screech of tyres as the Peugot pulled up alongside them and the President's soldiers dressed to impress with dark glasses, leapt out and made a grab for the camera. Phillips' suggestion that the guards should 'piss off and let us get on with it' was greeted with a jab up the nostril with a Russian Kalashnikov rifle and the ITN men were escorted back to the Grand Hotel. They were left in no doubt that this was their very final warning, and until further notice they should consider themselves under house arrest.

For three days, Seymour and Phillips weathered the frustrations of sunning themselves at the poolside, while Hatfield made occasional telephone calls to either the State House, the Ministry of Information, or ITN in London, hoping for confirmation of the date and time for the Amin interview. The repetitive routine was broken only once, when the three men were eating a cold chicken lunch at a poolside table. Suddenly, both Seymour and the table were covered by a vast shadow as an enormous kite – a large bird of prey – swooped low over his head, snatched his chicken and flew off. 'Seymour's face was a study,' said Hatfield. 'He watched in blank amazement as this enormous shitehawk disappeared over the hotel roof with half a chicken in its talons.' To Hatfield, it was not only the high spot of his trip to Uganda, it also marked retribution for Seymour's 'one-up-manship' a few days beforehand in Nairobi.

Eventually the crew was contacted by Imajong who told them that they should be ready to leave the hotel at 6 am the following morning, as His Excellency Idi Amin, President of Uganda, was now ready to talk to the world via Independent Television News.

State House at Entebbe is a throwback to the days of true

colonialism. Located on the edge of Lake Victoria, it is a mixture of a grand country seat and a small fortress, surrounded by colourful trees and manicured lawns. To the ITN men, it seemed an incongruous base for a dictatorial madman to inflict his will upon an ailing and strife-torn East African state.

They were greeted by an immaculately-dressed manservant who offered them coffee before showing them into the state breakfast room, where a table had been laid, complete with the presidential silver. After a full 'English breakfast' – one of the best ever – they decided to set up the interview in the garden, showing the State House in the background. Without lighting equipment, it would have been impossible to film the interview inside.

Amin had insisted on using his state chair for the interview, appearing inordinately proud of the splendid coat of arms carved on the back. He dismissed Hatfield's argument that, as long as Amin was sitting on it, the crest could not be seen: 'No matter,' said the dictator, 'it will make me feel more 'portant.'

The crew had been told that Amin was in his room, dressing for the interview. Their concentration on rigging the equipment was suddenly ruptured when the Ugandan President, dressed only in a shirt and a pair of voluminous underpants, appeared on the balcony in a state of great excitement. 'I am de black Hitler,' he screamed. 'Your BBC World Service say I am de Black Hitler,' waving his arms in a passable imitation of the Nazi leader. The previous day, Liberal leader, Jeremy Thorpe, had used the phrase in a parliamentary attack on Amin's regime. 'He seemed very proud,' recalled Phillips. 'It was obvious that he was some sort of Hitler groupie.'

Suddenly, Amin stopped screaming and frowned towards the crew. 'Not dere,' he ordered. 'We will do de talking by de pond.' Ten minutes later, the crew had re-rigged their equipment against a colourful backdrop of plants, fountains, and an ornamental pond and Amin, watched attentively by all his ministers and their families who had been summoned to the occasion, sat in his heavy state chair opposite Hatfield.

It was a dark, overcast sky, and Seymour was worried about his light readings: 'I put the light meter next to his face, and it hardly registered,' he said. 'If it had been much darker, we couldn't have filmed.' Phillips tested for voice levels and the interview was about to start when Amin held up his hand signalling to one of his ministers. 'It am de fish,' he said. 'Dey am destroyin' de train of t'ought.' Biting their lips to avoid laughing, the ITN crew watched disbelievingly for five minutes as the Foreign Minister of Uganda dabbled around in the pond with a fishing net to remove the six offending goldfish, and commit their souls to a nearby bush. 'Right,' ordered Amin, slapping his ample thigh in approval, 'now we am ready.'

The interview went well. Hatfield offered Amin the chance to respond to the recent 'Hitler' jibe, and the Ugandan dictator switched on his most winning smile, and made full use of the obvious worldwide PR potential. When Hatfield asked him about rumours of killings, the plummeting economy, and his forceful, if illogical, method of rule, he saw it as a chance to underline his loyalty to Britain: 'The Queen will understand why I have had to do this,' he said, emphasizing his point by gesticulating wildly, 'and my British brothers will also understand.'

Hatfield was happy with the way the interview was shaping; Amin, it seemed, was playing right into his hands. It now started to rain, however, and Seymour was beginning to have problems. He was operating his 16mm Auricon on a fixed tripod, and Amin was slowly disappearing out of frame. He looked up to see the state chair holding the nineteen-stone frame of the Ugandan President, slowly sinking into the damp, soggy ground by the fishpond. 'The more he waved his arms, the lower he sank,' said Seymour. 'We dared not stop him in case he ended the interview. By the time we'd finished, his knees were almost level with his ears. He looked quite ridiculous.'

After the interview, Amin seemed remarkably affable. Following the difficulties in arranging the interview, the ITN men were floored by the suggestion that they should tour Uganda by helicopter as Amin's guests 'to see how my people love me.'

The crew declined the invitation as diplomatically as possible, explaining that it was important to rush the film back to

London. This, Hatfield explained, would be to Amin's advantage, since the sooner they returned, the sooner his friends in Britain would have the chance to see him on television. Seymour and Phillips nodded in enthusiastic agreement, but were surprised by Amin's sudden change of mood. 'All right,' he said. 'Leave my country immediately.' The crew was driven straight to Entebbe airport, caught the next flight to London, and the highly topical Amin interview was shown in full on 'News at One' the following day.

Tailpiece . . .

Five years later, in 1977, Seymour was again back in Uganda, but this time the Ugandan authorities were falling over themselves to ensure that the ITN crew was afforded every facility.

Amin was celebrating the sixth anniversary of his coup with a series of unveilings, official openings and other events which would both boost his ego, and create further publicity. As a part of his anniversary gesture, he had invited a party of British cattle farmers to Uganda after obtaining their co-operation in purchasing breeding stock to improve the strain of Ugandan herds. For ITN it was an opportunity to return to Uganda and cover a British-interest livestock story, and see for themselves the extent of misery, poverty, and fear that Amin and Bob Astles, his British-born aide, had instilled in the Ugandan people.

Reporter Jon Snow had already met and interviewed Astalls in London, and with this level of contact he was the obvious candidate for the job. Seymour had already worked with Amin and, together with sound recordist Tony Piddington, he was booked on an East African Airways flight to Entebbe. Despite the booking arrangements, the flight did not bother to land at Entebbe, which may have emphasized the contempt with which Uganda was regarded by its East African neighbours, but it did little to pacify the crew. They had booked to Entebbe and their tickets clearly had 'destination Entebbe' marked on

Some of the men behind the news: Peter Sissons (above left), *whose life was saved by Cyril Page* (above right) *in Biafra; Alan Downes* (below left) *and Hugh Thomson, who have worked together in trouble-spots as far apart as Israel and Vietnam.*

When Chris Faulds (left) photographed the Saudi Arabian Airways DC-3, he didn't know he would be flying accompanied by six sticks of smouldering dynamite. Cameraman Paul Carleton (arrowed) found bullets flying during the siege of the Intercontinental Hotel in Jordan.

Alan Downes and Hugh Thomson in action during the Six-Day War; aboard the four-wheel-drive truck they bought to take them to the front line, and in a patrol boat in the Gulf of Eilat.

Vietnam: Sandy Gall and Alan Downes (above) *at Dong-Ha, where all accredited newsmen had to wear full combat gear.*
The last day in Saigon (opposite), *where cameraman Peter Wilkinson, soundman Hugh Thomson and Sandy Gall watch the evacuation, before seeking their own escape route.*

Idi Amin, President of Uganda at the time, has a pre-interview discussion with Keith Hatfield, watched attentively by Tom Phillips and Derek Seymour – who are seen below in the more relaxed surroundings of the ITN club bar.

David Nicholas (above left) *lived for two months with the worry that Mike Doyle* (above right), *Tom Phillips and Michael Nicholson were lost in the Angolan bush. Doyle's photograph of his colleagues captures their feelings at facing up to yet another day's trek – in all, they walked about 1,400 miles.*

Afghanistan, where the ITN crew disguised themselves as locals to cross the border from North Pakistan into Soviet-occupied territory. Cameraman Chris Faulds and soundman John Soldini record John Suchet's report of their clandestine assignment.

Reporter Desmond Hamill looks through the viewfinder as cameraman Sebastian Rich and sound recordist Nigel Thomson prepare to record Israeli action outside Beirut. Following their kidnap in West Beirut by an extremist Kurd faction, the same team moved to East Beirut – where they made the most of a chance meeting with Israeli defence chief Ariel Sharon.

The team that first made generally known what was happening in El Salvador: reporter *Jon Snow* (above left), soundman *Don Warren* (above right) *and* (below) cameraman *Alan Downes, seen here with Don McCullin. McCullin, a well-known war photographer, was injured when covering the fighting in spring 1982.*

Northern Ireland: closer to home, but just as dangerous. Chris Squires in the midst of an IRA attack on British troops in Londonderry, and (below) cameraman Peter Wilkinson and soundman Bob Hammond with the British troops in Belfast.

*It's not always possible to treat it as just another job – Peter Wilkinson caught
by a gas attack while filming in Belfast.*

them; why the hell were they going to Nairobi, they wanted to
know? And, more to the point, how were they going to get
back to Uganda? Students of East African politics will be
familiar with the meaningless shrug which successfully evades
most loaded questions, and the ITN men could only sit
helplessly as they crossed the equator and, eventually, landed
about 250 miles away from their destination.

Complaints at Nairobi got them nowhere as successive officials disclaimed all responsibility and seemed reluctant to
help the itinerant newsmen make alternative plans but,
eventually, after a combination of coaxing, threatening, and
bribing, they succeeded in chartering a small aircraft to fly
them and their gear to Entebbe.

For Seymour, the arrival at Entebbe brough back vivid
recollections of his last visit to Uganda, as the three men were
suddenly surrounded by Amin's special guard, dressed in
dark suits and wearing dark glasses. Their bags and equipment were seized as, protesting vehemently, they were
ushered towards a waiting Beechcraft. Once on board the aircraft, they were shown to luxurious seats and offered a drink as
they were given the official explanation. His Excellency, the
President of Uganda, was due to open a chemical plant in the
north of Uganda; the event was to be attended by representatives of many sympathetic countries and the ITN men were
expected to be there as Amin's personal camera team. 'You
have kept them waiting three hours already,' they were
told.

Seconds later, the substantial frame of the Ugandan President appeared at the doorway of the cabin. 'Good afternoon,
gentlemen,' he said. 'Welcome to Uganda,' and he shook hands
with the surprised, and somewhat perplexed, news crew.
Amin seemed unworried by the delay and was philosophical
about the snub by East African Airways. 'I owe dem much
money,' he said. 'If dey will not land in my country, why
should I pay dem?' This added a further burden to the finan-
cially troubled airline and prompted Kenya also to withdraw
its support. A few weeks later, East African Airways ceased
to operate.

By the time that Amin and the ITN crew arrived for the long-
overdue opening of the new chemical plant, foreign envoys

were getting more than a little hot under the collar. 'It was a sweltering day and Amin had insisted that they all wore suits and ties,' recalled Seymour. 'The atmosphere was a little strained, to say the least.'

For the next few days, the ITN crew was 'invited' to accompany Amin on all his ego-trips as he launched himself into an orgy of public appearances, hoping to convince international observers that he was a kindly benefactor, tragically misjudged by the outside world. For the ITN crew, it was a difficult time. They had to be at their most diplomatic, fearing that refusal to comply with 'requests' from Amin or Astles could lead to expulsion and ruin their chances of any in-depth revelation of the true situation in the beleaguered state.

It was a comic reversal of the normal camera crew situation, as the dictatorial President held doors open for them, waited for their signal before he would embark on any public speech, and went out of his way to ensure that they were fed and watered.

Relief came in the form of the OAU Conference, which Amin was due to chair in Zambia, and the crew was dispatched to Lusaka in the expectation that the potentially volatile mix of African states would provide some newsworthy footage.

On the second day of the Conference, news filtered through to Lusaka that one of Amin's personal aircraft carrying the party of British cattle farmers on a tour of North-East Uganda had been reported missing. Grabbing the chance to present himself as the great humanitarian, Amin immediately left for Entebbe where he personally supervised the search operation. The missing aircraft, which had made a forced landing after engine trouble, was discovered the following day with most of the passengers unharmed, and the ITN crew dashed back to Entebbe, landing just half an hour before the rescued Britons arrived.

Snow and the crew sent back a straight news piece on the rescue operation, reporting that it had been supervised by the Ugandan President. Amin saw it as an exercise in self-glorification and let it be known that he was delighted 'wid de rescue and wid de publicity', and sent his thanks to the crew who were staying in a British-owned hotel on the edge of Lake Victoria, not far from Amin's State House.

They were engaged in a game of Scrabble when they were approached by the proprietor. 'The President wants to know,' he said, 'if would like some special blankets tonight?' Seymour was puzzled. 'Who needs blankets in the middle of the tropics?' he asked. 'You've got to be joking.' It was delicately explained to the three men that the President was offering a selection of his human blankets 'to keep them warm at night' and he would be pleased if the men would like to take advantage of the offer of some female company. This offer posed an immediate threat to their delicately-poised relationship with Amin. To refuse was to run the risk of offending him, but to accept might involve them rather too closely with some of Amin's friends or relations – which might not augur well for their pensions. And a dose of Kampala clap was reckoned to be amongst the most dangerous of all social diseases. They declined the offer, and returned to their Scrabble.

CYPRUS

☙☙☙☙☙☙☙☙☙☙☙☙☙☙☙☙☙☙☙☙☙☙☙☙☙☙☙☙☙☙☙☙☙☙☙☙

'I'm from ITN . . .'

Not many crews can claim that running out of petrol helped them tumble across a world exclusive. Indeed, most major news triumphs are born from meticulous planning, reliable contacts, or the newsman's well-worn maxim of simply being in the right place at the right time.

It was a mixture of the lot which led to the ITN exclusive of the Turkish invasion of Cyprus when, twenty-four hours ahead of the rest of the world, they showed dramatic film of reporter Michael Nicholson standing in a field outside Kyrenia describing the scene, as heavily armed paratroopers floated silently to the ground all around him. The result was a thoroughbred world scoop which led to ITN's footage being screened by an unprecedented eighty-seven television networks across six continents, while in the UK both ITN and national newspapers were flooded with calls congratulating the team on the best war coverage ever seen on television.

It was the summer of 1974 and political observers were becoming increasingly alarmed about the safety of Cyprus as the Greek military junta, having bulldozed its way to power on the mainland, was starting to impose its will on the island. Although Cyprus had its own established constitution and parliament, it now found itself being influenced and manipulated by the Greek Generals. They had already sent in their heavies in the form of the bullying National Guard, and the situation between the Greek and Turkish Cypriots was deteriorating rapidly.

In London, it was clear to John Mahoney, Foreign Editor at
ITN, that something was about to blow up, and reporter
Michael Nicholson was dispatched to Nicosia. His brief was
simply to send back general 'mood' pieces depicting the
mounting tension in Cyprus, and when he landed an
exclusive interview with Archbishop Makarios, London regarded it as a tremendous bonus.

Immediately after an interview of this sort, it is normal for
the cameraman to pull back and take a few side-angled shots
of both the reporter and the interview subject, which can be
used for editing purposes. Makarios willingly obliged and
Italian cameraman Mario Rossetti soon had his editing shots
in the can. During this post-interview session Nicholson, anxious to get the film back to London, casually asked Makarios
about the immediate future of Cyprus. Would he be missing
anything if he flew back to London that night? What about the
Archbishop's own safety – was his life in danger? Makarios
shook his head. Nothing, he assured Nicholson, would happen in the immediate future, and he felt perfectly safe thank
you. Fortunately, as proved later, the sound was also running
as Rossetti filmed this 'mute' editing shot.

Taking Makarios's advice as fairly reliable, the crew pulled
out of Nicosia on the afternoon of Friday, 12 July, and
Nicholson was back in London in time for the interview to be
included in 'News at Ten' that night. He then had a couple of
days off, and his mind was far from the troubles of Cyprus
when the ringing of his bedside telephone woke him in the
early hours of Monday morning. John Mahoney, aware that
he had just aroused Nicholson from his slumbers, could not
resist asking: 'Are you sitting comfortably?' There was a pause
of a few seconds before he added his stinging punch-line:
'Makarios has been assassinated.'

Under dictator Nicos Sampson, the Greeks had taken Cyprus, and civil war was imminent. A few hours later, Nicholson
was on his way back to London's Heathrow airport, accompanied by cameraman Alan Downes (already widely applauded
for his film coverage of military conflict in Vietnam, the
Middle East and Biafra), and sound recordist Bob Hammond.
No aircraft were being allowed to land in Cyprus, and the crew
flew instead to Tel Aviv, regarded as the most convenient place

to bide their time until Sampson and his junta deigned to re-open the Cypriot airstrips. On arriving in Tel Aviv, the ITN men chartered a light aircraft in the hope that they might somehow be able to sneak their way into Cyprus. It was the first of many attempts before they finally reached Nicosia.

That night, the world's news bulletins led with the Greek coup in Cyprus, and the reported assassination of Makarios. ITN were able to show their exclusive editing shot, filmed only three days beforehand, of the Archbishop giving assurances that his life was not in danger. (It was later discovered that the information was false; there had indeed been an attempt on Makarios's life, but it had failed and he had escaped into the mountains.)

The television news crew flew over Cyprus twice a day for the next two days, but were still refused landing permission. Frustrated in their efforts, they decided to try their luck in Turkey and, after flying over Adana, the pilot radioed that he was short of fuel and requested immediate landing facilities. The tiny plane was allowed to land, but the pilot and crew were immediately apprehended by security forces who gave them a comprehensive grilling for several hours, believing them to be spying on Turkey's massive, but secret, military build-up.

Finally, on the Thursday morning, they were given the go-ahead to land in Cyprus and, within an hour, other journalists from the world's Press arrived en masse in a chartered aircraft. The ITN crew immediately started to film random scenes of Greek troops in Nicosia, and were pleasantly surprised that none of the other television crews appeared to be doing the same. The reason was soon clear; Nicos Sampson, the self-styled (and virtually self-appointed) leader of the Greek regime in Cyprus, was giving a Press conference and, because Downes and Co. had flown in independently, they had some-how missed the official announcement.

Sampson's awareness of the value of media exposure stemmed from his days as a freelance photographer, and it has been freely reported that he once engineered his own 'exclusive' by arranging to have a British soldier shot while he recorded the murder on film. By the time the ITN crew arrived, the Press conference was almost over. In fact, it had been little more than a shallow charade with Sampson delivering a

statement steeped in propaganda and refusing to answer any
questions. Downes remembered the occasion well:

> 'As soon as it was over, we persuaded Sampson that we
> needed a special piece for British television. He agreed to
> do it for us, together with ABC and an Israeli crew.
> Nicholson was at his best and really screwed Sampson
> into the ground. He took over the whole thing and, at the
> end, Sampson was virtually steaming with anger.'

Nicholson's dominance of the situation was later confirmed
by the news that the ABC reporter had been rapped over the
knuckles for only asking one question.

Contrary to expectations, the Turks did not retaliate
immediately and Nicholson, Downes, and Hammond spent
most of the Friday evening in the bar of their hotel, the Ledra
Palace in Nicosia, musing just how long ITN would keep them
out there. The Sampson interview had been well-received and
Downes had filmed some impressive footage of Greek heavy
armament manoeuvres. Now, however, there seemed little to
do other than wait, watch and enjoy the produce of the
local grape.

For the second time in a week, Nicholson's dreams were
shattered by the telephone in the early hours of the morning.
When Foreign Editor John Mahoney had phoned with news of
the coup five days beforehand, his brain had automatically
gone into 'drive'; now, with a heavy head as a souvenir from
the previous evening, his brain was having difficulty in engag-
ing first gear as he struggled to comprehend the staccato
urgency of colleague Peter Snow's message from London:
'The Turks are about to invade Cyprus – they'll be landing in
the north at Salamis Bay.'

Nicholson mumbled his thanks, put his head back on the
pillow, and felt his eyes drooping when, from somewhere
within the recesses of his mind, an alarm bell sounded . . . the
Turks were preparing to invade! Suddenly, he was wide awake,
but the alarm was still ringing. Surely, the message had said
that the invasion was coming from the north, but Salamis Bay
was in the south, towards an area known as the panhandle. He
guessed by inference from his voice that Snow was neither at

home, nor at the office, so Nicholson had no way of checking
his facts. Instead, he telephoned fellow ITN reporter Ray
Moloney, who was also staying in the Ledra Palace and was
operating with a UPITN crew and told him of Snow's
message.

The logical route for the Turks would be straight across the
channel to the north but, after a brief discussion, it was
decided to cover both possibilities. Moloney and his crew
would cover Salamis Bay in the south, while Nicholson and
Co. would make for Kyrenia in the north.

If suspicions were aroused by the clandestine sight of
Nicholson, Downes, and Hammond, pushing their rented
Hillman Hunter silently out of the hotel car park shortly
before five in the morning, nobody bothered to question
them. As soon as they were reasonably sure that their departure would not alert rival newsmen, they leapt in the car and
headed towards the northern outskirts of Nicosia.

By now, logic told them that the landings could not be anywhere but Kyrenia and they were confident that they had a
head start on their rivals. A few minutes later, they noticed the
first tell-tale signs of invasion fear as, one by one, families
carrying children and a few meagre possessions, started vacat-
ing their homes on the edge of Nicosia. Soon, as the handful of
families became a steady stream of evacuees heading for
shelter or the relative safety of the hills, it was obvious that ITN's
advantage had already been reduced to a very slender margin;
the seaborne invasion of Cyprus had already begun.

Soon, Nicosia was behind them and, as he steered the car
along the bumpy, uneven road north, Downes began to dwell
on the tragedy that was befalling Kyrenia. An experienced
newsman, he still had time for emotional recollections and,
remembered clearly the serenity of the Kyrenia beaches which
they had visited after the interview with Sampson less than
forty-eight hours earlier. Most of all, he remembered the irony
of meeting four young Irish tourists who had decided to
exchange the anger and outrages of their native Belfast for the
calm of tranquil Kyrenia. Soon, it would all change.

Downes' ruminations ceased abruptly as he felt the car lose
power. It spluttered, picked up again momentarily, and then
coasted to a standstill. Expletives abounded for the next few

seconds as the three men leapt out, lifted the bonnet and peered beneath it.

Between them, they had considerable mechanical experience and could see that everything still appeared to be in the right place. They switched on the ignition and tried again before one of them noticed that the petrol gauge was on zero. Fearing the worst, they dipped the tank, and found it dry. More expletives were given an airing, but this time they were more colourful, and aimed mostly in the direction of Nicholson, who had been responsible for hiring the car. Unlike most countries, it appeared that the Cypriot car hire firms did not actually provide the car with petrol unless you specifically asked for it.

They surveyed the desolate landscape disconsolately. There was nothing, nothing at all, and the only sign of life they had seen was a village, about four miles back down the road. Downes eased his frustration by kicking the car, although he later admitted he would rather have kicked Nicholson and, pausing only to collect their camera and sound gear, they headed towards the village, hoping to find some petrol, or even another car. They realized that they were certain to lose the slight advantage they had but, with luck, they could still reach Kyrenia in time to film some of the action. Their mood was not helped when, after about fifteen minutes, BBC reporter Mike Sullivan drew up alongside and enquired what was wrong. Hearing that they had simply 'broken down', he sympathized with them, adding that he was, regrettably, unable to help.

Ten minutes later, a second BBC car passed. This one, however, did not stop. Instead, reporter Keith Graves hooted with delight, and slowing down enough to ensure that they would not miss his enthusiastic V-sign, disappeared in a cloud of dust towards Kyrenia. Strangely, the ITN men were cheered by the knowledge that two BBC crews were heading towards Kyrenia only minutes apart, almost certainly unaware of each other's existence. This was obviously another battle in the second war of Cyprus: 'Both the newsmen and the military recognized that the first was between the Greeks and the Turks, and the second between rival BBC news teams, all wanting the major slice of the action for themselves,' explained Alan Downes. 'They had at least four crews out there, and at the time, we only had two. There's no doubt that we were understaffed, but we were helped considerably by the fact that the BBC reporters seemed to be working against each other.'

By the time they reached the village, time had become their biggest enemy. There was no sign of a garage and, out of pure desperation, they tried to steal a Morris Minor, but were chased off before they got it started. Then a head popped out of a first-floor window and shouted at them: 'Hello. Aren't you 'News at Ten'?' Nicholson looked up and nodded blankly. 'I was a Law student in Edinburgh,' explained the beaming face in perfect English. 'It's my favourite programme.'

The three men had just started to ask about obtaining a car when their train of thought was diverted by the distant drone of heavy aircraft. Over a dozen C-130 Turkish troop transporters were flying towards them at about five thousand feet and, as they watched, a stream of half a dozen little mushrooms dropped out of the leading aircraft. Then more . . . and more . . . 'Christ!' yelled Nicholson, 'they're landing.' The Cypriot was totally unperturbed. He had been expecting it for days, he said, and was fairly certain that he knew the exact spot where the paratroopers would land, a few miles away. Then he added, almost as an afterthought, 'Would you like a lift?'

Barely able to believe that such good fortune could be born out of disaster, the three men climbed into the Cypriot's bright green Beetle and, obeying Downes' simple instruction to 'Follow those parachutes', the driver headed towards the dropping zone. Their spirits soared again, boosted by the knowledge that not only would they be first to film the landing, but also that the aircraft were coming in behind rival crews heading for Kyrenia, and were unlikely to be spotted.

Downes later summed up their reaction to this unprecedented slice of luck: 'It was one of total incredulity which gave way to complete euphoria,' he said, adding the tag: 'Ideally, they could have been a bit closer, but you can't have everything.' They had almost reached the dropping zone when the driver's legal training clearly pricked his conscience and, to the alarm of the crew, he pulled into the forecourt of a local police station. 'I must check if it is in order to proceed,' he said meticulously, preparing himself for a confrontation with the duty sergeant.

Realizing they could not afford to be around if the answer was negative, the crew took their chance; they grabbed their gear and ran. Within minutes, they were approaching the field where a couple of dozen armed Turkish soldiers were grappling with their parachute release buttons, while hundreds more drifted towards the earth.

Instinctively, Downes and Hammond started to film and record the historic scene as the three men walked slowly towards the invaders. Nicholson was, at first, unaware that Downes' camera was running as he approached the nearest Turkish soldier and, shaking his hand, came out with the immortal line which was to become a catch-phrase back at the ITN bar: 'Good morning, I'm Michael Nicholson from ITN. Welcome to Cyprus.'

Nicholson, now realizing that Downes was filming individuals in close-up, advised him to stop, fearing that the invaders might mistake the shoulder-held 16mm CP16 camera for some kind of weapon. Downes, however, could not be discouraged. He knew that any kind of long lens could look like a weapon, and recalled the tale of the *Paris Match* photographer who was blown apart by a tank shell in Hungary, in 1956, while trying to take action close-ups. This, however, was too good to miss and nothing was going to stop him shooting as much footage as possible.

By now, half a dozen Turkish Cypriot children from neighbouring farm cottages, had run into the field and, totally oblivious of any danger, started to offer water to their protectors. Nicholson was now moving freely among the invading force, trying to make it as clear as possible that they were a friendly news team. Downes recalled it with a degree of humour:

> 'They were completely bemused by this incredible figure who kept rushing up to them, shaking them by the hand, and saying "Welcome to Cyprus". It was a very clever move because, although the Turks were understandably a bit on edge, it caused no alarm and gave me more time to film them.'

Eventually, they were approached by a Turkish Major who ordered them to stop filming, and insisted on inspecting their 'official papers'. Both Downes and Hammond handed over their Scotland Yard press passes and, after a cursory inspection, the officer stuck them in his pocket and marched away to concentrate on the invasion of Cyprus. 'We never saw them again,' said Downes. 'He's probably got them to this day, and he's quite welcome to them.'

Taking care to keep out of sight of the Turkish Major, the crew continued filming for several more minutes before the landing area came under attack from distant Greek field artillery. The three men flung themselves into a ditch and stayed down during the twenty-minute bombardment; but the Greeks' aim and range lacked accuracy and, although they all described it as 'a bit of a hairy experience', nothing landed close enough to endanger their lives.

By the time they emerged from their ditch, there was not a Turkish soldier in sight and the field was deserted. 'It wasn't easy to lose an entire battalion of paratroopers in a field,' said Downes, 'but we managed it. We had no idea which way they went and we never saw them again.'

Still enthusing about the slice of luck which had given them such invaluable and exclusive footage, they walked through the late morning heat to Gonyeli, a distant village where a handful of Turks were converting a small cottage hospital into a casualty station. They shot a few seconds of film before they were again alerted by the familiar sound of heavy Greek artillery. Seconds later, shells started exploding in and around the village and the three sprinted for the safety of a nearby kebab house.

The Greeks' aim had improved considerably since the shelling of the landing area earlier that morning, and the crew dived for the only cover they could find, lying face-down among the ashes beneath a large three-sided barbeque stove. Ten minutes later, the bombardment ceased as suddenly as it had begun, and the three men emerged from their cover, looking like a trio of Jolson impressionists waiting to audition.

They were still wiping off their 'make up' a few minutes later, when the Cypriot proprietor appeared from somewhere within the bowels of the kebab house, and welcomed them warmly in excellent English: Were they familiar with Neasden, he wanted to know. He had heard it was a splendid place and seemed inordinately proud of his son, who ran the town's Wimpy Bar.

Any further thoughts on North London hamburger houses were brought to a premature halt by the unmistakable sound of heavy helicopters approaching. They rushed outside and saw about eight Turkish troop carriers preparing to land in a field less than half a mile away. Again, they could hardly believe their luck; if filming the paratroop landings had been the golden prize, it now seemed that they had taken the silver too!

Downes filmed the entire landing from the steps of the kebab house. It was a skilful operation, with each helicopter taking only seconds to land, disgorge its human cargo, and take off again. Then, only minutes after the last helicopter had lifted itself above the tiny village to return north, the Greeks began their bombardment of the landing area. 'I couldn't believe it,' said Downes. 'It was as though they had held their fire until the helicopters had left, and then started to blast seven tons of you-know-what out of it.'

The shelling around the village intensified and those without proper shelter sought refuge in the small makeshift hospital. The three men decided that they would probably stand a better chance by remaining in the kebab house until the shelling subsided, frequently diving for cover among the ashes of the enormous barbeque grill. More than once, as the ground shuddered beneath them, they were convinced that the tiny restaurant had been hit.

It was mid afternoon when, with little chance of securing any transport, the three started the long walk back towards Nicosia. The searing heat combined with the indiscriminate shelling to make it a particularly uncomfortable journey. To keep the noise to a minimum, they walked silently in their bare feet, seeking cover in the ditch every time that a distant, shallow-sounding 'thud' signalled the dispatch of another twenty-five-pound shell. It was a long, tiring walk and the ITN men had almost reached the 'green line' demarcation area, when they were offered a lift back to the Ledra Palace by a party of rival journalists, travelling in the comparative luxury of a battered jeep. They were grateful for the ride, although they parried the casual, but loaded, questions about where they had been and what they had filmed. 'Got anything?' they would be asked, and the three would intimate with a grunt, a grimace, or a shrug, that things had not really been too interesting.

They arrived in Nicosia early in the evening to find the Ledra Palace still open, but in total darkness. The top floor had been severely damaged by a rocket and holiday-makers – many of them British – were huddled together, cursing their luck as their sunshine holiday island slid deeper and deeper into the grip of civil war. The Greek waiters, smartly clad in white shirts and bow ties the night before, now wore olive green uniforms and displayed a reborn sense of urgency as they tore the wrapping from brand-new cases of arms and tried, mostly unsuccessfully, to assemble mortars and light machine guns, and to load rifle magazines.

The previous night, a second ITN crew had arrived at the hotel with reporter Christopher Wain, after filming activity in a small Turkish-Cypriot village. The first they knew about the invasion was around six o'clock in the morning, when they were awakened by firing. The camera crew, John Collings and soundman Tony Piddington, rushed to the roof of the hotel to film the action as waves of Turkish aircraft came over and were later able to shoot footage of the Greeks as they prepared to defend the hotel. Without leaving the confines of the Ledra Palace, they had successfully recorded military action on both sides of the green line, and filmed distraught, terrified holiday-makers diving for cover in the hotel lounge, as bullets smashed through the windows to embed themselves deep in the walls. It was all good stuff, and cameraman John Collings was justifiably pleased with it.

They were discussing the best way of getting it back to Wells Street, when Nicholson, Downes, and Hammond arrived at the hotel with news of their catch. Suddenly, the 'Useless if Delayed' message, which accompanies all ITN film, took on a whole new meaning. Now it was obvious that getting the film back to London was top priority.

The opportunity presented itself when news filtered through that the United Nations had negotiated a thirty-minute cease-fire starting at nine the following morning to allow holiday-makers to escape from the Nicosia war zone. This, they thought, might just allow them the chance to get their film and stories out to the British sovereign airbase at Akrotiri, on the far side of Limassol, in the hope that it would be flown back to the UK fairly swiftly.

It was a long shot, but it was worth a try, and if anyone could talk the RAF into helping, it would be the ITN 'fixer', Alex Valentine. Valentine was a colourful Italian-Scot with a pedigree which included reporting stints for both Reuter and ITN, and had also met with considerable success as a producer of 'World in Action'. What he did not know about Cyprus was not worth knowing and, as an additional plus, he seemed to have the Akrotiri base in the palm of his hand.

It was decided that the reporters should waste no time in recording their stories and that Collings, Piddington, and Wain would then attempt to burst out of Nicosia in their rented Morris Marina Estate, and head for the Akrotiri base sixty miles away. It was unlikely, however, that they would find the luxury of petrol en route, so it was imperative that they start their journey with a full tank. After raiding the hotel kitchen for sizeable tin cans, and tearing a piece of rubber piping from the plumbing system, Downes and Hammond emerged with some makeshift syphoning equipment and proceeded to steal four or five gallons from a friendly-looking blue Ford Cortina.

With a tankful of petrol, a white sheet tied to the roof, and a couple of Union Jacks fluttering from the front and back to offer clues of their neutrality and nationality, if not their identity, their escape chariot was as ready as it was ever likely to be. Several canisters of film and the recorded stories from Nicholson and Wain were packaged inside two pillowcases, courtesy of the Ledra Palace, and Collings sat back to wait for the blast on the whistle which was to signal the start of the cease-fire. He felt not unlike a Wells Fargo driver enjoying a last finger of rye before being given thirty seconds' start on a mob of marauding Apaches.

At 9 am exactly, a high-pitched blast on a United Nations whistle (cease-fires, commencing, for the use of) signalled a fleeting end to hostilities and the start of a carefully co-ordinated team effort which was to result in one of the most remarkable 'world exclusives' in the history of television news.

As Collings, Piddington and Wain moved unobtrusively towards the car park, they sensed that the same idea was dawning on other news teams but, by the time their rivals had started to think about a source of petrol, Collings and the ITN men were already on their way. They had travelled less than three hundred yards before they were stopped by the Cypriot police. Waving his Press pass, Wain explained that they were merely going round the block to visit colleagues in the nearby Hilton Hotel, and they were waved through.

Later, they were stopped at a roadblock and were on the thin end of a heated argument with 'irregular' Greek soldiers, when the cavalry appeared in the form of the Grenadier guards, who were in Cyprus as a part of the UN Force. They were cheerily waved through and advised to take the most direct road to Akrotiri, as it was occupied by Turks whose military superiority at the time allowed them to be more accommodating to newsmen. Twenty minutes later, an NBC team, also heading for Akrotiri, were stopped at the same checkpoint. This time, no cavalry appeared, and they were turned back at gunpoint.

Nearly two-and-a-half hours after leaving Nicosia, the ITN Marina Estate coasted to a halt by the sentry gate at the airbase. Although it was common for news teams to send film back to London via the RAF, the duty guard still insisted on inspecting their ID papers and confirming their names with the base public relations officer.

The guard's doubts were given some weight by the fact that their personal luggage had been stolen on their arrival in Cyprus, and they had not shaved or changed their clothes for three days. They had not eaten for twenty-four hours either, and whatever dubious thoughts lay behind the sentry's offering of a bunch of grapes, it was well received. The grapes tasted even sweeter when their car was waved through the gate with orders to report to the CO's office, where they explained the urgency of the situation to a sympathetic officer. 'I suppose you want us to act as postman for you?' he asked.

The Royal Air Force has long held a reputation for offering practical assistance to the bona fide media, whether it be ITN, the BBC, or even a foreign news organization. There were obviously no exclusive deals to be done, but when the ITN men heard that a Hercules was due to leave Akrotiri for the UK late that afternoon, they had every reason to feel confident that they would still have the edge on the opposition.

After a couple of brief telephone conversations, during which the sympathetic officer emitted a lengthy series of grunts, punctuated only by the occasional 'Uh-huh', he turned to them apologetically. 'Sorry,' he said, 'got it wrong. There's a VC10 leaving for Brize Norton in twenty minutes.' He paused, adding almost as an afterthought: 'Any good to you?'

Barely able to believe their ears, the news team nodded, confirming that yes, that would be rather convenient, thank you very much, and within half an hour a pair of Ledra Palace pillowcases, containing exclusive film of the Turkish invasion of Cyprus the previous day, were winging their way to England by courtesy of the Royal Air Force.

From the base at Akrotiri, Wain was able to contact ITN via the Ministry of Defence, and tell them that the precious package was on its way to Brize Norton, and was scheduled to arrive at about 7.30 pm, London time. Normally, the arrival of unprocessed, unedited news film, somewhere in the heart of the Oxfordshire countryside on a Sunday, just two-and-a-half hours before the ten o'clock bulletin goes on the air, would earn an automatic 'tomorrow' tag. This situation, however, was far from normal, and a chartered helicopter was dispatched to Brize Norton to fly the film to Battersea where it would be met by two dispatch riders (in case one broke down), and rushed to the ITN headquarters at Wells Street.

The package arrived at nine o'clock and was in the processing room within seconds. Twenty minutes later, two senior editors and the duty producer were piecing together the historic film sequences and, with only minutes to go before the ten o'clock bulletin, the report was ready for transmission.

In an extended bulletin, devoted entirely to Cyprus, ITN viewers witnessed one of the most sensational exclusive war stories ever to be shown on television. Other networks managed to get their material through twenty-four hours later, but most of it was shot from long distance, and lacked both the impact and quality of the ITN coverage. It is a fact that many of the television companies with crews in Cyprus were among the eighty-seven networks to purchase the ITN report. In addition to reporter Nicholson, both Downes and Hammond received wide acclaim for their work.

The morning after the bulletin was screened in the UK, a representative of the United Nations in Cyprus visited the Ledra Palace, to advise the total evacuation of the hotel. The Turks, claiming that Greek forces were using it as a firing base had given the UN fifteen minutes' notice to evacuate all civilians before they bombed the building.

The Press contingent needed no second bidding, and their departure from the car park bore the mark of the classic start at Le Mans. All, that is, except the correspondent of one Fleet Street daily, who could not understand why his blue Ford Cortina would not start. Downes offered him a lift.

Nicholson remained in Cyprus for a couple more days, before flying to Athens to pursue the Greek angle. Both Downes and Collings remained for a further week, filming the fighting, and the mass evacuation of British holiday-makers and ex-patriots who were ferried home from Akrotiri.

Downes and Ray Moloney also went back to Gonyeli to update their coverage of the tiny hospital and, after shooting a few seconds of film, took a break at the kebab house. They were halfway through their coffee when the proud father of Neasden's Wimpy king excused himself. He had something to show them, he said, and would be back in a few seconds.

When he re-appeared a few moments later, he was struggling to maintain his grip on an unexploded twenty-five-pound shell which had burst throught the back wall and lodged itself behind the kitchen on the very day that Downes and the others had sheltered from the attack. Downes, this time accompanied by Moloney, hit the familiar patch of floor behind the grill and again experienced the familiar taste of burnt charcoal and ash.

Seconds from death

By early August, the Cyprus issue had come off the boil. The UN had negotiated an uneasy peace between the Greeks and the Turks but the media, sensing that it would not last, continued their presence on the island.

Cameramen Downes and Collings and their crews were now back in London and ITN was wondering how long they could afford to keep their replacement teams languishing in the comfort of the Nicosia Hilton. True, they had sent back some refugee stories between the swimming and sunbathing sessions, but their watching brief was beginning to wear a bit thin.

Peter Wilkinson was one of the replacement cameramen and had flown into Nicosia with soundman Tom Phillips and reporter Keith Hatfield. Their first duty call had been to the Ledra Palace Hotel which, although severely damaged, was now the official headquarters of the United Nations force. By now the Canadians were featuring strongly in the UN presence, and the crew found a forceful contact in the Canadian liaison officer known generally as 'Major Chickenshit'. 'It was his favourite phrase,' explained Hatfield. 'If we dared suggest that the Turks might be preparing for an invasion, he would snap "Chickenshit". Even if we commented that it was a bloody hot day, his reaction would be the same – "Chickenshit".'

They persevered and Major Chickenshit eventually became a trusted source of information, although he was noticeably more forthcoming after a session at the bar where he would sting the ITN men for 'a double B and B' – not the recognized Benedictine and brandy, but bourbon and bourbon. He was drinking quadruple measures. The major's capacity for bourbon was equalled only by his perception of the situation in Cyprus, which was again beginning to smoulder. At a confidential meeting, he told Hatfield that the truce was not expected to last more than another two days, and the UN had three squadrons of Phantoms on stand-by at Akrotiri, ready to repel a Turkish attack on Nicosia international airport. As though to justify this confidence, Chickenshit added that the airport was already surrounded by his own Canadian troops armed with swingfire anti-tank missiles.

The second ITN crew comprising cameraman Derek Seymour, sound recordist John Soldini, and reporter Martyn Lewis were summoned to discuss a plan of action. In the event of an attack by the Turks, they would cover the airport activity while Hatfield, Wilkinson, and Phillips would take the road to Famagusta, another prime target for the Turks.

They did not doubt that Chickenshit's bourbon-soaked crystal ball was working, or even that the next few days would see them all back in the front line, filming the second phase of the Cyprus war. All they could do was wait for the first bang, and continue sending back stories illustrating the fear and tension which had gripped the small island.

In war zones, pressmen will grab any excuse for a party. When they heard that Seymour and BBC sound recordist Ted Stoddard were planning a joint party to celebrate their birthdays, it became an eagerly awaited event, shining like a beacon in the social calendar. Tragically, it was a date which Stoddard did not live to see. He was killed when he stepped on an anti-personnel mine after the Greeks had booby-trapped a section of a major road to stem the imminent Turkish advance.

The effect it had on his colleagues at the BBC and on his compatriots working for rival organizations, was devastating. Alan Downes, like many ITN cameramen and sound recordists, knew him well: 'It was the first fatality in our immediate circle,' he said quietly. 'It really got to us. It was as though we'd all been leading a charmed life, and this broke the spell. As newsmen, we see death all the time – we are hardened to the sight of dead troops because we never knew them, and there is no reality about it. When Ted died, we realized that it could have been any one of us. We weren't immune after all.'

Nothing travels as fast as bad news in trouble-spots, and rumours that a British television news team recordist had been killed, reached both ITN crews, then engaged on separate assignments. Seymour, Soldini, and Lewis were about to clinch their first interview with the Commander of the Turkish land forces when an adjutant broke the bad news. Fearing that the victims were Peter Wilkinson and his team, they excused themselves immediately and sped back to the Hilton Hotel in Nicosia. Likewise, Phillips, Hatfield, and Wilkinson had heard the story and they, too, dropped everything and rushed back to the hotel for news of their colleagues. 'We got there at about the same time, and when I saw Tom Phillips we just fell into each other's arms, said Seymour. 'I was never more pleased to see the old sod in my life.'

The next two days were quiet and emotional. Stoddard's death had shown just how vulnerable they all were and safety, insurance, and dependants suddenly became hypersensitive issues. The sagging spirits were not helped by the uncertainty of the political situation. Though they were certain that the Turks would launch a major second offensive, nobody knew when or how it would come. What they needed, they decided, was a good morale booster, and the party to celebrate the Seymour and Stoddard birthdays went ahead almost as planned.

By now, the Hilton was being used as emergency accommodation for refugees as well as the Press contingent. Rooms were being shared but, because of the special eating arrangements made for the homeless, the restaurant was virtually deserted. Most of the waiters had been called up by the Greek army, while others had fled in fear, leaving behind them a skeleton staff to cater for the handful of people who still wanted the Hilton service.

Seymour's party included rival BBC crews and a dozen other newsmen and throughout the meal the cheap Cyprus wine flowed freely. They had the restaurant to themselves apart from a party of United Nations officers seated a discreet distance away.

The resident group who, in happier times, serenaded the diners in the plush restaurant, had joined in the exodus the night before, leaving their instruments to the mercy of anyone who fancied a go. Led by would-be percussionist Keith Hatfield, and Martyn Lewis at the keyboard, assorted newsmen tried to get a recognizable note out of anything they could find as they launched Seymour into his thirty-fifth year in the time honoured manner.

The United Nations foursome, perhaps preferring the impending hostilities to the combined talents of the television and Fleet Street newsmen, beat a retreat after the third rendering of the song, presenting the ensemble with an opportunity to broaden its repertoire. Brigadier F.R. Henn, Commander of the UN forces in Cyprus, left the restaurant with his entourage to the enthusiastic, if somewhat irreverent, strains of 'Kiss Me Goodnight, Sergeant Major'.

Three days later, Peter Wilkinson was cursing the surfeit of food and cheap Cypriot wine as he suffered the uncomfortable experience of the local equivalent of 'Delhi belly'. He was on the throne promising himself nothing stronger than Seven-Up for the rest of his stay, when a deafening explosion rocked the hotel.

The Turks had commenced their second invasion of Cyprus and had unleashed a salvo on a Greek National Guard base just a few hundred yards from the hotel. The first shell had missed and hit the upper floor of the Hilton. Chickenshit and his crystal ball had been right – peace talks had broken down a few hours before, and the explosion signalled the second wave of hostilities.

Wilkinson swiftly forgot his discomfort as he grabbed his camera and, summoning Phillips and Hatfield on the way, rushed into the street to film the rest of the action. Later that morning they headed north towards the Turkish strongholds. Before they had covered a mile, they were confronted by a Swedish soldier covered in blood from head to toe. He flagged them down, explaining he was one of the UN forces who had just come under attack from the Turks. The army personnel carrier in which they had been travelling had suffered a direct hit, and many of his colleagues had either been blown apart, or burned to death. He had stopped the crew to advise them to go no further if they valued their lives and, when Wilkinson explained they were a television news team on their way to film the action, the Swede could only shake his head in disbelief. 'Crazy,' he whispered, as the tears mingled with the blood on his face. 'Bloody crazy.'

The team continued north, eventually reaching the orange groves where heavy Turkish artillery was trained on Nicosia. The journey had been particularly uncomfortable and the memory of the charred bodies of the UN soldiers at the roadside was to haunt them for months. However, they already had some good Greek action in the can, and were now able to complement this with some dramatic footage as the Turks escalated their offensive.

By now, they had arranged a regular charter flight from Akrotiri to Tel Aviv, where their film was beamed by satellite to London. The News Desk was delighted with the reports – particularly since the BBC coverage of the second Turkish invasion had not been so comprehensive – and Wilkinson's film commanded a large slice of 'News at Ten' that night.

The following afternoon, they decided to put out feelers in the direction of Famagusta, where the Turkish quarter was still under seige from the Greeks. They had reached the tiny hamlet of Mia Milia on the outskirts of Nicosia, when the sight of a small house, strategically situated on a corner warned them to stop. Experience told them that it would be ideal cover for snipers and, although their grey Mazda was festooned with Union Jacks and white flags of neutrality, they decided to play safe.

Hatfield got out of the car, raised his hands and walked to the house. Through an open door, he shouted 'Bassim, Bassim,' (Turkish for 'Press') into the darkness, and seconds later was staring down the muzzle of a .45mm Thomson machine gun. In times of crisis, your average pressman can be relied upon to pull a master stroke, and Hatfield is no exception. He quickly produced the international symbol of friendship, a packet of two hundred Rothmans, and with an avuncular smile, the Turk casually swung the Thomson over his shoulder. Hatfield then produced a map and pointed to the Famagusta road, indicating that this was their chosen route. The Turk shook his head fiercely, but relented at the sight of another two hundred king-sized filter-tips. Clearly believing that anyone was entitled to risk their lives for four hundred cigarettes, he shrugged and sauntered back into the darkness.

The crew had already filmed action in Nicosia that morning and were anxious not to delay its dispatch longer than necessary. They decided to return to their hotel, prepare their story and dispatch it to Akrotiri with all haste. They would take the road to Famagusta the following day when another couple of packets of cigarettes might well improve their relationship with the Turk.

The following morning saw another four hundred Rothmans change hands and, for all the Turkish soldier cared, the three ITN men could have had the freedom of Cyprus. It was a day that none of them will forget, mingling the triumph of

exclusive film with the horror of being the intended victims of
a group of marauding Turkish murderers.

They had travelled about three miles along the forbidden
Famagusta road when they came across a huge stationary
Turkish convoy. Crouching in an adjacent field were hundreds of armed infantrymen, while APCs and tanks were
being ordered into position by the commander circling above
in a helicopter. They had stumbled across the Turkish front
line preparing to take Famagusta.

A young major on the ground made a cursory attempt to
stop them filming but was far too pre-occupied with military
manoeuvres to be able to enforce his decision. Wilkinson and
Phillips had a field day and, by the time the convoy was ready
to move, there is little doubt that Nicos Sampson would have
paid handsomely for a glimpse of the film.

There was a brief period when they came under fire from a
mortar position on a hill just outside Famagusta, but the
threat was quickly erased by machine gun fire from Turkish
APCs. Again Wilkinson and Phillips were in the thick of the
action – a point not lost on Hatfield: 'They were quite fearless
and shot some superb film. People tend to forget that the
crews have to risk their lives while it's so easy for a reporter like
me to hide behind a tank.'

The crew accompanied the triumphant Turks into
Famagusta, filming emotional scenes of the liberated Cypriots
and the ensuing celebrations before piling all their equipment
back into the Mazda and heading for Episcopie, a small town
about twenty minutes away where they would be able to
dispatch the film and Hatfield's hastily written report to
Akrotiri.

About two miles outside Famagusta, they came upon a
small village which appeared to be deserted. As they rounded
a bend they surprised three young Turkish soldiers holding
three men at gunpoint. Two were elderly Cypriots, the third
was Max Hastings of the London *Evening Standard*. Hatfield
remembered the scene vividly: 'They were in full battledress
and armed with M-16 rifles. They were only young but they
had madness in their eyes and their leader seemed to be
foaming at the mouth.'

Stripped of their money and their valuables, the men were

about to be shot, when Wilkinson and Co. arrived on the scene. Hastings at first thought that the arrival of the crew had saved his life; seconds later, it was clear that this was to be only a temporary respite. To the young Turks, the arrival of the ITN team meant only two things – more money to take, and more bodies to leave.

As the three newsmen were stripped of their wallets and watches at gunpoint, Wilkinson noticed that their bayonets were black with dried blood. If this was to be the end, he thought, he would prefer a bullet.

Hatfield got out of the car slowly, and produced his Turkish press pass thinking that it might help to cool the situation. The leader spat in his face before studying the document upside down. Another of the young thugs grabbed Wilkinson's Pentax camera and, tearing off the lens cap, held it the wrong way with the lens to his eye. By now, what little hope remained of a peaceful solution had vanished, and it was made very clear that they were at the mercy of a bunch of illiterate, marauding peasants, who had broken away from the main Turkish force, and were engaged in an orgy of looting, robbery, and murder.

Hatfield was pushed back into the car with Wilkinson and Phillips accompanied by one of the old Cypriot men and an armed deserter. Hastings was ushered back into his own car, with the second old man and a guard and, with the armed leader gesturing to them to follow him, they moved forward at funeral pace. 'Their leader was a real bastard,' recalled Wilkinson. 'It was obvious that he was looking for somewhere to kill us all, and he waved us into a small alley with empty garages and storehouses.'

Hastings' car was in front and, as Wilkinson watched him bounce down the eighteen-inch drop from the roadway into the alley, it was obvious that, once in, there would be no way out. Wilkinson decided to play for time by pulling out the choke to flood the carburettor. As the engine spluttered to a stop, he turned to Phillips in the back of the car. 'Hit him as hard as you can,' he said, 'and we'll make a run for it.' To Hatfield and Phillips, however, the odds didn't seem too attractive. The young leader seemed a bit trigger-happy and would probably gun them down before they covered five yards so, with Wilkinson out-voted two to one, the plan was aborted.

Their wisdom proved prudent; seeing that the car had stopped, the young leader ran up to Wilkinson and, pointing his loaded rifle at his temple, ordered him to start the car. Hatfield, sensing that the illiterate Turk was not bluffing, suggested that they ought to go along with the request and, after a few seconds, the engine kicked itself into life. The car lurched forward down the eighteeen-inch drop and, with Wilkinson leaning on the horn in the vain hope of attracting somebody's attention, the crew slowly followed Max Hastings to almost certain execution.

The leader was ushering the two cars through into a large deserted garage, when Wilkinson looked to his left and saw a Turkish tank draw to a standstill near the road they had just turned off. Still hooting frantically, he waved his arms and saw the machine gun in the turret swing towards them. Within seconds, a Turkish tank commander, with an armed guard, was striding down the alley to investigate.

Terrified by the sight of authority, the young captors surrendered immediately, tying white handkerchiefs to their bloodstained bayonets. They were stripped and handcuffed, and their bounty laid out on the cobblestones. Apart from the money and valuables taken from Hastings, the old men, and the ITN crew there were a dozen watches, assorted wallets and a thick wad of bloodstained notes with a bullet hole through the middle. The tank commander spoke good English and apologized to the crew, assuring them that the young deserters would be dealt with in the proper manner. Wilkinson restrained himself as the young leader was taken away at gunpoint; but even now, many years later, he regrets not having done something to show his feelings. 'I wanted to kick him right in the balls,' he said, 'just to let him know how much we'd enjoyed his company for the last couple of hours.'

They dispatched their film to Akrotiri after being given an armed guard to Episcopie, and then drove back to the Nicosia Hilton in relative silence. Being only seconds away from death tends to stem the natural flow of conversation, and the three men kept their emotions very much to themselves until they reached their hotel. Sitting in the corner of the lounge,

Wilkinson reached for his diary. Against Tuesday, 15 August 1974, he wrote the simple sentiment:'It's good to be alive,' before settling at the bar to help Phillips demolish a litre bottle of Drambuie with ice.

ANGOLA

꙰꙰꙰꙰꙰꙰꙰꙰꙰꙰꙰꙰꙰꙰꙰꙰꙰꙰꙰꙰꙰꙰꙰꙰꙰꙰꙰꙰꙰꙰꙰꙰꙰꙰꙰

Missing – believed lost

The risks of the job are an accepted way of life among camera crews. While it is a fact that ITN has not lost a man in action since its formation in 1955, luck as well as good planning has played its part in maintaining this record. Many of the crews have been only feet away while colleagues from other television companies, newspapers, and magazines have fallen victim to a sniper's bullet, a bomb, a landmine, or even an assassination squad.

For years, reporter Peter Sissons carried the dubious distinction of being ITN's only near miss after being shot through both legs while covering the Biafran war. However, in 1978 he was upstaged in spectacular fashion by a three-man news team who were feared dead by even their most optimistic colleagues after being lost in the Angolan jungle for four months, during which they walked nearly 1,400 miles while hunted by armed Cuban pursuers.

Michael Nicholson, who had four years earlier scooped the world with his eye-witness account of the Turkish paratroopers landing in Cyprus, and four years later would earn high praise for his reporting of the Falklands affair, was serving a four-year spell as ITN's resident reporter in Johannesburg. He had been joined by former sound man Tom Phillips, now a cameraman, and his sound recordist Mike Doyle, who had both undertaken a six-month stint in South Africa. Their brief, which originated from London-based senior Foreign Editor Mike Morris, appeared quite straightforward: they were to fly from Johannesburg to southern Angola to interview Dr Jonas Savimbi, leader of the Unita Nationalist forces fighting a long, drawn-out campaign against the communist-backed Angolan government. According to the assignment desk, the job would take about a fortnight – three weeks at the most – and the standard briefing was followed by assurances that their main problem would be nothing more serious than the discomfort and irritation caused by an ever-present pestilence of flies.

The Angolan bush was not new to Nicholson. He had interviewed Savimbi three years earlier when, together with cameraman Alan Downes and soundman Jon Hunt, they had tumbled across a world scoop which was to have an immediate and lasting effect upon the balance of the political forces within Angola over the next few years.

Like many emergent African nations, Angola found itself a victim of the constantly changing political pattern of the early 1970s. The painful experiences of both Namibia and Rhodesia in their struggles for independence, were soon to be matched in the world headlines by news from Angola, Zaire, and Zambia, where the political climate was also undergoing change. Formerly known as Portuguese West Africa, Angola had adopted its new identity in the early 1950s. Still under the influence of the Lisbon government, things remained relatively stable there until 1975 when, having undergone a bloodless revolution, the Portuguese withdrew totally, leaving the fledgling independent state in the hands of Agostinho Neto, leader of the Marxist MPLA government which drew its abbreviated title from the Popular Movement for the Liberation of Angola.

The main opposition to Neto's regime came from Unita – a well-organized guerilla army led by Jonas Savimbi, a well-educated Svengali-like Nationalist who felt very strongly that Neto's communist-backed government was not good for, nor wanted by, the majority of the Angolan people. Savimbi had the sympathy of the West, but not much else, although it was rumoured that both Zambia and South Africa were providing limited practical assistance with food and fuel. The Neto government was also facing opposition from the FNLA troops headed by Holden Roberto. The FNLA was based in neighbouring Zaire, where Roberto had strong family connections –

President Mobutu was his brother-in-law.

The introduction for this first interview with Savimbi in 1975 had been effected by Evan Davies, brother of 'Maigret' star Rupert Davies. Evan had enjoyed a colourful career, which included a spell as Winston Churchill's bodyguard and had, more recently, seen him head an anti-terrorist operation in Aden. Now, he was representing a financial syndicate which was preparing to back Savimbi in the event of a Unita victory.

This offer of financial backing for the rebels was to be ITN's main story from Angola, and Nicholson, Downes and Hunt were to pick up what other pieces of local 'colour' they could find. Never, in their wildest dreams, could they have imagined the importance of the world exclusive which was just a few days away when, together with Evan Davies, they flew into Angola via Lusaka on that bright October morning in 1975. After being met by Unita officials, they were guided discreetly past customs and immigration officials to a small, private aircraft lent to Unita by Lonrho. An hour later they landed at Huambo, Savimbi's temporary headquarters, but were disappointed to discover that the Unita leader would not be joining them for another twenty-four hours.

The interview was purely routine to the crew, but when they asked to film the Unita rebels in action, Savimbi refused adamantly and not even the combined persuasive efforts of Nicholson, Downes, and Hunt would change his mind. Eventually, however, he agreed that the crew should be allowed to film some recently captured towns and villages on the southwest coast. This compromise would prove to be one of the worst decisions that Savimbi would ever make.

The crew, together with a handful of pro-Unita journalists and photographers, boarded an old coach and embarked on a tour which cameramen Alan Downes recalls without enthusiasm: 'We had been shown a couple of towns that either the Unita or FNLA forces had taken at least a week beforehand,' he said. 'The news value was nil and it was all very frustrating. To make matters worse, the food was bloody awful and we could hear the screams of the goats as they were being slaughtered with blunt instruments on the hotel stairs.'

Then suddenly, as the coach rounded a bend, Downes

witnessed a sight which set his heart thumping with an excitement which tells a newsman only one thing – they had chanced upon one of the hottest stories of the year. For there, spread out along the road, were at least a dozen Panhard armoured cars, and the unmistakable sight of heavily armed South African troops – which both Savimbi·and the South African government had vehemently denied existed in Angola. The bus, however, did not stop. Now they knew for sure that South African troops were backing Savimbi's stand against the MPLA, but how could they prove it?

After a short while they reached the next town which had been captured by the Unita rebels but, by now, the ITN team was not bothering to listen to the proud claims of the colonel who was their Unita guide. They simply had to get back to film the presence of the South Africans, but how could they do it? Surely, having seen the troops, they must now be taken back to Savimbi's camp by a different route? Even Alan Downes had little faith in his half-hearted assertion that 'it might be the only road back'.

They could hardly believe their luck when, after boarding the coach for the return journey they saw it was following exactly the same route. Immediately the team implemented its plan of action: Alan Downes had already taken the front seat next to the driver with his camera casually perched on his shoulder, ready to film through the coach windows, ensuring that neither the Unita guard nor the troops were aware of his action, while Jon Hunt sat behind him, chatting idly. To anyone behind them, it appeared that the two men were having a perfectly normal conversation. It was unlikely that they would be able to stop the bus at the critical moment, but Nicholson was going to have a bloody good try.

After ten or fifteen minutes they again reached the spot occupied by the troops – unmistakably South African with their fair hair, shorts, and long socks, and the team moved into action. Downes switched on his camera, still resting casually on his shoulder, Hunt continued chatting, while Nicholson suddenly leapt to his feet and ordered the coach to stop. 'Ask them if we can take some pictures,' he yelled, in mock excitement. 'They will not allow it,' said the Unita guard. 'Let me try,' insisted Nicholson. 'At least let me talk to them.'

It worked. The coach stopped and Nicholson walked slowly towards a young South African officer, with Downes filming surreptitiously through the front windscreen. The South African shook his head and Nicholson returned after about twenty seconds, clearly angry. Obviously, they would not allow any pictures, but where the hell had Downes been, Nicholson wanted to know. Why had he not followed Nicholson and filmed the introduction just as they had done the previous year in Cyprus when they scooped the world with the Turkish paratroop landings? Downes was adamant in his view: 'They would never have allowed it. They would have taken the film,' he argued. As it was, he had at least twenty seconds of usable footage which proved beyond doubt the extent of the South African presence in Angola.

When they challenged Savimbi with their evidence the following day, he shrugged pathetically. Believing, quite wrongly, that the film had already been flown out of the country, he admitted that the South Africans were actively supporting Unita in the field. 'When friends are hard to find,' he said, 'you are forced to accept help wherever you can get it.'

Seeking ratification of their story from another source, the crew contacted a Reuter reporter, who later joined Nicholson in a fight over south-western Angola, discovering further pockets of military activity. The Reuter man filed his copy to coincide with ITN's exclusive footage of the build-up of South African troops.

When Alan Downes' film was shown worldwide just twenty-four hours later, it heralded the complete withdrawal of all South African troops from Angola and weakened Savimbi's military strength and dented his credibility. Downes was philosophical about it: 'I liked Savimbi very much, and he seems to be fighting for all the right things. But I'm a news-man, not a politician. It's the job of ITN crews to gather the news, not to justify or condemn it.'

It was a bright balmy morning almost three years later when, on Sunday, 5 August 1978, Tom Phillips, Mike Doyle, and

Michael Nicholson boarded a scheduled Swissair flight from Johannesburg to Kinshasa, the capital of Zaire. Doyle and Phillips had only recently been teamed together, although both were extremely widely travelled and veterans of many war campaigns. Apart from a brief trip to Cairo to cover one of the endless strings of Middle East peace talks which abounded in the late 1970s, their work together so far had been confined to fairly run-of-the-mill diary assignments in the UK. When they were offered the chance of a six month attachment to Johannesburg, both men jumped at it. Their life-style would differ greatly from the standard 'four-on four-off' roster in London, and they would be on hand to cover anything that was required.

Now they were off to Angola to interview Dr Savimbi, who was trying desperately hard to drum up European support for his Unita rebels. Nicholson had already given them details of his meeting three years before, but now the political emphasis had changed, and the Soviet Union had increased its level of support to Neto's MPLA government. Further communist aid came in the form of thousands of highly trained Cuban troops who were flown into Luanda to act as 'advisers' to Neto's government.

Over recent years, relationships between the official governments of Angola and Zaire had been far from congenial, and both were known to be 'sympathetic' towards rebel groups in each other's countries. Now, however, a sudden slump in Zaire's economic fortunes had convinced Mobutu that it was time for a little political juggling. A rebellion, eventually quashed with the aid of Belgian and French paratroopers, had closed the lucrative copper and cobalt mines which were once responsible for two-thirds of Zaire's overseas earnings, and Mobutu was about to start wooing Europe for economic aid. Neto, meanwhile, was also courting Mobutu, seeking a reciprocal agreement to stop supporting the rebel groups which were causing irritation to both leaders.

Savimbi, on the other hand, was not prepared to wheel and deal. He had 12,000 trained troops fighting a successful guerilla campaign, with a further 10,000 'reservists', although it later became apparent that these were little more than thinly

trained women and children. But Savimbi held two major
trumps: his Unita forces had gained control of the Benguela
railway which was the main artery for the all-important copper
mining areas of Zaire and Zambia, linking them to Angola's
Atlantic coast just south of Luanda. His second ace was his
charismatic personality. He had sewn the seeds of his dream
years beforehand while studying economics in Lisbon. Now
he believed fervently in his cause and his followers believed
passionately in him. He also believed that the time was right to
seek the help of the media to canvass support for Unita in
the West.

It was against this background of patchwork politics that
Doyle, Phillips, and Nicholson were to forge an inseparable
bond and share a remarkable true-life adventure which would
have been more suited to a fictional TV thriller than a news
bulletin. Their plane touched down on time in the midday
heat of Kinshasa after an uneventful flight. They were met in
Zaire by a party of plain-clothes security officers who relieved
them of all their baggage and guided them swiftly though the
airport terminal, avoiding both immigration and customs
control. The three were taken to a car and driven to a hotel in
Kinshasa where they were signed in under false names and
their baggage was returned, minus all identification marks.
Clearly, if anything went wrong, there would be nothing to
show that Nicholson, Doyle, and Phillips had ever set foot
in Zaire.

At about four in the morning, the shrill of a telephone
brought a premature end to what was to be their last night in a
bed for four months. The message was clear and simple. 'We
are ready to leave.' Within fifteen minutes, the three were
being ushered into a car, and driven back to Kinshasa airport
where, after a furtive exchange of passwords and signals, a side
gate was opened and the car eased smoothly and silently into a
large dark hanger.

Through the gloom the three recognized the outline of a
twin-engined Fokker Friendship. There were signalled aboard
and, as they groped their way down the dark gangway,
immediately realized they were not alone. They had been
delivered into the hands of their 'escort' – a dozen armed
Unita rebels who were to guide them on the first leg of their

journey to a rendezvous with Savimbi, deep in the Angolan bush.

At first light, the Fokker nosed its way out of the hangar and almost casually took off for Lubumbashi, Zaire's second town near the Zambian border. On landing, the aircraft was quickly dispatched to the quietest corner of the airport. After an agonizing four-hour wait, during which the ITN crew and Unita soliders were warned not to move for fear of attracting attention, the aircraft refuelled and headed south-west towards a disused grass airstrip near the Acobango River, deep in southern Angola. Mike Doyle recalled the landing clearly: 'It was early evening and the sun was going down. Suddenly, in the half-light these shadowy silhouettes appeared from the bushes. It was a weird, rather unreal sensation, and would have made a super photograph.'

Eventually, they were allowed to disembark and set foot in Angola for the first time. The reception party included a couple of girls who prepared a bowl of 'mealy' – a thick porridge-like substance which, recalled Doyle, looks like Polyfilla and tastes like Polyfilla. They had a couple of tins of spam, and one of the Unita soldiers produced a jar of pickled onions, but the crew picked at it without much enthusiasm after the long journey.

After an hour or so, a distant rumbling heralded the arrival of one of Unita's military trucks. Doyle and Phillips sat in the front, safeguarding the valuable camera and recording equipment, while reporter Nicholson travelled in the back with the Unita guides. 'It was an interminable journey,' recalled Doyle. 'Six or seven hours of just bouncing through the bush on the roughest tracks imaginable.' Eventually they reached a make-shift camp where the rebels skilfully fashioned simple but effective platform beds from stakes and binding.

This was their base for the next three days, during which the men became increasingly impatient. 'Where was Savimbi, and why weren't they moving?' they wanted to know. Communications, however, were difficult since the Colonel spoke no English and only a smattering of fractured French. Although he successfully conveyed the message that they would move 'when it was safe', this did little to ease the impatience of the news team.

Eventually, on the fourth night, they were awakened to be told that they were moving at last, and were now on their way to meet Savimbi. They were guided silently and swiftly through the bush for about half an hour to a clearing where two lorries were waiting for them. The first, full of armed Unita rebels, moved out followed about twenty minutes later by the second truck carrying the ITN crew and more armed Unita forces. For an hour, it was an uneventful trip. The sun was just beginning to break when, in the words of sound recordist Mike Doyle, 'All hell broke loose'. The lorry had driven straight into an ambush, and suddenly the peace of dawn was shattered with the scream of rockets, tracer shells, and the crack of rifles. Nicholson and the Unita guards in the back of the truck ducked for cover, while Doyle and Phillips crouched in the cab with their camera and recording equipment. As the driver swung the lorry towards the safety of the bush, Phillips had the presence of mind to switch on his camera and film dramatic footage of the action.

The MPLA forces had dug themselves in only seventy-five yards from the track but, incredibly, missed their target. The only Unita casualty was a minor leg wound suffered by one of the guerillas travelling in the back of the truck. The first lorry had safely passed along the track some twenty minutes earlier, and it soon became clear that the MPLA's specific target was not so much the Unita rebels, but the ITN crew themselves. Divisions of Savimbi's guerilla rebels had been in regular radio contact with each other, but their code had now been cracked by the Cubans. Not only did they have a fairly accurate indication of Savimbi's whereabouts, they knew that Western journalists were on their way to interview him.

Neto's directive to his MPLA forces in the south was simple: stop the newsmen reaching Savimbi. According to Mike Doyle's assertion, they failed in their objective only 'because they must have been bloody awful shots'. What the MPLA did not know, however, was that they almost succeeded in killing the ITN men and their Unita guides with one of the oldest ruses in the history of warfare. After the government forces had been repelled by the Unita marksmen, they went to inspect the site where the ambush took place. The fleeing MPLA had left behind them all the tell-tale signs of a panic-inspired withdrawal, including half a dozen tins of Plumrose ham. Clearly delighted by the prospect of devouring the mouth watering spoils of war, Nicholson grabbed a can and proposed an early lunch break. He was about to open it when it was savagely snatched from his hand by the Unita Colonel who inspected it intently. Nicholson was starting to protest vehemently about the apparent loss of his lunch, when the Colonel triumphantly pointed to half a dozen tell-tale pin pricks, and shook his head excitedly. Each tin had been injected with a deadly poison.

Savimbi, with his lair almost discovered and his Unita code cracked, had to pack up his camp and move swiftly, as MPLA action escalated in southern Angola. Obviously, the scheduled meeting with Savimbi was no longer on. If the crew was to succeed in its mission, it would now have to locate the Unita leader as he dodged from camp to camp in the Angolan jungle, while at the same time staying out of range of MPLA and Cuban pursuers who, having missed their prey once, would be anxious to make amends.

It was obvious to Phillips, Doyle, and Nicholson that they had no alternative but to place themselves completely in the hands of their Unita guides. They had no hope of getting out of the bush on their own and to fall into the hands of government or Cuban forces would have meant certain death, justified by the claim that they were Unita mercenaries. So, accompanied by the Unita Colonel, four armed Unita rebels, and two girls, the three began their historic trek through the Angolan bush – a journey that was to cover nearly fifteen hundred miles and take over one hundred days before it culminated in a dramatic rescue operation masterminded by ITN colleagues and two English civil pilots.

The Unita Colonel's immediate aim was to get the three men and himself removed from the scene of the action as swiftly as possible. Setting a cracking pace, they marched for about six hours without knowing either their destination or the direction in which they were travelling.

That night they slept under trees after eating a handful of rice which their Unita leader had managed to obtain from a sympathetic village. Early the following morning, they set off again at the same pace, but this time the terrain was mostly black sticky swampland and, by now, the conditions had begun to affect the fifty-year old Mike Doyle. When the group eventually stopped to rest in the shade of a large tree some six hours later, he pulled off the new boots he had bought specifically for the mission to reveal an ugly array of blisters on both feet. Nicholson immediately cut and drained them with a pair of scissors, but it was obvious that Doyle would not be able to put his socks and boots on again.

Doyle could see that his condition presented a major threat to the safety of the party, and suggested that they should leave him in the safety of a nearby village, and return for him at a later date, but the Colonel quashed this suggestion immediately, drawing his forefinger menacingly across his throat. The gesture was plain enough; if Doyle was left behind, his life expectation would be about an hour. Instead, the Unita officer negotiated with the villagers, and returned with six oxen hauling a large hollowed-out tree trunk – a primitive form of transport for moving supplies. With his feet wrapped in a blanket, Doyle was transferred to the sled where he travelled with the cameras and sound recording equipment.

Feeling rather like a down-market Father Christmas in the wrong setting, the sound recordist was dragged in the tree trunk for the rest of the day and recalled the journey without enthusiasm: 'It certainly gave my feet a rest, but a bum's-eye view of six stinking oxen rather detracted from the comparative luxury of the situation. In fact, they were kicking up so much dust and filth that I found it difficult to breathe.' To make matters worse, that night was spent in a filthy black burnt-out jungle camp where Phillips and Doyle – both self-confessed heterosexuals – had to snuggle up together beneath a single blanket to keep warm as the night temperature plummeted.

The following morning brought another setback. Cameraman Tom Phillips had drunk contaminated water the previous night, and now had such acute stomach pains that he could not move. The Unita Colonel was again forced to adopt alternative measures to keep the group on the move, and later that day salvation appeared in the shape of a Mercedes Unimog. This large powerful jeep-type vehicle ploughed through the bush like a steamroller as it transferred the ITN crew and its mentors to their next destination. This gave the crew tremendous heart. At last, the Unita forces seemed to be in control of the area and they must now be close to Savimbi. This was the eighth day and it now seemed likely that they would be able to complete their task and return to the safety of Johannesburg within another week or ten days. Their hopes proved to be shortlived.

The MPLA offensive in the south had widened and Savimbi had again fled, leaving instructions for the group to follow. It was becoming increasingly obvious to the news team that they would not, after all, get out of Angola as quickly, or as easily, as they had hoped.

The following morning, the crew, with a strengthened armed guard, were ushered into the back of a lorry for an uncomfortable journey which was to last for thirty-six hours, as they moved in wide arcs to the east and west. By now, the newsmen were tired, hungry and, most of all, frustrated. However, as long as they were with their Unita keepers, they felt that they were safe. The nightmare journey came to an end when the lorry was becoming persistently bogged down in the mud. From now on, there was no alternative but to march.

Doyle, meanwhile, had been attempting to walk again without much success. Still unable to get his boots over his blistered feet, he had adopted a pair of soft moccasin slippers and, after cutting open the back, found he could just about shuffle along at a snail's pace. He was carried on the back of a burly Unita guard, later discarding his soft moccasins which kept slipping off his feet. He was prepared, he said, to walk barefooted, but this suggestion was vetoed by the group's new Unita leader. Eventually, Doyle agreed to wear a pair of Nicholson's shoes which were about four sizes too large and fitted over his injured feet with room to spare. After several days on the march, however, Doyle's feet could take it no longer. His toes had taken such a hammering inside Nicholson's borrowed shoes that they were severely bruised and every toenail had turned black. The contaminated filth from swamps had also been retained in the shoes and his feet were, quite literally, starting to rot. His shoes were removed and an effort made to clean his feet. A brief conference, conducted mostly in sign language, was held between Nicholson,

Phillips, the Unita Colonel, and a guard carrying the group's first aid box, and a decision was made. A sharp knife and scissors were produced and, in the middle of the steaming Angolan jungle, Mike Doyle underwent the nightmare experience of having all his toenails removed. The Unita Colonel, who by his actions made it clear that he would rather be fighting the MPLA than acting as a wet-nurse to a team of British newsmen, showed a little compassion by commandeering a pair of soft canvas boots from one of the girls, and giving them to Doyle. He wore them until his incredible adventure ended, more than three months later, and still holds them amongst his most valued possessions.

Although the new Unita man could speak and understand English, he was reluctant to show it, and questions on Savimbi's whereabouts and the projected meeting were met with little more than a grunt or a monosyllabic 'soon'. The sufferings of the three Englishmen were compounded by hunger, the realization that they were moving further and further away from their supposed destination, and the endless stream of flies which abound in the tropics. 'They were everywhere,' recalled Doyle. 'They got into your eyes, up your nose, in your ears, and God knows how many we swallowed. We just had to switch off our minds and march mechanically, with our eyes focused on the man in front of us.'

Under the prompting and guidance of the Unita Colonel, the small group continued its zig-zag pattern north often marching through the intense heat of the afternoon in the bid to save time. As before, daily radio contact with other Unita groups was maintained and as before, any enquiries from the frustrated British trio were met with a curt grunt or a meaningless nod. With their spirits at their lowest ebb, the three men followed their leader blindly from camp to camp, from waterhole to waterhole, despairing of ever meeting Savimbi. Doyle was still suffering considerable pain from his feet, and eventually, during the heat of a mid-afternoon, he crashed to the ground from sheer exhaustion. They had been in Angola for more than a month, and they had trekked for over three weeks since abandoning their lorry in the swamp. 'I'd had enough,' recalled Doyle. 'It was a sweltering afternoon and nobody in their right mind should have tried to march through that heat. I was unfit and I just keeled over.' Although he was revived with water, it was obvious that he could not go on. The group set up camp and Doyle lay on the ground not caring whether he lived or died. 'I was exhausted, and I'd lost the will to go on. If someone had brought down the final curtain there and then, I couldn't really have cared.' He remembers the Unita medic hovering over him, holding a king-sized hypodermic needle which was full of a thick liquid which, Doyle thought at the time, resembled petroleum jelly. Pausing only to brush the patient lightly with a piece of cotton wool as a perfunctory gesture of basic hygiene, the medic then proceeded to inject the entire contents of the syringe into Doyle's upper right arm. Then a remarkable thing happened. Within a few minutes, the ailing soundman began to feel stronger, and had recovered the will to live. Within an hour, he felt fitter than he had for two days and, two hours later, he had made a complete recovery, apart from the discomfort of his feet. 'I've no idea what it was – I wish I knew,' he said afterwards. 'From that moment on, I never looked back. It was, quite literally, a miracle cure.'

The amazing improvement in Mike Doyle's condition provided a brief morale-booster for both Phillips and Nicholson but, after more endless marching and the same non-committal reply to questions about Savimbi and their destination, the temporary lifting of their spirits was again dragged down. True, they had a very vague idea where they were and where they were heading after crossing a couple of rivers at first light, but the scale of the map they carried was too small to determine their position with any accuracy.

Each day became a carbon copy of the day before, with endless marching and a growing sense of despair. To their credit, the Unita party managed to secure food regularly, but it was monotonous. They day would begin with strange-tasting tea, drunk gratefully from an empty baked bean can, and a rock-like biscuit. Lunch was inevitably a handful of rice with rough-looking corned beef and this was normally served in the evening too, although the monotony was occasionally broken by the addition of a spoonful of jam.

They were close to breaking point one evening, when the tight-lipped Unita Colonel approached them as they swallowed

the last few grains of the meagre rice ration. Without the
slightest trace of emotion, he gruffly delivered the message
they had waited so long to hear: 'We see Savimbi tomorrow.'
To the three British newsmen, these four words represented
the best after-dinner speech they could wish to hear.

The following day, they continued their trek through the
jungle with spirits high, although experience warned them to
be prepared for yet another disappointment. Their mental
warning light, however, was not necessary. After marching for
most of the day, they came across a large camp in a clearing.
Standing in the centre, surrounded by hundreds of suppor-
ters who had come from miles around to pay homage to the
man they regarded as their saviour, stood Dr Jonas Savimbi,
leader of the Unita rebels in Angola.

Since arriving in Angola on the evening of 6 August, Mike
Doyle had kept a copious diary, chronicling the departure and
arrival times at various camps, and estimating, where possible, the direction and distance travelled. This not only proved
to be invaluable and irrefutable evidence when recounting the
story later, but also provided the crew with an almanac of
dates as one identical day merged into the next. This diary
shows that, between abandoning the lorry in a swamp after the
arduous thirty-six hour journey, and eventually locating
Savimbi, the crew had trekked northwards for thirty days and
had, by this time, spent a total of forty-two days in Angola.

Back in London, ITN executives were disturbed, rather than
worried. It was now mid-September and a job which they
thought would take three weeks had, so far, taken six, with still
no word from the crew. However, they were all experienced
men, and it seemed likely to Foreign Editor Mike Morris that
the escalation of MPLA activity had hampered their progress.
There was also a shift in the political attitude of Zaire where
President Mobutu, although sympathetic to Unita, was now
being wooed strongly by Neto's MPLA government.

Morris was also aware that most things take twice as long to
achieve in Africa as anywhere else in the world, but this did not
prevent him from flying to Paris to seek first-hand information
on the men's whereabouts from Unita's chief European

representative, Chitunda. He returned home with a promise from Chitunda that the men were safe, although he could not say exactly where they were. Meanwhile, the Foreign Desk had been sending messages to their team via Unita offices in both Brussels and Kinshasa but, although they had no way of knowing at the time, nothing was getting through.

A week later, there was still no news, and Morris again flew to Paris, this time accompanied by deputy editor Don Horobin. 'This was a measure of the anxiety we were all beginning to feel,' said Morris. 'Normally nothing on God's earth can coax Don to get on an aeroplane.' Again there was nothing positive from Chitunda, except the loose assurance that the men were 'still safe'. Although ITN Editor David Nicholas shared Morris's inward concern for the safety of the three men, all they could do was keep quiet, cross their fingers and, for the time being at least, play the waiting game.

After living the nomadic life of guerilla rebels for the past six weeks, Nicholson, Phillips, and Doyle found their five-day stay at Savimbi's camp to be relatively luxurious. The beds were makeshift but adequate, limited water was available for washing, food was plentiful, and there was the bonus of real orange juice. A rejuvenated Mike Doyle had his feet bathed and treated every day, while women in the camp offered a primitive, but willing, laundry service.

Savimbi, not underestimating the value of sympathetic exposure on the Western television networks, was co-operative. He allowed the men to film freely around the camp, but like the 1975 interview, would not permit the crew to accompany the Unita rebels on a raid or film their movements. The Unita forces, however, claimed that they were creating havoc to the Benguela railway, a vital link between Angola and the copper mines in Zaire and Zambia. If the crew fancied a march of between six and eight weeks towards the north, Savimbi's men would be quite happy to blow up a section of track for ITN's benefit. Hardly surprisingly, the offer was declined by all three, and most vehemently by Mike Doyle.

As the crew prepared to pack up and leave Savimbi's camp,

the Unita leader dropped a bombshell. The route planned for their escape from Angola was now occupied by Neto's Cuban-backed government forces, who also controlled the airfield earmarked for the first stage of their homeward journey. Savimbi, however, assured them that he had adopted a secondary plan, and the crew would be taken south to the Namibian border, where they would be met by sympathetic South African troops who would guarantee their safe conduct back to Johannesburg.

Accompanied by an armed guard of about twenty Unita rebels, led by the same tight-lipped Colonel Chindondo, the three started their trek south, confident that it would be only a matter of days before they, together with their exclusive film of the Savimbi interview, were safely home. None of them had any reason to suspect that they were barely half way through their ordeal, and that they would be pinned down in Angola for another two months.

The first indication that all was not going according to plan came on the fourth day after leaving Savimbi's camp. They had marched south for two days, before reaching a semi-permanent encampment where they remained for another two days. The border to Namibia was only another two days march south and, from then on, they assured themselves, it would be all plain sailing. Their bubble was cruelly burst by Colonel Chindondo who looked even more sour than usual after returning from his daily radio contact with other Unita rebel groups. It was one of the few occasions that he chose to speak English: 'The South Africans will not accept you,' he said. 'We cannot go to Namibia.'

Whether this sudden reversal of policy by the South Africans was linked to events three years earlier is open to conjecture. Certainly, the South Africans were more than a little put out by ITN's proof of the extent of their support in Angola, and Michael Nicholson was part of that team. On the other hand, Nicholson was now a trusted journalist based in Johannesburg, and it is unlikely that they would have afforded him that facility if they were still seething over the ITN disclosures.

More likely, perhaps, are the two theories provided by Morris, who suggests that either Unita's message did not get

through to the right people, or one South African officer –
possibly involved in Angola three years beforehand – took it
upon himself to block the entire operation. Whatever the
reason, the sudden gravity of the situation was not lost on the
crew, and suddenly a large question mark appeared, not only
over their immediate future, but also their ultimate safety.

The following morning, instead of heading south towards
their proposed exit route, they were marched north in the
hope of finding an alternative airstrip which was not in the
hands of the MPLA. As before, however, the pace was fast but
geographical progress was slow, as the group zig-zagged from
east to west, and on one occasion found themselves crossing
the same unmade road for the third time. After four more
days, they met a division of Savimbi's rebel army moving
south and this temptation to return to guerilla action proved
too strong for Chindondo. Leaving the ITN men in the charge
of a junior officer and a handful of armed rebels, he grunted a
brief 'goodbye', and was never seen again.

The new leader was no more communicative than his pre-
decessor, and persistent questions from the three about their
destination and the ultimate plan met with little or no response. Eventually the group reached a permanent campsite,
where a hut was built for them, and rough platform beds provided. This was to be their home for the next seventeen days,
during which their frustrations were magnified by the ever-
present swarms of flies which made it impossible for them to
leave their hut between six in the morning and six in the
evening.

They hung sleeping bags over the doorway to stop the flies
getting in and, at mealtimes, their food was served beneath
this makeshift curtain. The food was again edible and seemed
plentiful, and they were delighted to be supplied with one
bowl of hot water each day – a luxury they had not experienced since leaving Kinshasa. The three would rise early, and
spend an hour outside their hut before returning to escape
flies. In the evening, too, they would spend an hour or two
around a fire in the compound, but it was the hours in
between that were proving to be the major threat. These long
periods of inactivity, especially towards the end of this
seventeen-day period, stretched the relationships between the

three men to the limit. 'It was dreadful for all of us,' recalled
Doyle. 'We had feared this might happen, so we had actually
discussed the dangers in advance. The slightest little thing
could upset us: perhaps Tom would brush his teeth in a different way, or one of us might cough in an irritating manner.
But we wouldn't allow anything to develop – we'd just bite our
tongue, or walk away, cool off, and forget it.'

There was nothing to do except talk. When they left Johannesburg, Doyle had taken the precaution of packing Dennis
Morris's book *The Washing of the Spears,* but this had been
thrown away by Nicholson in an effort to cut down baggage
weight in the early days of their trek, and he now fully
understood the folly of his action. Apart from Mike Doyle's
diary, they had exhausted their last scraps of paper weeks ago
and, although there was plenty to write about, there was nothing to write on. There was no way that they could record their
experiences on film either, for the lengthy interview with
Savimbi, coupled with the rapid changes in temperature
between day and night, had taken their toll of the batteries.
Although they also carried an older 16mm clockwork camera,
this, together with a limited stock of film, was to be kept for
emergencies only.

So the men talked and talked. They talked about previous
assignments, themselves and their colleagues. Doyle even
read snippets from an old diary to the most attentive audience
of two. They played word games, discussed relationships,
meetings, politics, and even added a little imaginative taste to
their standard rice-based meals with tales of the best
restaurants and hotels they had visited on their world-wide
assignments.

They recalled, too, their journey to the airport in Johannesburg back on that warm, balmy Sunday morning, to catch the
Swissair flight to Kinshasa. They were running late because
they had been detained by a South African news bulletin
claiming that Savimbi was under house arrest in Kinshasa.
Unable to obtain confirmation of this report, they decided to
push ahead as planned and Doyle, at the wheel, was driving a
little too enthusiastically in his bid to make up time and was
stopped for speeding. Never one to lose his cool in such a
situation, he quietly and politely provided all the relevant

details to the police officer, and all three were continuing their journey within ten minutes. But now it was obvious to both Nicholson and Phillips that their current dilemma was exclusively Doyle's fault; if he had not been such a gentleman and had instead unleashed a fusillade of East End verbal fury on Johannesburg's young officer, followed by a bang on the jaw for good measure, they would now be languishing in the comfort of a Johannesburg jail, not lost in the Angolan bush!

For Phillips and Doyle, however, the high spot of their sojourn was the morning spent calculating the amount of overtime they could charge for their current assigment if they ever got back to fill in an expenses form at ITN's Wells Street headquarters. This, of course, was pure hypothesis since both men had accepted a six-month Johannesburg secondment on the understanding that jobs would be covered as and when it became necessary. The true value of the operation was simply that it passed a few more hours.

Finding ways of filling in the endless daytime hours was more important to Doyle than the others. He was having trouble sleeping and the days seemed inordinately long. Phillips, on the other hand, had the ability to close his eyes and catnap for a couple of hours, almost at will. In an effort to fill the long hours, Doyle would set himself half a dozen menial tasks every day, the result of some proving to be more practical than others. However, he did produce one highly successful innovation when, much to the delight of his colleagues, he solved a biting sanitation problem. In the absence of flush toilets, the ITN men had to make do with a rather more primitive facility of a pit in the ground covered by branches. In the middle of the branches would be a hole over which, somewhat precariously, the men would perch while answering the calls of nature. 'After a week every fly in Angola had discovered this pit and the whole thing was proving rather unsavoury, and most uncomfortable,' remembered Nicholson. It was then that Doyle had the brainwave of transforming one of the unwanted canisters of film into a makeshift toilet cover to keep the flies out. With the aid of some sealing tape which he fashioned into a handle, he provided Angola's first-ever 16mm negative sanitary aid. It fitted perfectly and proved highly effective for the remainder of their stay.

Eventually, after seventeen days at the camp, they received the heartening news that they would be on the move again the following day. Things seemed to be happening at last and their optimism was further strengthened by the camp's senior Unita man who assured them, in barely understandable broken English, that they would be taken home from the next camp. As they prepared to leave the camp the following morning – their seventy-fourth day in Angola – the ITN men were in high spirits.

Back at Wells Street, fears for the safety of the men were running high. Nothing had been heard for over ten weeks and if Britain's recent shift in its political attitude towards Angola was making life difficult for the Unita rebels, it was clearly creating considerable problems for Messrs Nicholson, Phillips, and Doyle. Morris had already made a third trip to Paris where, as he later described it, he had spent a fruitless week 'sitting on Chitunda's head' in an effort to glean some positive information. By now, it had become clear that the Unita representative knew little or nothing about the location of the missing men, and it was a very worried Morris who returned to London to lay the foundations for ITN's own rescue operation.

The Foreign Office seemed reluctant to show any interest in the matter and, despite repeated requests for guidance, Morris's difficulties were exacerbated still further by 'the ignorance and obstruction' of junior officials.

Although nothing was known for certain, it was assumed that the three men were being escorted south towards either the South African or Zambian border but, with the escalation of MPLA and Cuban activity, there was no knowing how long these relatively peaceful areas would remain safe. Clearly, if there was to be any hope of getting the three men out alive, the time had come to act.

Unita had already offered the services of their Zaire-based Fokker Friendship on the understanding that ITN would equip it with weather-scanning radar and other vital spares. This, at least, was a start, and Morris decided to fly to Kinshasa as soon as the necessary equipment was available. Meanwhile, it was decided to dispatch reporter Tony Carthew to Lusaka where, masquerading as a private businessman, he would make discreet enquiries about hiring a private aircraft to fly to Angola as soon as the missing men had been located. The type of light civil aircraft available in Zambia did not have the range, and Carthew's problems were doubled when it became clear that he might have to charter a second aircraft for refuelling purposes.

On 18 October, three days after Carthew had arrived in Lusaka, Morris flew into Kinshasa with Unita's vital radar equipment. Coincidentaly, it was later established that this was the same day that the three ITN men were moved on from the camp where they had been hidden for seventeen days. The Unita party which greeted Morris on his arrival at Kinshasa were friendly and optimistic about the rescue chances. They were also delighted with the radar equipment but expressed some suprise when they discovered that Morris intended to remain in Zaire to plan and monitor the rescue attempt. They had expected him to act as a messenger, simply delivering the equipment and returning to London. Morris, however, was adamant, insisting that if Unita was re-equipping their aircraft at ITN's expense, he would be remaining in Kinshasa, close to both the Unita representatives and the Fokker Friendship. His strong case lost some ground the following morning, however, when the Unita men came to him claiming that the radar equipment did not work.

Confident that they were on the last leg of their journey, the mood of the three newsmen was almost buoyant as they marched away from the camp which had been their shelter for the past seventeen days. At last it seemed that someone, somewhere, knew what they were doing, and it would only be a matter of a couple more days before they were flown back to the safety of Johannesburg, or Kinshasa, or Lubumbashi, or anywhere.

The next few days, however, were to be among the most arduous and unpleasant of their trek. More than two weeks of inactivity had left its mark, and tiredness – an enemy they had

not encountered before – became a major problem. 'By the
time we sat down to rest, we were absolutely buggered,' admitted Doyle. 'Mosquitoes and scorpions were everywhere and
we didn't even have the strength to knock them off when they
started running all over us.' There was, however, one respite, a
few minutes of levity during which they forgot their tiredness
and their frustrations. They had been walking two-and-a-half
days when they were alerted by a shout from behind them.
Turning round, they found themselves confronted by an
excited Unita soldier running towards them brandishing
Doyle's patent 16mm negative sanitary aid. Handing it to the
men, he proudly informed them that they had left behind
their 'important film', and he had tracked them for more than
two days to return it. Nicholson recalled the moment
vividly:

> 'He suddenly appeared, looking very pleased with him-
> self, waving this crap-encrusted can of film. We told him
> that it was the important interview with Savimbi, and that
> his leader would be very pleased with him. It was a
> moment of total incongruity which broke the tension
> completely.'

A few moments later, a proud Unita rebel was returning to
his camp knowing that he had greatly helped Savimbi's cause,
a soiled canister of film had been committed to the Angolan
bush for ever, and a weary party of television newsmen and
guerilla rebels were again proceeding towards their goal.

Spurred on by thoughts of a bath, clean clothes, and resuming contact with the civilized world, the three men forced their
tired limbs to keep moving until, close to exhaustion, they
reached their destination – the large, well-equipped camp
where they believed they would be spending their last night,
two at the most, in this tropical hell. Their strength and their
spirits were fortified by what Phillips described as one of the
most welcome meals he had ever had: 'dried potatoes, dried
carrots and mashed corned beef, but bloody magnificent!'

But their gastronomic pleasures were shortlived. An hour
later, their stomachs turned to lead when they again heard the
bad news which by now had become so familiar to them; the

MPLA and Cuban forces were closing in and there was no chance of reaching the airstrip. Their only hope, they were told, was to head south again to an airstrip which was in the control of Unita forces. There was a moment's silence after Phillips's question, 'How far?' as the camp commander appeared to struggle with some mental calculations. 'If you march fast like Unita soldiers,' he said, 'you could do it in three weeks.'

'Set up the beers'

By now, ITN executives and staff were beginning to fear the worst. Morris and Carthew had been in neighbouring African states for several days but no positive news had filtered back, and it was hardly surprising that other news crews were becoming agitated by the lack of news about their colleagues. In the camera crews' room they talked of little else and feelings were running particularly high. 'Were the men still alive? If so, where were they? What is being done? Send us out there – we'll find them! Why is there no information?'

Morris was in daily contact with London, but even editor David Nicholas was beginning to doubt his quiet assurances that everything was going to plan. Morris had, by now, developed a strong relationship with the Unita men, and felt he could trust them. He was assured that the men were safe, but that was all, and all he could do was strengthen his bonds with his hosts while he continued to play the waiting game.

Inevitably, Fleet Street had also picked up rumours of the missing newsmen but, thanks to the co-operation of national newspaper and agency editors, ITN managed to kill the story. 'To admit our crew was missing in Angola, where a civil war was escalating, could only have jeopardized their safety,' Nicholas later explained.

Meanwhile, Carthew had made some headway in Lusaka before a cruel twist of fate forced him to blow his cover and take him completely out of the game. Without warning, Rhodesia launched an intensive three-day air and ground offensive on Nkomo's Zapu guerilla movement around Lusaka, claiming their action was retribution after a civil aircraft had been shot down. Urgent reports were needed back at Wells Street and, being the only international newsman in Lusaka at the time, Carthew reverted to his more accustomed reporting role. His presence ensured that ITN had first reports of the action, although he later had considerable difficulty in convincing rival foreign correspondents that his presence on the first day of the attacks was 'purely coincidental'.

The news that another three-week march lay ahead of them, did nothing to improve the mood of the Unita guards. They had been trained to fight, they argued, not to act as porters and guides to three nomadic newsmen. For the first time since they had linked up with the Unita rebels, Phillips, Doyle, and Nicholson sensed an air of hostility towards them.

Thoroughly dejected, with their spirits at an all-time low, they continued their trek south for three days, hardly able to muster the energy – or the will – to speak. Again, the three men spread themselves out, staring only at the marching boots in front of them, lifting their heads occasionally as they passed a deserted village, a burnt-out tree trunk, or that straight, unfinished sand-covered road – all by now familiar landmarks. They slept rough for two nights, providing simple targets for the mosquitoes and, late on the third day, reached the permanent Unita encampment where, four weeks earlier, Chindondo had told them that they would not be allowed to cross the Namibian border.

The following morning they again went through the familiar routine of filling their water bottles under the malevolent gaze of their rebel guards, and prepared to continue their trek south. This, remembered Doyle, was a particularly tough and uncomfortable slog, alternating between the open savannah areas which provided no protection from the sun, and the steaming humidity of jungle swamps with the endless swarms of flies adding to their discomfort. Normally, a day's march would take them past at least one, maybe two, waterholes, where they would fill their flasks. This day, however, the hottest, most uncomfortable day of all, there was no water. By early afternoon, both Phillips and Nicholson had exhausted their flasks but Doyle had drunk little of his. 'It was a mental excercise that I would impose on myself,' he said later. 'I would be dying for a drink, but I would keep saying "just another half hour" – then, I would do it again. It was as though I had to prove to myself that I still had some will-power.' When Nicholson and Phillips discovered that Doyle still had more than half his water supply left by the late afternoon, their first reaction was to throw a large rock at him, before their common sense was restored, and they gulped down the water gratefully.

For four days they marched through the tropical heat, following their guides with the blind faith of helpless children. By now, the affliction of the flies had reached almost epidemic proportions. Whenever they ate, they were forced to pull their grime-encrusted combat jackets over their heads to cover the food and their mouths, but after a minute or ninety seconds, this became insufferably hot.

The heat and flies were also beginning to affect the Unita guards. Nerves became frayed, and, for the first time, the rebels became openly aggressive, arguing among themselves and waving their arms about menacingly. These gestures left the ITN men in no doubt about the reason for these ill-tempered exchanges: exasperated by the lack of guerilla action, a handful of their guard was in favour of killing the news crew who were nothing more than a liability. Savimbi, however, had promised the three men safe conduct out of Angola, and proved to be a man of his word. In a radio message, he insisted that his soldiers continued to protect 'their important visitors', quickly dispelling further thoughts of massacring the ITN crew. Savimbi had already given his interview, and was aware that the news team provided an important opportunity to exhibit Unita's activities to the out-side world. Doyle, Phillips, and Nicholson could be forgiven for thinking that the only thing that stood between them and certain death, was a couple of thousand feet of exposed 16mm film.

They had completed a week of their estimated three-week trek when they arrived at yet another camp which, like its senior Unita officer, was totally new to them. The men recall

him as a portly, larger-than-life figure with an unkempt bushy
beard, a Davey Crockett-style hat and a small brass cow-bell
around his waist. With little regard for his wild-West predilec-
tion, or his military status, he was immediately christened
Tinkerbell.

Under Colonel Tinkerbell, life became almost pleasant for
the next couple of weeks, as they headed south-east towards
Zambia, away from the immediate dangers of Neto's government forces. Although they kept moving at a fast pace, their
route took them close to rivers where they were able to cool off
and wash. They were in more pleasant surroundings and the
attitude of the Unita guards changed noticeably as they felt the
imminent danger of confrontation with the Cubans was passing. 'It was no holiday,' recalled Doyle, 'but at least it wasn't as
bad as it had been. We had three days without food when
Unita's supply lorry didn't turn up, but after what we'd been
through already, that was really no problem – there was always
plenty of water!'

Tinkerbell added a degree of credibility to his Davey Croc-
kett image by appearing with a horse one morning, and was
able to check the ground ahead of the main party. He also
diligently maintained regular radio contact with the camps
ahead, ensuring that he gave the widest possible berth to any
isolated pockets of MPLA activity.

In a more relaxed frame of mind, the rebels afforded themselves the luxury of an afternoon's hunting, and returned with
a wildebeest which kept the party in meat for three days. 'It
was a sensational treat,' said Doyle. 'They gave us the best cuts
and it tasted just like fillet steak. Unfortunately, we ate so
much rich protein in such a short time that we were all
horribly sick and, by the third day, we didn't care if we never
saw another piece of meat again.'

By now, it was early November and the party had to cope
with yet another discomfort – the monsoons. At the first sign
of the rains, the three TV men had been given waterproof
groundsheets and every night when they struck camp, their
routine was the same. Doyle would find some suitable shrubs
and stakes and peg out his groundsheet as a makeshift cover,
while the other two would lay theirs on the ground for the
three to sleep on. Phillips would go in search of wood, while

Nicholson had the responsibility of lighting the damp brushwood.

The advent of the rainy season increased the problem of the mosquitoes, and the three men were forced to cover themselves completely for protection. 'Even spare socks were used as gloves to stop our hands being bitten,' said Doyle. 'And if that wasn't enough, we were also in among the tsetse flies which stung like needles.'

Again, the pattern of the days blended into one endless march, all the time keeping within the cover of the trees. Mile followed mile, day followed day, with only the occasional meeting with a Unita Unimog to break the monotony. These were used primarily as supply vehicles, distributing food and ammunition to the rebels wherever it was needed. It was thanks to Tinkerbell's constant radio contact and navigational instructions that they were found at all.

Then, one afternoon, long after time had ceased to have much meaning, they walked into a clearing surrounded by a dozen or so corrugated iron huts. The three men remember it clearly. It was the first time they had seen huts built from corrugated iron – a legacy from the days of the Portuguese regime, when they had a large army camp at the nearby airstrip. It was very quiet, with only a handful of Unita soldiers in evidence. Nicholson was able to converse with the senior officer – a young lieutenant aged about twenty-two who could speak French. They were assured that plans were in hand to have them flown out 'as soon as possible'. Phillips and Doyle were allocated one large hut, while Nicholson had another to himself and, for the next two days, the men relaxed, swimming and washing their clothes in the nearby river. The French-speaking lieutenant spent most of the time in his hut making contact with Unita forces on his short-wave radio. He would appear once a day to tell the men forlornly: 'No news.'

The following morning brought a welcome change to their routine and a cause for celebration. It was presented to them by Mateus, the most friendly and approachable member of their Unita entourage, who had assumed responsibility for their food and general well-being. He had managed to obtain some rice, mealy and jam from which, with the aid of a battered round tin, he had managed to conjure a cake which he presented to them with a hug and a smile. His well-rehearsed two-word speech was clearly understood by the ITN news team. 'Happy Anniversary,' he said. They had now been missing in Angola for one hundred days.

The wait seemed interminable. Mealtimes punctuated the endless bouts of swimming, washing, sleeping, sunbathing and, when they could think of something to say, talking. And, day after day, the young lieutenant's message was depressingly repetitive: 'Pas d'information.' Then, on the morning of the 106th day, came the news that they had believed they might never hear. Brusquely and officially, they were told that a plane was coming from Kinshasa and they should be ready to leave at four pm. The former Portugese airstrip was less than two miles away – merely a few paces to the three men who had already walked an estimated 1,400 miles in their efforts to avoid capture, castigation and almost certain death at the hands of the MPLA and Cuban forces.

They walked through torrential thunderstorms to find Unita soldiers clearing hundreds of large rocks from the neglected grass airstrip, and this kept their hopes buoyant. Could this really be it? Were they on their way home at last? For two hours they waited, soaked to the skin but high in hopes. Then, a few minutes after they had heard the radio crackle into life, they were confronted by the young rebel lieutenant. Addressing himself to Nicholson, he said that 'the plane had broken down' and would not, after all, be landing. The rescue attempt was off. For the three men it was almost the last straw. 'We felt so depressed during that walk back to the camp' said Doyle. 'To be so near and yet so far once again. We despaired.'

After three more days of swimming, washing, eating, and sunbathing in conditions far removed from the five-star luxury it suggests, they were again spurred into action by the young lieutenant. He had received an order to get his three charges down to the airstrip immediately. Understandably sceptical, the ITN men again gathered their meagre possessions and, with the trusty Mateus carrying the camera and sound gear, retraced their steps back to the forlorn-looking landing strip.

They were beginning to steel themselves against yet another disappointment when the sharp ears of the Unita soldiers picked up the distant noise of an aeroplane. But this was not the drone of the Unita Fokker Friendship they had been expecting, instead this was definitely identified as the sound of a jet aircraft. Nicholson, who had walked further down the runway to climb onto the roof of a derelict Portugese army hut, shielded his eyes as he looked hopefully into the setting sun. The Unita guards, on the other hand, were perturbed by the unfamiliar noise as it came nearer and nearer.

Taking cover, they flicked off their safety catches and trained their rifles towards the approaching aircraft.

By the end of October, the atmosphere at ITN had become almost unbearable. There was still no news, tempers were becoming frayed and crews, now believing that they would never see Doyle, Phillips, or Nicholson again, were talking openly of 'a cover-up' and the pressure was on ITN to make a positive press statement. Morris, however, was against the idea. His relationship with the Unita men was now even stronger, and he was able to persuade them to help him obtain definite proof that the three men were still alive.

They agreed to transmit a priority message to Savimbi's camps in southern Angola, seeking the answer to a question which only the three ITN men would know. Morris remembered that Nicholson had recently acquired a new pet and quickly scribbled out the chosen message: 'What is the name of your new dog? Wells Street.' The Unita men were true to thier word. This was the only message which ever filtered through to the men but, ironically, when Nicholson scribbled his answer 'The name of my new dog is Badger,' the Unita radio operator was convinced it was a coded signal and refused to send it. 'In that case,' snapped the furious reporter, 'just tell them to set up the beers.'

A couple of days later, Morris received an unintelligible message which, far from providing the proof he was seeking, filled his mind with doubts. He dispatched a copy of the scrambled letters to ITN, where it was pinned to the Foreign

Desk notice board, inviting anybody to attempt to decipher the code. It fell to a lady called Barbara Gray to rekindle their hopes by pointing out that it was not a code at all, merely the transposition of several letters. 'It's easy,' she said. 'It says "Set up the beers".'

It was a euphoric moment. At least the crew was still alive and Morris's convictions had been ratified. However, the Angolan situation was worsening daily and the fact that they were still alive at the beginning of November was no guarantee that they would actually get out intact.

The Unita men, however, tried hard to dispel Morris's doubts.'Everything is going to plan,' they assured him. The ITN Foreign Editor then had no way of knowing that his Unita contacts were simply keeping him at arms' length while the ITN men, led by Tinkerbell, completed their three-week trek to their final camp in southern Angola. Even when they arrived, it took some days for the message to reach Kinshasa.

By this time, Rhodesia's activity in Zambia had ceased, and Carthew, with his identity now known, had flown to Kinshasa to help Morris finalize plans for what appeared to be a straightforward rescue operation.

The Unita pilots who had been co-opted for the rescue flight were Angolans, both very experienced at locating the small grass airstrips which abounded in southern Angola. With their co-operation, the rescue flight was set for Wednesday, 22 November – the 106th day. The message was dispatched to the corrugated encampment where the young lieutenant had imparted the good news to the ITN team, who were later led through torrential rains, only to return to their camp, bitterly disconsolate, some hours later.

The lieutenant's information that 'the plane had broken' was remarkably accurate, for the Unita Fokker had been severly damaged the previous day in Zaire, when a wrongly feathered propeller was sheared from its engine casing. Although Unita had dispatched the message with all speed, it had taken twenty-four hours to reach its destination.

If this was bad news, there was worse to come. Back in Kinshasa, Morris and Carthew learned that Unita could only keep the three men at their present camp for another three days. The window was closing, and if the rescue flight had not been implemented by the third day, the men would again be moved on.

Carthew was desperate. He now knew the men were at the former Portuguese airstrip in the south of Angola, but had no aircraft and only a limited time to get them out. To make matters worse, he had been banned from South Africa while working for the *Daily Mail* several years beforehand and was, therefore, unable to fly direct to Johannesburg to muster help. A frantic exchange of wires to and from London resulted in fellow reporter John Suchet – a temporary replacement for Nicholson – receiving a brief to contact a specific company in Johannesburg with its own HS 125 exceecutive jet. He had been given the lead by colleague Peter Snow who knew the company from his previous assignments in South Africa. After locating the two English pilots, Suchet explained the situation in detail, making no attempt to minimize the risk factor, before asking for their co-operation and practical assistance. Captain Roy Matthews and his colleague Johnny Adams discussed it together briefly, before agreeing to undertake what they later described as the 'most lunatic mission of their lives'. Both men had broad experience of flying over southern Africa, and were ideally qualified for the job.

Once Morris and Carthew received a wire in Kinshasa confirming the flight was on, they settled down to work out the logistics of the flight plan. First, the jet would have to fly from Johannesburg to Lubumbashi where it would refuel, and then cross to Kinshasa to rendezvous with Unita leaders, Carthew, and the rest of the rescue team. The plane would then return to Lubumbashi to refuel before the dash down to southern Angola where, if all went according to plan, they would pick up the itinerant newsmen and return with all haste. The timing of the landing in southern Angola would be crucial, scheduled for between 6.30 and 7 pm, when the light begins to fade but is still strong enough to allow an experienced pilot about ten minutes to touch down and take off again.

The flight plans to be filed by Carthew would be false, claiming that the executive aircraft would be confining its movements within Zaire, commuting only between Kinshasa and Lubumbashi. Although the plan was complex, everyone agreed that it was sound enough in theory. In practice, however, two administrative gremlins appeared, not only endangering the entire operation but at times reducing it to the level of farce.

When Captain Matthews brought the HS 125 down in Lubumbashi for its scheduled refuelling stop en route to Kinshasa, he produced the standard credit card used by pilots throughout the world. To his amazement, the authorities refused to accept it, and both men had to empty their pockets to scrape together enough money to purchase enough fuel to get them to their destination.

Once in Kinshasa, Unita accepted responsibility for all subsequent refuelling costs from their own coffers. The Unita funds comprised mostly local currency in low-denomination (one-zaire, five-zaire or ten-zaire) notes. With ten zaires equal to about twenty-five US cents, it was immediately apparent to Carthew that the transaction for something like seven thousand dollars-worth of fuel would present a few problems. He was right. A seemingly endless stream of willing helpers brought out notes in sports bags, carrier bags, boxes and newspapers, and proceeded to count it on the runway as Carthew, Morris, and the two English pilots watched in amazement. It was a performance that they would witness twice more before the job was over.

That night, in a room of the Intercontinental Hotel, Kinshasa, the two English pilots joined a Portuguese pilot and his navigator, a rebel Unita major, and two ITN news men, for a final briefing on what was to become one of the most dramatic rescues ever attempted. At this meeting, they were given the co-ordinates for the tiny airstrip in southern Angola, revealing for the first time their exact destination.

For the past twenty-four hours, Carthew and Morris had repeatedly refused Unita's requests to allow them to fly out wounded Unita rebels on the return journey. Such folly, they explained, could lead to everyone getting shot as either gun-runners or mercenaries. Now, Carthew was also to be excluded from the rescue bid at the direct intervention of ITN boss, David Nicholas. 'We don't know for certain that they're alive,' he explained. 'If we've already lost three, we'd be bloody silly to make it four.'

Disappointed, but understanding the motivation behind

the decision, Carthew flew with the rescue team only as far as Lubumbashi, where he again supervised the refuelling and subsequent exchange of thousands of low-denomination Zaire notes. Then, pausing only to stow a few bottles of beer on board for Doyle, Phillips, and Nicholson, he stood and watched as the insignificant little jet screamed down the runway before lifting its nose towards the sky.

He knew that the flight to the old airstrip would take exactly one hour and ten minutes. Allowing no more than ten minutes to pick up the three men, turn around and take off again, they should be back in just two-and-a-half hours. Tony Carthew began to count.

Nicholson saw it first from his vantage point on top of the disused army hut. As it came nearer, he recognized the outline of the HS 125 and, waving his arms excitedly, ran back to his colleagues screaming 'It's ours. It's for us.' As the executive jet swooped low over the airfield, and banked away preparing to make its approach, Phillips and Doyle stood in silence, not daring to believe that rescue was only minutes away. They watched in awe as it completed its circle and appeared to hover momentarily before hitting the ground with such force that several dials on the control panel spun crazily and jammed. Then, regaining its poise, the shaken aircraft bounced down the pitted, uneven grass strip and came to a halt two hundred yards away.

Together, the three men dashed towards the plane blind to any thought other than their imminent escape from their four months of hell in the steaming, fly-infested bush. As the cabin door opened and the steps extended, willing hands reached out to haul them in. It was Phillips who realized first. 'Christ!' he screamed above the high-pitched hum of the engines. 'We've forgotten the gear!'

Ignoring the pleas of Captain Matthews and the others on board, the three men turned their backs on the rescue plane and dashed back to the bush to collect their bags, cameras, and recording equipment. Then, pausing only to shout a single word of farewell to the young lieutenant, the Unita rebels with whom they had lived for so long, and the amiable

Mateus, they humped the baggage back to the aircraft. By running back for their equipment, they had lost several valuable minutes and might well have jeopardized the entire operation, according to their rescuers. It was Doyle's simple answer which summarized the feelings of all three: 'We couldn't leave that lot behind – not after all we've been through.' Coaxing every ounce of power from the engines, Matthews pulled back on the stick and the HS 125 rose like a rocket. Then, turning to his three new passengers, casually said, 'By the way – there's some beer in the fridge – courtesy of ITN.'

Back at Lubumbashi airport, Tony Carthew paced around nervously, glancing at his watch every few seconds. Every minute had seemed like an hour, and the tiny Hawker-Siddeley jet was now almost fifteen minutes overdue. Anticipation of a joyous reunion began to give way to fear of failure. Were the three men still alive? Had the rescue party managed to locate the old airstrip? Perhaps the tiny executive jet had been spotted and attacked either from the ground or by the Russian-built Mig fighters which formed the basis of Neto's air force? All were frightening, but very real, possibilities.

Then, he heard the familiar whine of a small jet aircraft preparing to land, and instinctively knew that they had made it. In his enthusiasm, Carthew virtually chased it down the runway as it touched down and eventually came to a standstill. He had realized that his three colleagues would probably want to leap from the aircraft and celebrate their newly found freedom, but he had to stop them at all costs. He had filed flight plans between Lubumbashi and Kinshasa for himself only and the sudden appearance of three Englishmen who had just been plucked from the Angolan bush would not only raise a few eyebrows, but also some insurmountable problems. As soon as the cabin door opened, Carthew clambered inside and his emotional joy at the reunion with his colleagues was forcibly tempered by the need to keep them out of sight.

During the flight back from their pick-up point, the three missing newsmen had been relatively quiet, realizing that they and their pilots were still far from safe. Now they wanted to celebrate, but at Carthew's insistence the real party would have to wait until they were back in Johannesburg. He had already persuaded the airport authorities to re-open the small bar at Lubumbashi, and purchased a dozen litres of beer – some for immediate consumption, and some to keep them company on the final stage of their journey. Unfortunately, however, there was an acute bottle shortage in Zaire at the time and the bar staff insisted that, while they had not minded re-opening the bar they would rather like the empties back before Carthew left Lubumbashi.

Carthew left the celebrations on board the cramped aircraft for a few minutes to Telex an urgent message to London; a message which was to spark off one of the wildest impromtu celebrations ever seen in the world of television. It read, simply: 'I have all chickens safely back in the nest. All look reasonably fit. ETA midnight Jo'burg – Carthew.'

By the time the HS 125 had refuelled, the three men had drunk as much beer as they could take, and transferred the rest into as many cans as they could find. These were seen off with little trouble during the flight, after which they proceeded to drink the contents of three magnificent crystal decanters (conventional fittings on many privately owned jet aircraft). After four months without alcohol, it took rapid effect. 'They were very emotional, talking, drinking, and even shedding a few tears of relief.' said Carthew later. 'By the time they got to Johannesburg, they were absolutely pissed, but the moment they got out of the aircraft, to be met by an ITN crew, they seemed to regain full control of themselves.'

They touched down shortly after midnight, as Carthew had predicted to London and, later that day, Sunday, 26 November, ITN viewers saw three slim, suntanned newsmen climb from their aircraft – Doyle and Nicholson with magnificent grey beards, and Phillips clean-shaven – to be confronted by their colleague Sandy Gall, brandishing a bottle of Dom Perignon champagne. After the brief initial interview, Sandy Gall announced he was worried. The Dom Perignon he explained, had already travelled a considerable distance in the boot of his car and, in his view, ought to be drunk immediately.

Carthew was also worried, but for a completely different reason. Approaching rapidly, and carrying a large black book, was a sombre-looking man wearing the unmistakable stamp

of a South African immigration official. After the heady and
emotional experience of playing a significant part in the successful rescue operation, Carthew then had the deflating
experience of being refused admittance to South Africa. He
was on the black list, explained the official and that was that.
He could not even be swayed by the champagne.

For Tony Carthew, the next hour was among the most
frightening in his life. Captain Matthews, after flying virtually
non-stop for twelve hours, was ordered to stable his jet and fly
the black-listed reporter across Johannesburg in a single-
engined light aircraft to Jan Smuts airport, where they had
facilities for detaining 'personae non gratae.' The weary English
pilot was in no physical condition to fly, but was forced to
comply with the orders of the immigration officer. With a
shrug, Carthew boarded the small, single-engined aircraft half
an hour later and, after nudging the pilot to keep him awake
'on at least two or three occasions', was duly delivered into the
hands of the authorities at Smuts airport. He was detained
until later that day, and then escorted to a London-bound jet
which enabled him to give a detailed account of the dramatic
rescue operation on ITN's 'News at One' on Monday,
27 November.

For Doyle, Phillips, and Nicholson, the return to their
Johannesburg base was euphoric. Sandy Gall chauffeured
them home, dropping Doyle and Phillips first, then
Nicholson, before returning to his hotel in search of a further
supply of champagne. The newly reunited Mr and Mrs
Nicholson decided that they would spend the rest of the night
celebrating with Phillips and Doyle and, not bothering to
change, started to walk the half mile or so to the rented house
which ITN provided for the crew. Nicholson recalled their
arrival clearly: 'We could hear this deafening music coming
from the house, and it was obvious that they were having a
party. I peeped through the curtain at once end of the room,
and I could see Mike dancing stark naked with a bottle of
champagne in one hand and a glass in the other. From
another window, I could just see Tom – he was also dancing
naked, and pouring champagne over his head.'

Convinced that they were about to crash an instant orgy,
Michael and Diana Nicholson entered the room with some

trepidation. Doyle and Phillips were dancing alone, drunk and totally oblivious to anything around them. Nicholson joined the early morning revellers, but made the mistake of keeping his clothes on. When the giggling trio linked hands and jumped into the swimming pool his invaluable and carefully protected passport, with dozens of visas holding memories of hundreds of news stories around the world, was still in his pocket. He retrieved it half an hour later to find a sodden, blurred, and irretrievable mess. But, like his colleagues he would not need a visa stamp to recall the greatest story of his life for, ironically, according to their passports, they had never been there.

John Holland, now a sound recordist, was a lighting technician in 1978. Like all crewmen, he was desperately worried about the fate of his missing colleagues, but felt powerless to make any positive contribution. On the night of Saturday, 25 November, he together with his wife Maureen and two friends, drove into London to see the hit African musical *Ipi Tombi*. He had heard rumours of a rescue attempt, and the ethnic sight of the African dancers on stage magnified his hopes still further. After the show, he drove the few hundred yards to Wells Street and, walking through the swing doors, asked the security man, 'Any news?' 'They're all in the newsroom.' was the reply and, sensing something had happened, Holland sprinted up the stairs to the first floor.

He did not need to be told. The popping of champagne corks and the cheering of the newsroom staff confirmed that Carthew's message had arrived. Barbara Gray, who had unscrambled the puzzling message, and Annie Scott, manageress of the ITN Club Bar, the camera crews' 'second home', threw their arms around him sobbing, 'They're safe.' Holland, court jester of the camera crews with a quip for every occasion, was uncharacteristically silent as he walked slowly back to his car with tears in his eyes.

AFGHANISTAN

සේ

A guest of the Russians

When news filtered through that the Russians had invaded
Afghanistan in the last days of 1979, it sent a chill down the
spine of most politically-aware people in the Western world. It
was a draught which took the edge off the Christmas celebrations as inevitable comparisons were made with the fate of
Hungary in 1956 and Czechoslovakia in 1968. The move was
seen as another aggressive step by the Soviet Union in its quest
to inflict its communist doctrine on its weaker neighbours, but
many political observers were puzzled by the timing of the
invasion. For a major power due to host the Olympic Games
for the first time in its history in six months' time, the move
was hardly diplomatic. As the Russian grip became tighter, the
thirst for information became greater, and television newsmen
from most major networks throughout the world were hastily
dispatched to Kabul in the quest of news.

The Russians were as reluctant as ever to open their doors to
the world and made access difficult for news crews. Although
ITN camera teams succeeded in reaching Afghanistan to film
some very dramatic and revealing footage during the ensuing
twelve months, their methods of entry were, by necessity,
devious and mostly dangerous. They were interrogated,
imprisoned, threatened, bombed, and almost poisoned, and
the two crews who successfully disguised themselves as
Afghans to cross the border from Pakistan risked certain incar-
ceration on spying charges. The Russians do not take kindly to
being hoodwinked by European newsmen.

The invasion of Afghanistan started on 27 December but the news was not confirmed nor its implications fully digested, for another twenty-four hours. It was that sleepy period between Christmas and the New Year when most of the Western world lapses into its annual festive coma and, by the time the shock waves penetrated, the Russians had control of Kabul airport and scheduled flights into Afghanistan were virtually non-existent.

The ITN crew – cameraman Derek Seymour, sound recordist Tony Piddington, and reporter Martyn Lewis – were briefed on New Year's Eve, and the morning of 1 January 1980, saw them heading west down the almost deserted M4 towards Heathrow airport. They had been booked on a flight to New Delhi which was considered the best springboard from which to catch one of the rare flights into Kabul. A dozen other news crews had the same idea. Delhi's Intercontinental Hotel was like the International Press Club as newsmen spent four days milling around the bar and making several fruitless visits to the airport. On the few occasions that a flight left for Kabul, passport control officers diligently obeyed their two-word dictum: 'No Press.'

Seymour and Co. had now been joined by Claes Bratt, a Swedish cameraman working for UPITN in Bangkok, who had flown into New Delhi to provide any assistance the crew might need. He had completely dismantled his CP16 camera, wrapping the components in the contents of his overnight bag, and, with his passport describing him as a 'student' he was able to move around the airport without arousing any suspicion that he was a media man.

On the morning of the fifth day, the ITN crew doggedly retraced their steps back to the airport, knowing that it was almost certainly a wasted journey. Other crews, who relied on telephone enquiries, were told that there were either no flights or no seats available for the Press. On arriving at the airport, the spirits of the four men were slightly lifted by the news that a flight was scheduled to depart for Kabul later that morning, but they viewed their chances with some pessimism. On previous excursions, they had tried to adopt a fairly low profile, but felt sure that they had already been rubber-stamped as members of the Press contingent. Their case was not helped

when an Indian family buttonholed Lewis in the airport
lounge and asked for his autograph, explaining that they lived
in England and were regular followers of 'News at Ten'.

They queued at the desk of Ariana Afghan Airways, and
purchased tickets without any problems, but even at this stage,
they were not optimistic about their chances of being allowed
on the flight. They still had to clear the main hurdle of
passport control and emigration. There were no other
newsmen in evidence, however, and they quietly felt that this
might help their cause.

The four spread themselves out in the queue, with Lewis at
the front. He presented his passport and ticket for inspection
by the Indian official who stared long and hard at Lewis. 'You
are a British reporter,' he said. Lewis turned on his full innocent
charm and pointed to the false description against the
'occupation' entry in his passport. 'No,' he protested. 'I'm a
company executive here on business.' When, after a few more
anxious seconds, Lewis was allowed through, he was as
surprised as anyone. After a few paces, he turned and looked
questioningly towards his colleagues. Seymour realized the
importance of getting even just one man into Kabul and,
nodding discreetly, mouthed the monosyllabic order 'Go'.

Claes Bratt was next. With his worldly goods (not to
mention a CP16 camera) tucked neatly in his overnight grip, he
appeared the archetypal Scandinavian student, bumming his
way through the East, and he was waved through without a
second glance. The God of Bureaucracy smiled on Seymour,
too. His job definition, in common with most of his
colleagues, is director-camerman. For obvious reasons there
are times when cameramen, like reporters, have to travel
incognito, and for this reason his passport described his
occupation simply as 'Director'. Assuming that he was dealing
with another businessman, Patel of passport control dropped
his third brick in as many minutes, and allowed him through.
Piddington, however, was a doomed man. With the description
'television technician' clearly marked in his passport, his way
was barred, and his assertion that he was really a TV repair man
on holiday cut little ice with the officials. He trudged back
displaying all the disappointment of a volunteer conscript
having failed a medical.

With three out of four on the aircraft, and not another television news crew in sight, the ITN men had every reason to feel pleased with themselves as the medium-range Ariana Boeing nosed its way through the clear blue skies towards Afghanistan. As Seymour reflected on their good fortune, he had no way of knowing that within forty-eight hours his role would be reversed, and instead of looking through the view-finder, he would be looking into the camera, telling the world how he had been captured by the Russians, interrogated and imprisoned after being caught filming front-line manoeuvres. Nothing, in fact, could have been further from his mind as the aircraft bounced down the Kabul runway, before finally coming to a standstill outside the passenger terminal.

As they passed through customs, Seymour and Lewis were surprised to see David Phillips, a former ITN colleague, now working as field producer with the American NBC network. Phillips was awaiting the arrival of his own news team and was clearly disturbed to learn that they had not been on the flight. The reasons for his agitation was soon evident; he had located the exact position of the Russian front-line build-up but, without a camera crew, this intelligence was useless. On the other hand, the ITN men had the gear, but not the information, and the logical deal was struck. In return for full co-operation from Phillips, NBC would receive an edited copy of the story, enabling them to transmit at the same time as their rival network, ABC, with whom ITN have an automatic exchange agreement.

Anxious to capitalize on their obvious advantage, the four men did not bother to check into a hotel. Instead, they took a taxi from the airport and, under direction from Phillips, headed towards the Khyber Pass, on the far side of Kabul. After forty-five minutes' drive along a straight and seemingly endless road, they saw the first signs of Russian military presence and slowed down for a closer look at the heavy Soviet armaments parked by the roadside. Despite the temptation to stop and film the column, they decided to push forward to get as close to the front line as possible. It was a logical plan; they could always film the Russians on the way back and, in the event of trouble, they would be facing the right way for a speedy dash back to Kabul.

Within ten minutes, they were at the breathtaking entrance
to the Khyber Pass, but they had little time to admire the
scenic splendour. Instead, their attention was focused on the
Russian troops feverishly engaged in digging slit trenches
across the hillside.

Lewis had picked up a smattering of Russian a couple of
months beforehand while covering the annual Soviet military
parade in Red Square. He waved in a gesture of friendliness,
and the troops waved back in acknowledgement of his greeting 'Dobroye Utro' and then resumed their digging with an air
of mechanical resignation. The uniform was the only thing
that distinguished them from Afghan peasants, thought
Seymour, as he continued filming the Soviet movements.

He had shot nearly five minutes of the film before a Russian
APC thundered towards them. An officer, flanked by two
armed soldiers, leaped out and waving his arms, made it clear
that Seymour and Bratt had incurred Soviet displeasure. 'No
films,' he snapped. 'Stop now.' There are times when
cameramen, certain of their ground and confident of their
rights, can argue the toss and continue filming at their own
risk. Standing in the front line of Russian-occupied territory
was not one of them. Instead, they switched off their cameras
and sound gear and gazed somewhat quizzically at the
Russian officer who now seemed unsure of his next move.

After ten minutes, the atmosphere seemed to relax slightly,
and Seymour took the chance to play what turned out to be an
ace card. Making some excuse to return to the car, he and
Bratt swiftly switched the half-used film magazine for a new
one and tucked the original under the driver's seat. Then, with
the camera pointing towards the ground, they ran off approximately the same amount of footage on the new magazine. It
was a slim chance, thought Seymour, but if the Russians
attempted to ruin the film by removing it from the magazine,
they could play with the useless one while the all-important
footage was concealed in the car.

Another ten minutes ticked by and the men were getting
restless. 'If we can't film, we'll go back to our hotel,' they
suggested, but this proposal was greeted with a definitive
'Niet'. The crew was getting colder, more impatient and less
certain of their destiny. Then, after a further wait of twenty

minutes, a Russian Colonel arrived in a jeep, and the two officers conversed in furtive tones, occasionally looking towards various crew members in turn. After five minutes, they seemed to reach a decision. Seymour was ordered to stow the camera gear in the boot before he and Phillips were ushered into the back of the taxi with the senior Russian officer seated between them. Lewis and Bratt were bundled into the army personnel carrier, and the little two-vehicle convoy headed down the long, straight road towards Kabul.

Seymour and Phillips sat in silence. There was little to say in the presence of the Russian, and Seymour, seated immediately behind the driver, was more concerned with keeping the film magazine concealed. At the start of the journey, the sudden forward momentum of the car had sent it skidding out from beneath the driver's seat, narrowly missing the Russian's right shoe. Looking anywhere but downwards, Seymour delicately guided the film back to its hiding place and wedged his foot against it to ensure that it stayed there.

After reaching Kabul, it became clear that the Russian officer was looking for a particular destination as he ordered the taxi driver to turn first right, then left, all the time peering intently from the car windows. His knowledge of local geography was non-existent and the driver, following the Colonel's erratic directions, had already shaken off the APC 'tail' carrying Lewis and Bratt. It was later established that he had been searching for the Russian Embassy. They continued their aimless tour through the streets of Kabul for another hour before passing what appeared to be a cross between an Afghan prison and an army barrack. Making a snap decision, the Russian ordered the taxi to drive in through the large iron gates.

Giving the film magazine a final nudge with his foot to ensure it remained well hidden, Seymour obeyed the order to get out of the car and was immediately hit by the biting cold. It was now late afternoon and the temperature was around ten degrees below freezing. That night it would sink to twenty degrees below.

Although the men were uncertain of the Russian strength in Kabul, the sight of Soviet tanks and other heavy armaments in the barrack square suggested that it was a formidable presence. As Russian troops opened the boot and seized the film gear, Seymour was reflecting on the dramatic footage he could have taken if the camera had been in his, rather than Russian, hands. He was brought back to reality by a tug on his arm and the two men, together with the taxi driver, were quickly propelled towards the main building. Clearly, the Soviets had not assembled their strength in Kabul for the benefit of Western eyes.

Seymour and Phillips were taken to a small room where they were confronted by an Afghan interrogator who, in perfect English, drilled them with the standard questions familiar to anyone who has ever seen a low-budget movie: 'What were their names? Where were they from? What were they doing? Why were they filming the Russians? How did they get into Afghanistan? Surely, they must have false documents?' Seymour and Phillips answered all the questions truthfully. As experienced television newsmen, they knew the penalty of lying. After fifteen minutes they were led to the nearby 'slammer suite' and thrown in separate cells. Their rooms were classic design: eight feet wide, twelve feet long, one tiny barred window, a door with a small grille, and a single hard wooden chair.

For two hours, Seymour sat alone wondering whether he and the rest of the team had finally overstepped the mark. After all, the Russians had been in Afghanistan for only a few days. World opinion was running at fever pitch, and an ITN television crew had suddenly popped up filming their front-line manoeuvres. He was concerned, too, about the film magazine hidden beneath the driver's seat. If the taxi left now, they would not have a hope in hell of finding it.

Eventually, his cell door creaked open and the Afghan with the Oxford accent re-appeared with two minions carrying a small square wooden table, and another chair. Placing a sheaf of papers and a pen on the table, he ordered Seymour to chronicle his entire life history with full details of his education, jobs, countries visited, dates, his personal family background, and, most important, details of how and when he arrived in Afghanistan. The Afghan interrogator paused in the doorway and narrowed his eyes to add a touch of Gestapo-style menace to his parting line: 'It is most important

Mr Seymour, that you leave *nothing* out.'

Seymour laboured at it for hours, giving a full and accurate picture of as much of his thirty-nine years as he could remember. He had not been asked to do prep. like this for nearly twenty-five years, and he found it not only a valuable exercise to alleviate the pressure, but also an amusing way of passing the time. He paused occasionally to ease his aching wrist and wonder if David Phillips had been asked to do the same.

It was 10.30 pm when the Afghan returned, again with an armed Russian guard, and sat in the empty chair opposite the cameraman. He studied the wad of notes in front of him dispassionately, before looking up. 'Now,' he said, 'we will ask you some questions.' Although Seymour was tired, cold, hungry, and more than a little worried, he was amused by the high drama of the situation. There was even a single, bare electric light bulb directly over the table, adding further authenticity to what had now become a classic interrogation scene.

The session lasted for over five hours, with a brief break halfway through. The Afghan had tried desperately to find a flaw in Seymour's story but, in spite of firing his barrage of questions in a haphazard, rather than chronological, order had failed to do so. Eventually, at four o'clock in the morning, the questioning ceased, and a guard appeared with an old mattress and blanket which he threw in the corner.

Still wearing his anorak, gloves, and boots, Seymour put his head down, but found it difficult to sleep. He eventually dozed off only to be awakened an hour later by the sound of tanks revving up immediately outside his cell. Further sleep was out of the question and he climbed on a chair to peer out of his tiny cell window. He was surprised to see the taxi exactly where they had left it, and could only assume that the driver had also been questioned about how and when he had picked up the ITN men. For the next hour, he watched the growing activity in the square as more tanks spluttered into action creating welcome heat for the men inside. He was amused to see that the Russian tank crews appeared to have shaven heads beneath their leather helmets.

His early morning watch was punctuated by the arrival of 'breakfast' – something resembling hot, sweet tea in a chipped mug, and a piece of dry unleavened bread, neither of which made any impact on his appetite. Seymour resumed his vigil, watching tanks, APCs and other armaments shuffle around the square in a meaningless game of military chess, before his attention was attracted by a lone soldier, marching purposefully towards the taxi. Opening the doors, he groped around for a couple of minutes before emerging triumphantly with the all-important magazine of film.

Seymour's heart sank to his boots; the lone thought that they might have actually scored one over the Russians had helped to keep his spirits afloat but now, all was certainly lost. He guessed that there were no processing facilities in Kabul, and the Russians would be unable to view the filmed evidence, which would have inflamed them even more. It was more likely that they would simply expose the film by tearing it from its magazine, thus rendering it useless.

When the taxi driver was released, half an hour later, Seymour realized that the question of the destiny of the film had been purely academic; if the Russians hadn't found the film, it would have been almost impossible to trace. Inevitably, the disappointments of the past few days boiled to the surface. Having at last gained entry into Afghanistan and been the first to film the Russian presence, then coming so close to duping the Russians by switching films, he now realized that the ultimate achievement of his endeavours would be a fat zero. He kicked the wall in anger and swore loudly.

The hours ticked by agonizingly slowly until mid-day when the Afghan interrogator re-appeared and Seymour was subjected to yet another futile questioning. This time, however, he had added a question of his own. The gastronomic shortcomings of his Afghan breakfast were playing hell with his guts and access to a toilet was a priority, if not a necessity. He was escorted by a Russian soldier to a door at the far end of a nearby corridor, where the sight and smell almost made him throw up. Afghan toilet habits differ widely from the accepted Western standards of hygiene. Instead of sitting on the seat, they stand on it, adopt a crouching position and aim. Most of them miss. Enraged by the thought that he should be expected to use such a putrid facility, he exploded, insisting on a cleaner, more civilized alternative. Within ten minutes, the foul toilets had been completely hosed out for his benefit, although the pungent stench of pollution remained as a permanent feature of the place.

He had returned to his cell only a short time before the door again clanked open and he was summoned into the corridor where he saw Phillips for the first time since they had been parted the previous evening. Their greeting was more like city gents meeting on a tube train, than television newsmen incarcerated in an Afghan jail: ' Morning, old boy,' said Seymour, and Phillips continued the charade with the retort: 'Fine day – a bit nippy though.'

At gunpoint, they were marched to the room where they were originally interrogated, and Seymour's heart leapt as they walked through the door. Scattered over the floor, apparently unharmed, was all the camera and sound equipment which the Russians had removed from the car boot the previous night. To the left, instantly recognizable by the muddy footprints where Seymour had successfully concealed it with his boot, was the unopened magazine containing world exclusive film of the Russian invasion forces.

Restraining himself from making a frienzied dive for the magazine, Seymour first picked up the camera and inspected it. He could tell immediately that the Russians had been tampering with it; the film loops were loose, and they had obviously been trying to ascertain how it worked. As he casually bent forward to pick up the prize magazine of film, the Afghan tapped him on the shoulder. 'You are extremely lucky,' he said. 'You left that in the taxi. If we hadn't looked, you would have lost it.' Seymour nodded his thanks, first to the Afghan and then to the Russian guard who had retrieved it. The Soviet guard nodded back and smiled, obviously pleased to have been of service.

They were now free to go and, after receiving a parting warning about future dangers of filming Russian troops or armaments, they were escorted back across the barrack square to the main gate where one of the guards deftly removed Seymour's Seiko from his wrist, clearly believing it to be justified payment for the return of the film magazine. With barely an hour's sleep in the past thirty hours, Seymour could hardly stay awake. Once back at the hotel, the bed attracted him like a magnet and he was about to put his head down when the telephone rang. It was a rather heated Lewis. 'Where the bloody hell have you been?' he demanded.

Lewis and Bratt had got off very lightly. After being bundled in the APC, they had been searched and relieved of their maps which were apparently more detailed and sophisticated than anything the Russians possessed. Lewis had also been deprived of his pocket-sized battery tape recorder which his captors regarded as the richest of prizes. For Lewis and Bratt, however, these losses were tempered by the thought that they were probably the first Western journalists to have a first-hand sight of the interior of a modern Soviet personnel carrier.

The mood inside the APC had been more relaxed than in the taxi ahead, and Bratt freely distributed his cigarettes to the driver and the officer. This helped thaw the atmosphere still further and, in reply to Lewis's questions, the two men were told that they were being taken to the Soviet Embassy for interrogation. When the constant meanderings of the taxi ahead eventually separated the two vehicles, the driver of the APC continued his aimless mystery tour of Kabul, looking for the Embassy with more hope than conviction. When they passed the Intercontinental for the second time, Lewis suggested that it would be easier for everyone concerned if they were to stop the charade, and allow both himself and Bratt to return to their hotel. Certainly, it seemed that the Russians were not too keen to spend the rest of the day ferrying the two men around the Afghan capital, and Bratt clinched their freedom by parting with his last packet of cigarettes. Not many British newsmen can claim to have been dropped off at the entrance of their hotel by a Russian armoured personnel carrier.

Lewis immediately contacted the British Embassy to report their brief detention. Showing uncharacteristic excitement about the incident, they dispatched an envoy to the hotel immediately and both Lewis and Bratt were persuaded to stay at the Embassy overnight. 'Folly to stay at the hotel,' they were warned. 'The Russians have failed with you so far – they'll probably come back.' Unaware of Seymour's situation, Lewis left a message for him to contact the British Embassy as soon as he arrived at the hotel. Only when the message was still there the following morning, did Lewis have any real doubts about the safety of his colleague and when he eventually contacted him at about 2 pm that afternoon, his fierce question was motivated more by relief than anger.

'In the slammer,' answered Seymour, 'and I'm knackered and hungry.' Once he was over the surprise, and had heard a graphic account of Seymour's 'lost' twenty-four hours, Lewis's reaction was positive. 'It should make a great piece,' he said and, for the first time in fifteen years as a cameraman, Seymour knew what it was like on the other side of the lens.

Seymour took the interview and the film of the Russian front-line build up to New Delhi the following morning. At this stage, he still had no idea whether the Russians had exposed the film, and offered a silent prayer as he passed both magazines to the agency who would rush them to London.

The ban on newsmen entering Kabul had now been relaxed and, after picking up the rest of the ITN camera equipment, Seymour linked up with Piddington and the men braced themselves for a return to the Afghan capital. His fears about the film were put to rest twenty-four hours later when the crew received a cable from colleague Tony Carthew in Delhi congratulating them on both pieces. Their ruse had worked; the prize magazine of film which had been in Russian hands for four hours, and which contained intelligence of their front-line position and strength, had been handed back, un-opened.

The relaxation of restrictions on the admission of Western newsmen into Afghanistan was purely temporary. When the Russians got wind of the extent of anti-Soviet propaganda being screened across the European and American networks, they again put up the shutters, preventing the media from reaching Kabul by the recognized route. This presented a problem for the ITN Foreign Desk. The activities of Seymour and Lewis had already whetted the appetite of British viewers, but subsequent attempts to film the Russian presence in and around the Afghan capital had met with little success. By early February, Kabul airport was firmly closed to anyone but bona fide businessmen or tourists, and ITN decided it was time that three of their news staff took a 'holiday'.

Cameraman Bob Hammond and sound recordist Don Warren were given a special briefing and booked on a flight to New Delhi. From there, masquerading as tourists, they would try to catch the first available flight into Kabul just as Seymour and Lewis had done a few weeks beforehand. Unlike their colleagues, however, they would not be taking the bulky CP16 camera; instead, Hammond was equipped with an old-fashioned clockwork 16mm autoload which was smaller, and therefore easier to conceal, while Warren was issued with a slim, high-quality cassette recorder and miniature microphones, which could be hidden beneath his shirt. By issuing such unconventional equipment, ITN was doing its best to ensure not only that the crew would be able to operate more effectively, but also that the rather amateur appearance of their gear would support their claim to be tourists. For reporter John Suchet, who completed the team, entering Kabul in the guise of a tourist was relative child's play compared to his two subsequent assignments when, on both occasions, he and his crew crossed the mountainous Pakistan border disguised as Afghan rebels.

The crew were all experienced men. Warren had covered trouble spots all over the world, while Hammond, formerly a sound recordist, was part of the team which scooped the world exclusive with the Turkish landings in Cyprus in 1974. As a cameraman his coverage of the Iranian revolution, which led to the fall of the Peacock throne the previous year, helped him become the first ITN man to gain the Royal Television Society's coveted 'Cameraman of the Year' award. He described his winning portfolio of three films as a contrast of 'hot, cold, and wet' stories. The first incurred considerable danger, covering the Iranian uprising, the second being lowered by helicopter into the freezing Kent countryside to film motorists stranded in snowdrifts, while the third providing the uncomfortable experience of sitting in a powered rubber dinghy at the mercy of the Atlantic waves while filming Green Peace efforts to prevent the dumping of nuclear waste by the British Atomic

Authority's disposal craft *Gem*.

Now, at the behest of the Foreign Desk, he was en route to Kabul where he would do his best to convince the Afghan authorities that he was a harmless tourist, while filming further proof of the Soviet military build-up in and around the Afghan capital. An eyeball-to-eyeball confrontation with the Russians was not something that he was particularly relishing, but as long as they were careful and favoured with a little luck, he felt they could probably get away with it.

The ITN men arrived in New Delhi and booked themselves on a flight leaving for Afghanistan the following day. They had travelled separately to avoid suspicion and found little difficulty getting into Kabul. The tightening of Russian controls meant that visas were now necessary for entry into Afghanistan, but the crew had managed to secure the obligatory stamp, and proceeded to their hotel virtually unimpeded. Hammond's passport contained the bland description 'engineer' and, although the customs and immigration authorities had made a detailed inspection of their luggage, the men had not been subjected to a full body search and were allowed through with both the camera and cassette recorder undetected. They congratulated themselves on their good fortune. The authorities were very touchy and had even impounded Western newspapers from baggage in addition to issuing stern warnings about the use of still cameras.

The hotel lounge was full of Russians and Eastern European officials, all trying to fade nonchalantly into the background. This made them seem even more furtive, and Hammond remembers thinking that if this had been an audition for natural-looking film extras, he would not have hired any of them. Keen to put their 'tourist' label to the test, they dumped their baggage in their room and planned their first 'tour' of Kabul.

Taxis, however, posed a threat; many drivers were either government officials or informers who would flatly refuse to take passengers anywhere near Russian activity, and it was not easy to locate anti-Soviet sympathizers. Delicate enquiries eventually uncovered a 'friendly' clique of Afghans who put them in touch with a trustworthy driver, and they headed for the centre of Kabul. The taxi driver clearly knew his business;

within minutes they were approaching an armoured vehicle
which resembled a small tank. To avoid arousing unnecessary
suspicion, they stopped the taxi some distance away and,
telling the driver to wait, they walked casually towards the
Russians with a clear strategy in mind. Suchet, armed with
several packets of chewing gum, would distribute it liberally to
children around the armoured vehicle and try to engage the
Russians in casual conversation, with the aid of European
cigarettes. Next to him, Warren would pick up any dialogue
on his concealed microphone, while Hammond would be
unobtrusively filming the action from thirty yards away, pray-
ing that Suchet would be able to divert the Russians' attention
long enough to enable him to get some decent footage. It
worked for a couple of minutes and, by the time Hammond
was spotted, Suchet's liberal distribution of gum had attracted
so many children that the vehicle was unable to move. They
made their way back to their taxi, pleased with the results of
their first encounter with the invading Russians, but acutely
aware of the high risk of filming.

From their sympathetic contacts, the ITN men were also able
to glean valuable information about the location of Russian
armaments. They learned that there was a large mobile
artillery unit at an open camp about five miles to the north of
Kabul and, realizing the importance of keeping the lowest of
profiles, they discussed their tactics during the short drive
towards the base the following day.

It was a vast mobile camp and a handful of optimistic
Afghan traders were trying desperately either to sell to the
Russians or to 'exchange' luxury items like sunglasses for
packets of cigarettes. The crew was able to move freely without
arousing any immediate suspicion, and Hammond vividly
recalls the sight of female Russian soldiers bargaining fiercely
to pin down the Afghan traders to the lowest prices. In spite of
the trading, there was still an uneasy atmosphere around the
camp, and the Russian guards were quick to react to anything
or anybody which aroused the slightest suspicion.

It was a large compound housing up to four hundred Soviet
troops, and rich in military vehicles. To Hammond and the
others it was a prize not be missed. They mingled with the
crowd and, while Hammond filmed surreptitiously over

Suchet's shoulder, Warren wandered around with his microphones and cassette recorder concealed beneath his shirt. 'The equipment was very basic,' Hammond recalled later, 'and we were very restricted in our movements, but we managed to shoot some reasonable film.' It seemed that their luck was still holding out. Already, they had found two 'straight' taxi drivers, and they could not have wished for better material than the Russian troops and armaments which surrounded them. They had even been spotted by a couple of Russians who had elected to turn a blind eye, obviously too immersed in their own business to want to become involved with the transgressions of a group of tourists. It seemed almost too good to be true, Hammond thought to himself.

Then, suddenly, he knew it was all over. A peasant trader had spotted his camera, and, shouting excitedly to attract the attention of a Russian NCO, he pointed enthusiastically towards the three men and mimed a camera action. He had obviously seen it as an opportunity to score a few points for himself by putting the finger on the crew, and had achieved his objective with consummate ease. The crew started to walk away casually, but were soon halted in mid-step as a Russian guard fired a couple of rounds over their heads. He rushed towards them, grabbing Hammond's camera. Warren started to protest, but the Russian's only response was to tear open his shirt and reveal the concealed cassette recorder. The ensuing eerie silence was broken only by the scurrying of military boots as the NCO was joined by more Soviet guards.

They were searched, and their passports were impounded: then, with threatening jabs in the back from Soviet rifles, they were propelled towards the wall of a nearby shelter and ordered to stand a few feet apart, with their hands above their heads. Soon they were joined by their driver who was already marked as a collaborator, and two more Russians proceeded to strip his car for further evidence. Realizing that they could easily impound his licence, thus depriving him of a living, he broke down and sobbed.

For three hours, Hammond, Warren, and Suchet stood against the wall in silence, aware all the time that the Russians behind them were studying their passports and discussing their fate. They could also hear the movement of heavy trucks and tanks but any attempt to sneak a furtive glimpse was met with a smart rebuff by the Russians.

By mid-afternoon, the sun was sinking and the few Afghans who remained, hoping perhaps to witness a dramatic climax, were ushered away. To the three newsmen, this was an ominous sign, and when a truck pulled into the square a few minutes later, carrying between a dozen and twenty Russian soldiers with rifles, Hammond's stomach turned a cartwheel. 'It's a firing squad,' he told himself. 'They're going to chop us.' It was classic situation; the three men were lined up against the wall in the middle of nowhere, the sun was going down, and there were no witnesses. For the three men, it was a horrendous moment, and one which will live in their memories for ever. Suchet, who had a smattering of Russian, tried to engage an officer in conversation and was puzzled by his lack of success. 'It was almost as though he didn't understand,' said Hammond later. 'John's vocabulary was very basic and we later wondered if this so-called Russian officer had perhaps been co-opted from somewhere else.'

Fears that they might face a firing squad began to subside when four civilian Afghan defence officials arrived and scrutinized their passports. After about twenty minutes, the mood began to relax, and the three men were offered cigarettes which helped calm their nerves considerably. They were handed over to Afghan Foreign Office Ministry officials, who began to lose interest when the three men admitted being newsmen and it became apparent that Hammond, Warren, and Suchet were not spies. 'They gave us a severe bollocking and told us not to do it again,' said Hammond. Rather naively, the Afghans asked which cassettes and film cartridges had been used and, trying to look bitterly disappointed, Hammond pointed to two blank ones which were immediately impounded. The others were handed back to the crew, together with their passports.

They were driven back to Kabul separately, which gave them brief cause for alarm, before rallying in the bar of their hotel. With their cover well and truly blown, and the promise that things would become extremely uncomfortable if they were caught filming again, there seemed little point in remaining. When they flew out of Afghanistan the following day, it was with the knowledge that, for crews entering Kabul 'under cover', the risk factor had increased considerably.

Through the back door

For Suchet, gaining access to Afghanistan and levelling the score with the Russians, was becoming a challenge, if not an obsession. By March, scheduled air travel to Kabul was out of the question and, if he could find anyone foolhardy enough to fly a crew in by chartered light aircraft, it would probably be shot down within minutes of crossing the border. The only alternative, he decided, was to gain access by land. But how? He knew that Afghanistan was flanked on three sides by the borders with the USSR, Iran, and Pakistan; the first was an automatic non-starter and entry via Iran was equally unlikely, and would in any case only provide access to the south and west, whereas Russian action was concentrated in the north and the east. The logical route was through the Khyber Pass, but study of maps of Pakistan suggested alternative, less obvious routes, further north.

Suchet knew that several factions of the Mujahideen – the anti-Soviet Afghan guerilla movement – had their headquarters in Peshawar, and felt that there was a good chance that they could smuggle a crew across the border, disguised as Afghans. The Foreign Desk agreed to give it a try and, five weeks after returning from his six-day sortie to Kabul with Hammond and Warren, he was on a flight from Heathrow to Peshawar, via Karachi, with a brief to make contact with the Mujahideen and check the feasibility of the plan. ITN did not doubt that the rewards of the operation would be worthwhile, for no television news crew had ever penetrated Afghanistan through the Pakistan mountains.

Within a few days, London heard that the results of Suchet's enquiries had been positive, and the assignments desk summoned cameraman Chris Faulds and sound recordist John Soldini for a briefing. This was a logical choice since, like Suchet, they both had dark, sallow complexions which would make them less likely to stand out in a foreign environment. Soldini, with nearly twenty years' experience with ITN, was now in his mid-fifties but had the benefit of being an extremely fit man. Exactly ten years earlier, he had been a member of the joint ITN - Thames TV team which joined Chris Bonington's successful assault on the 26,500 feet South Face of Annapurna and was, therefore, considered well capable of coping with the mountain passes of northern Pakistan.

On 26 March Faulds and Soldini left Heathrow for Karachi, en route for Peshawar where twenty-four hours later, they joined Suchet at the Intercontinental Hotel. Suchet had established that there were five or six different factions of the Mujahideen in Peshawar and, although there was a strong rivalry between them, they were all united in the common cause to get the Russians out of their beloved Afghanistan. He had been successful in negotiations with one group, who seemed keen to take them across the border, but he was also keeping his options open with another two factions as a safety net, since views, favours, and promises tend to be very changeable in that part of the world. The three ITN men visited the chosen Mujahideen headquarters regularly during the next three days, trying to commit the rebels to a firm departure date. 'They seemed most co-operative,' remembered Faulds. 'They nodded enthusiastically and promised us the earth but, in retrospect, they probably didn't understand most of what we were saying.'

On the fourth day, the crew learned that they would be leaving the following morning and would be crossing the border through a small un-named pass about 100 miles to the northeast of the Khyber Pass. They would be dressed as Afghans, not only to fool the Russians but also to hoodwink the Pakistani police. The authorities were anxious not to upset the Russians by allowing free access through their country to Afghanistan, but felt that the story of the invasion and mass destruction of Afghan villages should be told. Consequently, while the Pakistani government appeared to adopt an obstructive policy, their less offical view was 'good luck' to anyone who could make it.

Later that day, the three men were taken to a store in Peshawar where the necessary clothes – turban, dirahan and lungi – were bought for them, together with blankets, while they hovered inconspicuously in the background. Every couple of minutes, the Mujahideen contact would give them a sidelong glance to establish their size, and after the accepted negotiation about the price, he ushered them out of the shop carrying what they desperately hoped was their passport to Afghanistan.

They were to report to the rebel headquarters in Peshawar at 4 am the next morning and, although they knew that the first part of their journey entailed a bus ride, they had been told little else. They dressed in their normal clothes to avoid suspicion if they were seen leaving the hotel and, assuming that they would be ferried to a base camp by car, had no compunction about packing their three suitcases with their Afghan outfits, camera, and sound gear, and anything else they thought they might need. They crept silently from the hotel and took a taxi to the rebel offices a couple of miles away, where the sight of the suitcases caused mild hysteria among the Mujahideen. Despite the language difficulties, it was made abundantly clear to the ITN men that it would be tricky enough guiding three Europeans through forbidden Pakistani and Afghan territory, without advertising the fact by carrying luggage.

Faulds, Soldini, and Suchet changed into their Afghan 'pyjamas' (as Faulds insisted on calling them) and transferred only the basic essentials from the suitcases to rucksacks. They had planned to take European clothes to lessen the chances of being regarded as spies if they were apprehended but these, together with much of their other more important equipment, were destined to remain at the rebel headquarters with their suitcases.

It seemed that they had overestimated the hospitality of their guides. Not only was there no base camp, but they also discovered that there was no car transport and they were expected to walk much of the way through mountainous territory. Time would prove that this was not the only Mujahideen promise to fall well short of expectations.

Accompanied by two guides, they made their way to the bus station and, feeling rather too conspicuous for comfort, tried to mingle with the crowd. 'We felt ridiculous,' said Faulds. 'It was as though we were attending some ghastly fancy dress event. I felt totally out of place.' Their guides were quick to warn them about the dangers of speaking – even among themselves – as there was a high risk that they would be overheard by the dozens of informers keen to curry favour with the local police. Even on the bus, the three men were separated to minimize suspicion. Sitting by themselves, their looks might only arouse mild interest; together they would kindle definite suspicion.

The guides paid the fares and, for three hours, the news team sat in total silence as the packed bus bounced along the uneven road towards the north beyond the Khyber Pass. Their silent thoughts were shattered only once by a loud bang which rattled the windows in the bus. Faulds, who immediately assumed it was a mortar shell, was extremely relieved to discover it was nothing more dangerous than a puncture. His relief gave way to a mixture of fear and embarrassment a few seconds later when all the passengers were shepherded off the bus while the driver replaced the offending wheel. He had his climbing boots on beneath his robes and, since most Afghans wear open leather sandals, he felt that this made him even more conspicuous. 'We stood out like sore thumbs,' he said. 'The other passengers were nudging each other and laughing. It was obvious that we were Europeans.' Fortunately for the three men, their embarrassment was not prolonged unnecessarily. The wheel was being changed briskly and efficiently, confirming Faulds' theory that, judging by the state of the roads, punctures were probably a regular feature of bus travel.

They continued their journey to the terminus at Gandow, a sizeable town on the road north, where they were told by their guides that they could change money into Afghan currency. They visited the local equivalent of the Bureau de Change – a financial entrepreneur operating from a humble hut – and again found themselves the butt of considerable humour, this time from children who seemed to find their appearance more than amusing.

Following their guides faithfully, they were led to another bus for the second phase of their journey which, although considerably shorter than the first, gave them some anxious moments. John Soldini, the darkest of the three and the one least likely to arouse suspicion, found himself seated next to one of those compulsive conversationalists who find it impossible to travel for more than five minutes in silence. The man was speaking in his native Pashto tongue and, not having the faintest idea what he was saying, Soldini stoically ignored the first four or five attempts to open dialogue. Far from having the desired effect, his apparent snub inflamed the man to such an extent that he became increasingly voluble and Soldini was much relieved by the eventual intervention of one of his Mujahideen guides.

The bus turned right into a side road which was little more than a dust track, and after half an hour it stopped at a road block. This, the men were informed, was the customs post and they should remain inside the bus and keep their heads well down. Their guides had taken responsibility for customs clearance, and for fifteen minutes they watched the activity around the customs barrier, with traders offering the local equivalent of 'duty free' and customs officials taking no more than a cursory glance at documents and baggage. The prospect of being rumbled by the customs officials had been worrying the men and, when the barrier was raised and the bus waved through, they breathed a sigh of relief, and allowed themselves to relax for the first time since leaving Peshawar.

Barely ten minutes later, the bus rumbled to a halt at the foot of the Pass and, grabbing their rucksacks, Faulds, Soldini, and Suchet followed their guides towards the rough pathway which would lead them across the border and into Afghanistan. Once across the border, they were confronted by a snorting old tractor towing a large flat trailer. Although it fell considerably short of the transport they had expected, they were grateful for the lift and clambered aboard together with a handful of other Afghans who had accompanied them from the bus. Faulds watched them chat among themselves as the tractor lurched into action, building up to a steady five miles an hour, and realized that, for the farming peasants of beleaguered Afghanistan, this transport of delight was about par for the course.

For two hours, they chugged through the valley, flanked by mountains on either side, until they reached the small village of Maserichina, which marked the termination of the agricultural taxi service. From now on, they would have to walk and for the first time Faulds realized with some consternation that neither of the guides was armed.

By early afternoon, they had resumed their journey, occasionally passing groups of Mujahideen rebels. Most of them were heading back towards Pakistan, suggesting to Suchet that they had suffered recent defeat, which was hardly surprising to anyone who glimpsed their vintage Lee-Enfield armoury. Apart from the discomfort of the afternoon heat, it was an attractive climb, reminiscent of a stroll through the Scottish Highlands. As they climbed higher, the altitude began to affect their physical condition and their mental state suffered a mild shock when their guides hailed a couple of passing peasants to ask for directions. When it happened again within half an hour, it dawned on the crew that these Mujahideen 'experts', guerillas who claimed that they could lead anyone through the Afghan mountains blindfolded, were lost.

By late afternoon, what little faith the crew had in their guides had drained away. They had stopped on three more occasions to ask the way, without much luck, and seemed content to continue their progress along the dusty footpath. Now, frustration as well as tiredness from the heat began to overtake the newsmen. They had not heard, let alone seen, any Russian activity and they now had serious doubt not only about the qualifications, but also the dedication, of their guides.

It was almost dusk by the time they reached a small village commune in the mountains, allaying the fears that they might be expected to sleep rough in the open. Even in March, Afghan nights can be uncomfortably cold. On the advice of their guides, they approached cautiously; Afghan villagers, they were warned, tend to be a bit trigger-happy when strangers approach their homes at night. The guides located the head man and, for over an hour, they were involved in a heated discussion as they tried to persuade the commune to offer hospitality to the crew. They had not eaten all day, and the prospect of food and a bed after their arduous walk was most appealing. As they sat in silence, they were able to follow the simple drift of the argument. The head of the commune, it appeared, did not want to be seen to be harbouring undesirables, and felt that the risk of reprisals was too great. The guides, on the other hand, argued that they were there to film important anti-Russian propaganda, and should be helped. Besides, they too, were weary and refused to go any further. It was probably this final selfish motive that eventually clinched the deal but, as a condition of their hospitality, the men had to sit outside the commune until it was dark. Only then would they be allowed to creep inside where they would be fed and given beds.

Faulds sat with the others on a rough wooden bench and reflected on the incongruous events of the day. It had started with the saga of the suitcases and the embarrassment of the fancy dress. His nerves had not been helped by either the puncture or the stop at the customs point, and then there had been the tractor ride. The next disaster had been the discovery that the guides were lost, and now he had to wait until it was dark before he could have something to eat. In spite of the compounded frustrations, he laughed silently though to himself. The fact that it was 1 April had not escaped him!

When a mixture of spinach, yogurt, and chapatas was laid out before them, they ate like starving men, and gratefully drank diluted yoghurt while they waited for nearly an hour for the tea to brew. This, explained their host, was due to heating problems. When it eventually arrived, it was hot, sweet, and black, and was served with large lumps of sugar which they were expected to eat as dessert. Their beds were rough wooden frames supporting a rope webbing, but they were adequate and the men slept soundly.

They were awakened before first light by their guides, who made it clear that they must leave the commune under cover of darkness to avoid being spotted. This, they added, had been part of the deal. The crew had little faith in the judgement of their guides and, since there were no stars visible, they had no way of determining their direction. By the time dawn broke, it came as no surprise to find that they were again lost. The guides, however, strongly denied it, insisting that they were in full command of the situation and heading towards the Russians, as promised. Faulds, feeling the effects of the previous day's marathon march, had lagged behind in the early stages but, by nine o'clock, had got his second wind. Suchet appeared to have no ill effects and Soldini, living up to his reputation as being one of the fittest men at ITN, took it almost at a canter. For eight hours they blindly followed their guides who, in spite of stopping another three or four times to seek direction, still insisted that they knew exactly what they were doing.

Soldini did not share their confidence, and told them so. To him, they behaved more like city folk than mountain guides, and he assumed that they were simply a couple of Mujahideen sympathizers who had welcomed the chance to get away from their more mundane administrative tasks. 'They were useless,' he said. 'They didn't talk or act like guides, and it was very clear that they didn't know their way through the Pass.' Later that morning, the guides' claim was given a fraction of credibility when they heard the familiar drone of a couple of light aircraft, but could not see them. 'They could have been helicopters,' said Faulds. 'In any event, it gave us a small boost and made us think that perhaps we were getting somewhere close to the action.'

It was sufficent incentive to have their camera and sound equipment at the ready, and they took the opportunity to film general background shots, and the occasional bunch of Mujahideen stragglers who, again, appeared to be moving *away* from the action. By the time they reached a village, which they later established had been their destination, it was shortly after mid-day, and the heat was becoming intolerable. They were not offered any food, which was obviously far too important to waste on strangers, but they jumped at the chance of a mug of tea. Soldini, who was allocated to one family, got his almost immediately but, for Faulds and Suchet who were the 'guests' of another, the forty-five minute wait seemed both unnecessary and torturous. Having experienced this dilatory approach to one of life's necessities twice within twenty-four hours, they could only surmise that there was either a shortage of matches, or water took considerably longer to reach boiling point in Afghanistan than anywhere else.

There was more frustration to come. By now, the enthusiasm of their guides had worn transparently thin, and they started making noises about returning to Peshawar with all haste. The crew argued that they had been promised access to Russian action, but nothing, it seemed, could budge the rock-like insistence of the guides. Even bribery – normally the passport to the impossible – failed and, after two hours of persuasion, cajoling, soft-soaping, and everything else short of physical threats, they gave in, accepting defeat anything but graciously. Before turning back, however, they insisted on shooting more footage of the valley areas which almost certainly contained small bands of resistance fighters and more dispirited groups of the Mujahideen heading back towards the Pakistan border 'probably for rest and recuperation', they decided. Again, the crew was surprised at the vintage of their rifles, most of which would not have been out of place in Flanders or the Somme. Even the rebels carrying highly prized Kalashnikovs could not hide their dejection.

It was a mood shared by the three newsmen as they loaded their camera gear on a rented donkey and, mouthing definite doubts about the guides and their parentage, started to head back towards the border. The whispered curses became noticeably more venomous and vociferous when, after walking for barely three hours, they reached the small commune where they had spent the previous night. The journey had taken them eight hours that morning and, suddenly, their minds were filled with doubts. Were the guides lost, or had the crew simply been the victims of a ruse to make them think that they had penetrated much further into Afghanistan? Certainly, this assertion was not impossible and later received considerable support when they heard that a French photographer was subsequently taken across the border by the Mujahideen, and spent three weeks hoping for some exclusive action shots, not realizing that she was never further than ten miles from Pakistan.

Having reached the commune by the shortest possible route, the party had saved time, and the guides were keen to push on towards the border. By now, it seemed that they were very familiar with the territory and the suggestion that they had been lost appeared incongruous. The crew, however, insisted on staying at the commune overnight, and this led to another inevitable sequence of rows as the guides tried to persuade the villagers to offer food and refuge.

The following morning, they finished their filming sequence with Suchet doing an 'into-camera' piece against the attractive backdrop of the Afghan mountains, and prepared to return to Peshawar. They left, as they had arrived, by a strange mixture of foot, tractor, and bus, affording themselves the luxury of a taxi ride for the last part of the journey from Gandow, only stopping to watch the driver change a wheel after the mandatory puncture.

In Peshawar, they were greeted by a Mujahideen official who was clearly perplexed by their early return. After listening to the crew's somewhat heated account of the three-day excursion, he agreed that they had perhaps been given the wrong guides. They had the option to try again with another rebel faction, but felt that they had a story to tell. Although they had not witnessed any front-line action, they had at least been the first camera crew to penetrate Afghanistan by slipping through the mountains of north Pakistan, and they had filmed some rather dejected-looking Mujahideen rebels.

Faulds was not sorry to change from his 'pyjamas' to the more familiar Western clothes but he was deeply disappointed by the results of the sortie across the border. He could not equate the attitude of their guides with the spirit which had motivated the Mujahideen – a bunch of ill-trained, poorly equipped mountain guerillas – to take on the might of the Russian Army. It seemed clear that, if David was to stand any chance against the bullying Soviet Goliath, he must first put his house in order.

The Mujahideen rebel resistance had become more active since Faulds and Soldini had first entered Afghanistan via the mountains of north Pakistan earlier in the year, and there had been a consequent dearth of news as the Russians successfully stemmed the flow of information. It was now June and, with the reported escalation of Russian air strikes against remote villages thought to be harbouring pockets of resistance, ITN decided that it was time to take another look.

Paul Carleton, a widely experienced cameraman with a track record embracing Jordan, Angola, Iran, and over one hundred sorties to Northern Ireland, was given an open brief to disappear for a month and, using his initiative, get as much action as possible. Together with sound recordist Jon Hunt and (almost inevitably) John Suchet, he was booked on a flight to Karachi with the parting edict that the crew was not, under any circumstances, to risk their lives by masquerading as Mujahideen rebels.

They entered Afghanistan twice during their four-week assignment, ignoring the order on both occasions when they disguised themselves as Afghans to spend four days with the Mujahideen. Although they narrowly escaped a plot to rob and murder them, their decision was totally vindicated by some of the most dramatic early news film to come out of Afghanistan.

In Pakistan, the Mujahideen can be located through its 'official' centres, which are normally spartan premises adorned with posters and slogans. Carleton and the crew made contact shortly after arriving in Peshawar in the north of Pakistan, and found them very willing to co-operate with Western newsmen. Their claim to have captured a considerable number of Russian armaments was of particular interest and, the following day, arrangements were made for them to fly to Quetta where they would be met and escorted into Afghanistan. On arriving in Quetta, the three men loaded their gear aboard a battered jeep which, by military standards, appeared to be well beyond pensionable age, and under a Mujahideen escort embarked on a long and arduous drive by road and dust track towards the Afghan border.

Eventually, after a journey which was, at best uncomfortable, and at its worst little short of murderous, they arrived at the Mujahideen camp located about twenty miles inside Afghanistan. Suchet had already seen the motley assortment of men and machines which constituted the rebel resistance, but Carleton and Hunt were both new to the territory and found the next hour a revelation. The officer-in-charge claimed to have been a former Afghan Army brigadier who deserted after the invasion rather than capitulate to the Russians. Although it was a highly laudable sentiment, there was something about his manner which made Carleton doubt the veracity of his claim to such high office, even in the Afghan army. These doubts were vindicated a few moments later when the officer proudly unveiled one the captured 'tanks' for the ITN men. It was an armoured personnel carrier, and the other 'heavy armaments' of which he had boasted were half a dozen obsolete howitzers, circa 1940. The guns had been positioned in pairs, so close together that if one had been fired, the other could easily have been blown apart.

To Carleton, it appeared little short of pathetic. He strongly doubted whether anything had been captured from the Russians and considered it more likely that a handful of Afghan defectors had simply driven their vehicles into the bush. He had already placed a large question mark over their competence as a guerilla force, and these doubts were substantiated as they watched an enthusiastic Afghan pour five gallons of petrol into the tank of a diesel-powered APC. It took him most of the afternoon to syphon the fuel out. 'They were like children playing with very expensive toys,' Carleton reflected later. 'It was rather tragic to see so much enthusiasm stifled by lack of professional knowledge.'

Accurate maps were at a premium, as Martyn Lewis had discovered in Kabul six months beforehand. If the Russians lacked the necessary detail on their charts, it was hardly surprising that the ill-equipped rebels had even less, and they eagerly copied the maps loaned by the ITN crew.

The men returned to Karachi knowing that if they were to film Russian activity and Mujahideen resistance, their best route would be across the mountains to the north of the Khyber Pass. They flew to Peshawar but soon found that their second sortie into Afghan country would present more problems than the first. The Pakistani authorities were still keen to avoid antagonizing the Russians and, as Carleton, Hunt, and Suchet had been earmarked as a television news team as soon as they arrived in Peshawar, they were consequently given a rather obvious 'tail' wherever they went. When they contacted the local faction of the Mujahideen, it was duly noted and reported, and the official secret-police vehicle faithfully trailed the ITN taxi back to their hotel, rather like a slow-motion sequence from 'Sweeney'.

The Mujahideen had again proved co-operative, and agreed to take the men across the Khyber Pass into Afghan territory. The crew knew that this would mean ignoring the ITN ruling on the use of disguise, and were aware of the reprisals if caught masquerading as Mujahideen rebels. They also knew that if they were to get the chance to film Soviet activity, there was no alternative.

They were told that they would be contacted within a few days and, meanwhile, they should adopt a low profile. Eventually, they were briefed for an early morning departure and, as they crept from their hotel at 3 am, they knew that the vigilance of the Peshawar secret police had not wavered, and they were still being watched. The watchdogs followed with dedicated concentration as the taxi drove slowly through the town before stopping outside the Mujahideen premises where, after making a great show of telling the driver that they would be only a few minutes, the three men disappeared from view. Once inside the building, they swiftly changed into their Afghan fancy dress and, accompanied by two rebel couriers, slipped out of the back door into a waiting car. The Peshawar secret police have still got a bit to learn.

A long drive through the dark lanes of northern Pakistan took them to a refugee camp in the foothills of the mountains which was to be their home for the next three days. Carleton remembered the camp not only for the discomfort and the relentless heat, but also for the lack of sanitary facilities which made it memorably unpleasant. Their stay was made even less bearable by the random appearances of the police who, smarting at the way they had been so easily fooled, now saw it as a personal challenge to apprehend the crew. Departure from the camp could not come too soon and, when the Mujahideen leaders announced that they would be leaving the following morning, the three ITN men were ready and waiting as dawn broke. They were to join a column of twenty-five armed rebels who would be responsible for their safety and the transportation of their camera and sound gear. They were also allocated a personal guide, an affable young man called Nor, who had been studying agriculture at Kabul University before his educational syllabus had been dislocated by the arrival of the Russians.

The arduous walk through the mountain pass under the scorching summer sun was an experience which Carleton, Hunt, and Suchet will not forget. For nineteen hours, they kept up the pace as the Mujahideen drove them relentlessly forwards through the maddening heat, with only the briefest of stops for rest. Thankfully, there was no shortage of water, and this almost led to their cover being blown. Spotting one of them preparing to relieve himself behind a tree, Nor was quick to point out that Afghans urinate in a squatting position rather than standing up. Although they were dressed in authentic Afghan guise, their facial features and fair skin immediately marked them as visitors, and they were led individually through the small villages with their heads kept well down to avoid arousing suspicion. Although he accepted the wisdom of the move, Carleton regretted it. He had eagerly awaited the opportunity to see the pretty little Afghan villages first-hand, and now he was actually there, he was being deprived of the experience.

The following morning, they reached the peak of the Pass, the accepted border between Pakistan and Afghanistan. The party took the opportunity to rest, thankful that at 10,000 feet it was noticeably cooler. While the three newsmen marvelled over the geological phenomena which presented them with the breath-taking views of Afghanistan across the valley, the Mujahideen distributed more of the rancid-smelling goat meat which had provided the base of their diet for the past forty-eight hours. 'It's foul. You wouldn't give it to a dog in Europe,' observed Carleton to his colleagues, but, realizing the importance of protein nourishment in the debilitating conditions, he forced himself to eat.

He was draining the last of his water to rid himself of the putrid taste, when his ears recognized the distant sound of high-powered jet aircraft approaching. He made a dive for the bag containing the dismantled CP16 camera and half a minute later was lying flat on his stomach filming three Russian MiG fighters as they screamed into the valley below him, strafing the villages with their accurate rocket fire. This was indeed a slice of good fortune; not only had the Migs arrived at exactly the right time, giving Carleton the chance to film Russian aggression against the defenceless villages, he also had the professional satisfaction of an artistic shot taken *above* the aircraft as they dived low into the bowels of the valley. If the three ITN men had realized the hell they would experience in the next eighteen hours, they would have basked in their good fortune a little longer.

They had no water as they started their marathon walk down the Afghan side of the Pass, but did not doubt the Mujahideen's promise that they knew the location of several freshwater springs. As they walked further down towards the valley, the temperature soared. It was approaching mid-day and Carleton was inevitably reminded of Noel Coward's cautionary lyric 'Mad Dogs and Englishmen'. There was no water. Three 'certain' sources had been found dry, and the temperature was soaring towards 120 degrees. Still the men walked and walked through the arid bush and the stifling heat. It was almost too hot to breathe without burning the lungs.

They walked for the rest of the day, welcoming the slight drop in temperature towards late afternoon but despite their optimistic claims that refreshment was 'just a few miles away' the Mujahideen failed to find any water. By now, all three were suffering from dehydration and heat exhaustion, and it was Suchet who collapsed first. He was almost unconscious but still had the strength to curse his luck venomously and inform whoever was listening that he had no wish to die miles from home in the mountains of Afghanistan. Although Carleton and Hunt were still on their feet, they shared Suchet's sentiments to the last letter and were far from confident that they could endure much longer.

Hunt stayed with Suchet while Carleton, armed with an empty canteen, went on alone in a determined search for water to revive his ailing colleague. Eventually he found it – a shallow pool, covered by a green slime and an assortment of dead insects. Every few seconds, a fresh drop of water would plummet down from the rocks above, making a temporary indentation in the emerald blanket. To Carleton, it was champagne. Burying his face in the pool, he drank deeply, caring neither about the slime, nor the insects which went the same way as the water. Then, filling the canteen, he hurried back to rejoin Hunt and Suchet. Disregarding Carleton's warning that 'it might be a bit dodgy', the two men gulped down the contents of the bottle and Suchet, feeling temporarily revived, was able to continue the seemingly endless walk until they eventually reached their target camp and the only reward they wanted. Clean water – as much as they could drink.

The following morning they were summoned by local tribesmen, disturbed by the condition of a pretty young mountain girl suffering from a badly-infected foot. She was about seven years old and her parents had brought her to the camp seeking advice on how to cure her condition. They had left their mercy dash very late; it was already clear to both Carleton and Hunt that the danger of gangrene was imminent, and that the girl was in urgent need of professional medical attention. 'It is essential that you get her to Pakistan,' Carleton told the parents, through an interpreter. They shook their heads grimly, explaining that they had no way of reaching Pakistan. The ITN men, already impressed by the bravery and striking beauty of the small girl with her big brown eyes, now felt partially responsible for her. 'We'll buy you a donkey,' said Carleton, neither thinking nor caring how he might justify the purchase of an ass on his expenses. Again, the parents shook their heads and shrugged. The interpreter's answer made Carleton's stomach turn over. 'They say it's not worth it,' he explained. 'She's only a girl.'

Without medical attention, gangrene would set in and spread with fatal results. Carleton remembered the supply of sixty oxytetracycline (antibiotic) tablets in his medical kit, and thought of his own young child at home. He looked at Hunt. 'We've got no choice,' he said. 'Otherwise she'll die.'

They sat the girl down on a stool and Hunt, with the aid of an unsterilized Swiss army penknife, performed crude surgery on the girl, squeezing as much poison as possible from the infected foot. Carleton could not hide his admiration for the girl. 'She sat there stoically, not murmuring, while the tribesmen stood around watching Jon perform one of the most disgusting operations I've ever seen.' Hunt cleaned the foot to the best of his ability before smothering it with antiseptic cream and applying a dressing. Then Carleton handed over his entire ration of antibiotics, telling the parents, again through the interpreter, to give the girl four tablets immediately, and four each day until the supply was exhausted. The mountain peasants could not believe their good fortune at being given the tablets. They saw the small packet as white man's medicine and, nodding their thanks, quickly headed back towards the solitude of their shack.

The reason for the swift departure became evident when they returned to the camp the following day, this time accompanied by a young boy with his arm in a splint. Again, Hunt and Carleton were summoned for their opinion. Someone had done a very good job, thought Carleton – as close to professional treatment as they were likely to get in that part of the world. 'Excellent,' he conveyed. 'Don't worry. It will be perfectly all right.' The parents nodded in satisfaction. 'This is our son,' they announced proudly. 'It doesn't matter about the girl, but the boy must get better.' Later, Carleton had his fears confirmed. The sixty antibiotic tablets had been given to the all-important son, achieving nothing for his broken arm, and the brave little girl with the beautiful brown eyes had died.

Later that day, the party moved deeper into Afghanistan, but were halted at a wide, fast-moving river. The Afghans, who had promised the newsmen safe conduct across the river, were now having second thoughts. The dangerous current would clearly present problems to anyone foolhardy enough to attempt a crossing and, after discussing the matter briefly among themselves, the Mujahideen leaders shook their heads. For Carleton, Hunt, and Suchet, it was obviously the end of the line.

They camouflaged themselves and hid in the bush, watching the ripples of activity across the river. Carleton, with his camera at the ready, prayed for some action, and he did not have long to wait. Within half an hour, they heard the familiar thundering sound of a large helicopter and, seconds later, a Soviet patrol gunship loomed into sight, obviously looking for Mujahideen rebels. The huge helicopter flew low over the bush, presenting Carleton with a close-up which filled his view-finder. Fortunately, the sun was behind him, and there was no danger of reflection giving away the position of his camera. With their spirits again high after the initial disappointment of not being able to cross the river, the crew took up a new position among the rocks, close to the river bank. The gamble paid off as a second gunship flew slowly past at the same level as the crew, some fifty feet above the water.

Barely able to believe their luck, they remained concealed among the rocks. If there was to be any action at all on the far side of the river, they now seemed to be in the best position to cover it. For over three hours they sat motionless in their hideaway, beneath the blazing afternoon sun. They were beginning to suffer from the effects of the heat and were doubting the wisdom of continuing their vigil when they heard the sound of heavy engines from across the river. Forcing themselves even lower among the rocks, they watched as a convoy of Soviet tanks came into view and moved slowly along the road parallel with the far river bank. They were less than three hundred yards away and Carleton was able to take in every detail through his view-finder. Suddenly, he froze as the column stopped immediately opposite their hideaway and, simultaneously, a dozen gun turrets swung menacingly towards his camera position. He continued filming, but now his head was filled with doubts. They were well camouflaged, even down to the twigs in their hair, but perhaps they had been spotted by one of the gunships. Carleton's brain raced to find a reason. Had the sun played a trick on them and somehow been reflected off the lens? He had been at pains to ensure this would not happen, but had he allowed his concentration to slip at some stage? Perhaps they had spotted some movements by the Mujahideen concealed in the bush behind them? Or was one of the tanks perhaps fitted with one of those ultra-powerful Russian telescopes that had picked them out as it scanned the bank opposite?

He stayed motionless, with his camera still running, until the tanks moved forwards again. It had been barely half a minute, but to Carleton, Hunt, and Suchet, it had seemed much longer. 'It caused a very slight stopping of the heart,' recalled Carleton later, 'we were lucky to have them so close, and the fact that they were kind enough to stop and pose for us really was a mammoth slice of good luck, although, at the time, it was a definite brown-trouser job.' Fate could not have been kinder. In the relatively short time they had been in Afghanistan, they had filmed a low-level rocket attack, had eyeball views of two armed patrol helicopters, and had a column of Russian tanks provide them with a brief cabaret. It was all great material, and the crew had every reason to feel pleased with themselves as they crept back to join the Mujahideen.

They had been back with the main party for only a couple of hours before their exuberance was punctured by Nor, their young student guide. The news team was carrying a large amount of money (a contingency fund in case of emergencies) and, by Afghan standards, appeared quite wealthy. Seeing the opportunity to make some easy money, a splinter group of the Mujahideen had decided that it would be quite fun to lure Carleton, Hunt, and Suchet down to a small village under some false pretext, rob them and kill them. These plans had been overheard by the faithful Nor and when, as predicted, a party of rebels invited Carleton and the others to accompany them to a village 'to see something interesting', they politely and firmly declined.

By now, they had had enough. They had been away for over three weeks and were keen to get their stories back to London, and if a breakaway group within the Mujahideen were planning to rub them out, it was definitely time to call it a day. Learning from their lesson a few days earlier, they stocked up with water before beginning the arduous walk back across the mountains into Pakistan. The more senior members of the rebel group appeared a little embarrassed as they prepared to start their trek back towards the refugee camp. In spite of their promise to take the ITN men across the river and deeper into Afghanistan, they had failed to do so. This, together with the fact that not a single shot had been fired by the rebels during the entire five days, was swiftly justified by the Mujahideen. 'Your safety was our priority,' they said, 'we could not afford to attract attention.'

During the march back across the Pass, Carleton had good reason to be thankful that the rebels had not been engaged in battle. He was inspecting one of their few Russian-built Kalashnikov automatic rifles and discovered that every third bullet was a tracer, and the rebel 'marksman' had no idea that he could be pinpointing his own position. 'He didn't even know what a tracer was,' said Carleton. 'They hadn't a clue about armaments or the effective range of their weapons. They were nothing more than a bunch of brave lunatics on a hiding to nothing.' Most were armed with obsolete Lee-Enfields, and Carleton even spotted an authentic Winchester.

As they continued their trek across the mountains, the ITN men became more and more fascinated by the behaviour of a young boy, aged about fourteen, who had tagged onto the party as it passed through one of the small Afghan villages. He always appeared to be running, and seemed obsessed about the safety of a large sack which he carried on his young shoulders. He was taking it across the border to Pakistan where he would exchange it for the equivalent of a few pounds. It would enable his family to eat for a month, he told them, as he allowed the crew to peep at the white powder inside the sack. It was refined cocaine, about one hundred-weight of it.

Eventually, they reached the stinking refugee camp where they had spent three days and nights before trudging across the Pass. This time, their stay was thankfully limited to one night only, and the following morning, still dressed in their Afghan disguise, they boarded a bus – nothing more than a rough conversion from a van – and headed for Peshawar. The camera and sound gear had been dismantled and secreted among their hand luggage, and the vital magazines of film were concealed beneath their loose robes.

After the trials of the past week, they were justified in believing that the very least they deserved was a trouble-free drive back to Peshawar. They were wrong. The presence of two uniformed policemen ensured it was a nightmare journey. Suchet, with his dark complexion, looked more bona fide than the others and Carleton with his newly acquired sun-tan, felt he could get away with it if he kept his head down and mouth shut. For the red-bearded Jon Hunt, however, there was an obvious problem and, with the others insisting that he had contracted some terminal disease and should on no account be disturbed, he pulled the robes over his head and lay down to 'die'.

Later that evening, after enjoying the luxury of a bath and dressing as Europeans for the first time in a week, Hunt keeled over in pain, holding his stomach. This time, he was not pretending and, by the time they reached Karachi the following day, Carleton too was doubled up with pain. The mixture of the contaminated water and highly suspicious meat was eventually taking its toll, and both Hunt and Carleton were later off work for several weeks with severe, and extremely uncomfortable, attacks of the Afghan trots.

Their clandestine coverage of the Mujahideen resistance in Afghanistan was highly praised, and the Russian activity on the far side of the river had provided the cream.

EL SALVADOR

The rebel connection

The horrors of the indiscriminate killings in El Salvador were first brought to the attention of the British public in 1981, after a series of exclusive ITN reports on the escalation of the civil war.

Traditionally, there had been little interest in the tiny Central American state but, by the time the elections had been held in the spring of the following year, the infamous activities of the government-backed 'death squads', culminating in the massacre of the four-man Dutch television team, had earned it a regular place in the headlines of the Western media.

During the autumn of 1981, reporter Jon Snow had made contact with groups based in London and El Salvador who supported the FMLN guerilla movement opposed to the Christian Democrat government headed by Napoleon Duarte. He had been to El Salvador two months earlier with cameraman Sebastian Rich and soundman Don Warren and, although it was 'unknown' territory, they had sent back twenty-five stories in thirty-two days, embracing the growing tension and the broadening of guerilla action. Now, thanks to Snow's contacts, the three men were being invited to enter the country illegally to film the FMLN activities before withdrawing and re-entering the country through the official route to report on the government's anti-rebel operation. The government's attitude to collaborators was inflexible and they would almost certainly be shot if they were caught among the rebels, but the high rewards of gaining such a world exclusive were considered to warrant the risk.

They flew from Heathrow to Miami and then on to Nicaragua where, they were told, they would be contacted. After a week of waiting, wondering, and hoping, they were eventually escorted from their hotel to a tiny airstrip where they boarded a light aircraft owned by 'charitable friends' and flown to a makeshift landing strip in western Honduras which, Rich remembered, resembled something out of a Tarzan movie. Here they were met by representatives of the El Salvador guerillas who were masquerading as refugees and, for the next three days, the ITN team lived at a refugee encampment, trying to look enthusiastic as they put together a few lightweight refugee stories to justify their presence to the watching Honduras police.

When, on the third day, they were told that they would be leaving that night to cross the border into El Salvador, they assumed that it was little more than a day's march. Instead, it was a long and exhausting slog, dodging armed patrols on both sides of the border and by the time they finally reached their destination, five days and ninety miles later, they had more than a little sympathy with their three colleagues who had been lost in Angola three years earlier. The guerilla guides were accompanied by members of their families and by the time they reached the Lempa River, the party was about twenty-five strong.

The fast-flowing river marks the border between Honduras and El Salvador and Snow, Rich and Warren expected, not unreasonably, to find some sort of frail boat or raft waiting to take them across. It was a clear night, and they could see the far bank but, despite assurances that transport was available for their equipment, they could see nothing. They were soon to marvel at their own naivety; when the 'craft' arrived it was a cylindrical water tank, measuring no more than five feet in length, with a hole cut in the side. Heavily armed gunships patrolled the river by day, they were told, and it would have been impossible to conceal even a small boat by the bank.

Women and children, together with the camera gear carefully wrapped in polythene bags, were packed into the rough metal cylinder and ferried across by guerillas who swam alongside, guiding the strange craft. The men stripped and

swam across the river, and three successful crossings in the old
water tank saw the passengers and equipment safely ashore.
Then, after a brief rest, they were off again, marching relentlessly on, covering as much ground as possible by night to
minimize the dangers of detection. They had little idea of
where they were, or even where they were going and had long
since lost faith in their guides' assurances that it was 'just one
more mile'.

Once, they thought they had actually arrived at their
destination, only to learn that the main guerilla force they
were meant to be joining had moved on another twenty
kilometres. When eventually they caught up with the main
force, they were barely one stage from exhaustion, and the
sight of a tatty hammock slung between two trees was like a
magnet to Rich. 'We were absolutely knackered,' he said.
'I slept for fourteen hours.'

The next two days were spent filming the life-style of the
guerillas – the everyday necessities like cooking, fishing, and
sewing – and the crew was even extended the privilege of a visit
to the guerilla 'bomb factory', a secret clearing where they
would fashion crude explosive devices from cans, nails, and
gunpowder. The language problem had been anticipated and
was a main reason why Don Warren had been assigned to the
job. An experienced soundman of many front-line campaigns,
he spoke fluent Spanish and was now fulfilling the key role of
liaison man for the crew. When he explained the importance
of moving to other camps to film more rebel activity, they
were taken to a large base outside Pena Blanca which was more
sophisticated than their first. This was more of a family centre
and, although it suggested a degree of permanence by
embracing rudimentary teaching facilities for young children
and rough training schedules for embryonic terrorists, the
guerillas were always alert to the dangers of discovery by
government patrols. Most of these 'teach-ins' and other meetings were conducted beneath a large and distinctive tree, a few
hundred yards from the village centre, reminding the crew of
an age past, when English children were taught in a similar
manner on the village green during the hot days of
summer.

The men were warned not to wander from the tracks and,

on the second morning, Snow narrowly missed being impaled on bamboo spikes when he disregarded the warning for reasons of natural privacy. He had taken barely three steps into the bush when the unnatural appearance of the ground in front of him made him stop. Gentle probing with his foot uncovered a lethal mantrap – a ten-foot pit containing a dozen bamboo canes, each sharpened like a spear and capable of inflicting fatal wounds. They later found a guerilla who had just finished building a similar trap when he slipped, avoiding death only by clinging desperately to a nearby tree. Even so, two bamboo spears had gone clear through his leg and the man was howling in agony. Rich was able to administer some of his supplies of morphine, and this help dispelled some of the final vestiges of reticence among the more suspicious rebels in the group.

The building of these mantraps was a regular feature of the rebel defences, but they would be forgotten when they moved from camp to camp, presenting a permanent hazard to their own guerilla comrades who might set up camp in the vicinity at a later date. Rich, with a young family of his own, was also aware of the dangers presented to children, and would actively discourage them from leaving the immediate camp area. He was able to divert their attention temporarily by giving them the last few feet of unexposed film and the reel bobbin – a habit which he developed during his career as a cameraman. 'Kids love anything new,' he said. 'If they've not seen it before, they automatically want it. It kept them happy for hours.'

They remained at the camp for five days, compiling a comprehensive report on the aims, motivations, and life-style of the hounded guerillas whose simple aim was the downfall of the fascist government. As they started the long trek back towards the Lempa River, and the border with Honduras, the ITN men congratulated themselves on their success; not only were they the first television news team to penetrate El Salvador through the mountains, they were also the first to live among and film the rebels as they prepared to escalate their programme of guerilla war against the government. Now all they had to do was get out of the country with their filmed evidence intact.

This time, they crossed the Lempa River by daylight – risking observation by the presence of prowling gunships – and Rich, boosted by the thought that they would soon be out of danger after their successful mission, decided it was time to give vent to his creativity. Instead of merely filming the water cylinder as it was guided across the river, he sensed that he could get some additional feeling for the scene by sitting in it himself, and filming the guerillas as they swam to safety. He was halfway across when he decided to change the angle of the shot by standing up, temporarily forgetting that the standard domestic water tank is not blessed with a keel. With no stability, it rolled like a barrel, hurling Rich and the camera equipment into the murky waters below.

Once back in the relative safety of Honduras, they continued their trek towards the refugee camp where they had first met their guerilla 'hosts'. They had been marching for four days and experience told them that they would almost certainly reach the camp the following day. When they reached a small tented village, the rebels were greeted like old friends and, had there been a red carpet in the Honduras bush, it would have almost certainly been rolled out for the television men who were given a VIP welcome. The head man threw his arms around them in a warm embrace talking excitedly and pointing towards a rough straw hut adorned with canvas. 'You will sleep here tonight,' he said.

He beckoned the men towards the building which Rich remembered was approximately twelve feet square. As he pulled back the canvas flap, they could see it housed a complete family. 'There were about a dozen of them spanning three generations,' said Rich. 'They were all asleep in hammocks.' The situation was obviously not new to the head man and he immediately set about finding resting places for his three revered guests. Two children were delicately lifted from one hammock, one from another, while Granny was elbowed from her slumbers and pursuaded to move in with Mum. The ITN men were not happy about evicting a family of poverty-stricken Hondurans from their hammocks, but the host had clearly made up his mind and they decided that it was probably better not to antagonize him. Warren, still a large man in spite of shedding weight, had one of the children's hammocks slung just a few feet above the ground, while the six-foot-four-inch frame of Snow tried to come to terms with the other. 'Don was lying in the hammock like a bent banana,' said Rich, 'while Jon virtually had to fold himself in half.'

Despite the discomfort, they fell into an uneasy sleep only to be aroused by an unfamiliar grunting. Rich lay silently, his imagination stretched to the limit, wondering if it was, after all, possible to do it in a hammock, when his mental meanderings were interrupted by a yell of horror as Warren felt something brush against him. 'What the bloody hell's going on,' he yelled, and sat bolt upright to see the family pig cavorting around the tent. His shout frightened the animal who charged out of the hut, grunting excitedly and waking up the chickens. 'It was like a chain reaction,' said Rich. 'The peace of the night was shattered in about thirty seconds. The noise of the chickens woke up the cockerel who, thinking it was morning, started to crow. That woke up the donkey and everyone else in the camp – the noise was unbelievable.' The men were aware of the dangers attracted by the noise, but could also see the funny side of the situation, and collapsed with laughter. The noise subsided after an hour, allowing the village to sleep for the remaining hours before the cockerel again performed – this time on cue.

The ITN men left the village that morning to find that the refugee camp was less than an hour away, and were surprised that their 'contacts' who had helped arrange the visit had been concerned for their safety. Like the ITN men, they had not realized that it would entail a five-day march in each direction and were beginning to fear that they had been apprehended by a government patrol. During the seventeen days, their rations had been limited to a handful of beans supplemented by sugar cane. They had been given the luxury of fish on only one occasion and the three men had each lost considerable weight. Now, weakened further by the five-day trek back to the refugee camp, they were ready for hibernation rather than sleep.

A week later, they were preparing to enter El Salvador again – this time by scheduled flight straight to the capital, San

Salvador. In the second stage of the operation, they were hoping to join the government forces in their hunt for the rebels, thus obtaining, exclusively for ITN, a complete package showing both sides of the growing domestic conflict.

After lengthy negotiations, they succeeded in persuading the military authorities to allow them to join a gunship patrol engaged in flushing out guerillas – a rare bonus made all the more pertinent with the knowledge of what was already in the can. They boarded the helicopter in San Salvador and after a thirty minute flight landed in a heavily-armed area which, at first sight, could have been anywhere in the Central American jungle. As the twenty armed troops leapt from the machine, the colonel in charge explained to the men, via Warren, that they were just a few hundred yards from a village which was just one of the many rebel strongholds recently captured by government troops. Rich climbed down from the helicopter with his camera but had only taken a few paces before he experienced the strangest sensation of déjà vu. He dismissed it immediately as imagination, but then both Snow and Warren caught his eye. They had sensed it too and when they saw the familiar and distinctive outline of the 'teaching tree' in front of them, the three men experienced that sense of tingling excitement which told them that Lady Luck had dealt them a once-in-a-lifetime hand; at almost incalculable odds, they had been flown to the same village where, two weeks earlier, they had lived among the guerilla rebels. Instinctively, Rich started to walk towards the village a few yards ahead of the main party, before an alarm bell sounded somewhere in the back of his head, and he purposefully changed direction. He cursed himself for his temporary stupidity, realizing that in just a few paces, he could easily have blown the luckiest coincidence that a cameraman would ever have.

Their elation at their good fortune was dampened by the knowledge that the guerillas, for whom they harboured a certain respect, were now almost certainly dead. There was no evidence of the bodies, but there was a smell of death in the air and the men guessed that the rebels, their women, and their children had been wiped out. Toys, cooking utensils, and other signs of everyday life in a small community lay scattered and broken, serving only as silent memorials to the families who had dared fight for their beliefs.

Snow interviewed the colonel against the effective background of a smouldering hut, knowing that it would provide a sharp and dramatic contrast to the film taken on their previous visit. While co-operative within the bounds of his brief, the officer was surly in manner, and it was clear that he had little time for the Press. He emphasized this after the interview: 'We know journalists have been here,' he said. 'If I find out who they are, I will kill them now.' The sinister emphasis on the word 'now' made Rich wonder fleetingly whether they were under suspicion and his heart plummeted to his ankles when the colonel triumphantly produced his proof – the bobbin from the end of the film reel with which Rich had successfully amused the children in the village.

But the colonel had not made the connection, and the three men could hardly contain their excitement at their success. Luck had played its part in presenting them with a world exclusive report, though this story could not be transmitted until the ITN men were out of the country. Meanwhile, there were other leads to follow.

Reports that the government-backed 'death squads' were executing active dissenters and leaving their bodies to rot at the foot of a volcano a few miles outside San Salvador, were at first regarded with some suspicion by the ITN men. They knew that the death squads existed but felt that the evidence would be disposed of in a less public manner. It was not until they were convinced by an anti-government contact, who claimed he knew the exact spot where the bodies had been dumped, that they pursued the story and, co-opting the man as a guide, drove to the volcanic area to the east of the city. They stopped the car a few hundred yards from a small volcano, still showing the signs of an eruption long since past, and proceeded on foot. As they approached, Rich could see a lake of black lava which, from a distance, appeared to be rippling gently. The guide said nothing; instead, he picked up a large stone and hurled it towards the pool which suddenly came alive as three dozen fat, well-fed vultures took temporarily to the air, angry at the interruption. Others did not move, too intent on feeding

on the human corpses, now barely recognizable, which were
scattered around the foot of the volcano. Skulls, picked clean
by the scavengers, bore the unmistakable bullet holes where
they had faced the death squad.

To Rich and Warren, both used to the sight of death in war,
it was a sickening experience. As the wind changed, the smell of
death and decomposing bodies became even more pungent,
and all three were glad when Snow's 'into-camera' report, with
its horrendous evidence, was completed and they headed
back towards the capital. Inflamed by their experience, they
told other pressmen in the hope that Duarte's dictatorial
regime would bow to the inevitable world outcry, and the
barbaric practices would stop. They even made their evidence
available to the government forces in San Salvador, but the
three beaming Colonels in charge of Press liaison could only
shake their heads and shrug. 'It is an extremist faction,' was
the official explanation. 'We have tried to stop it but we cannot
find them.' And, smiling, they agreed that it was a great
shame.

By now, the ITN men were regarded as the experts on El
Salvador and more news crews were arriving in the city daily.
'They would follow us if we walked across the street,' said .
Rich. 'Suddenly, it seemed that the whole world was interested
in the problems of El Salvador, and we had set the ball rolling.
It was certainly a tragic situation but, from a professional point
of view, it was my most satisfying job.'

The price of dissent

By March 1982, the world was watching with interest as El
Salvador prepared itself for the government elections. The
civil war had escalated considerably since Snow, Rich, and
Warren had returned home in December, and Napoleon
Duarte's regime was now under increasing pressure.

The ITN Foreign Desk wanted some pre-election coverage
and briefed a news team for a five-week tour of the Central
American states. They would first fly to El Salvador for a pre-
election 'mood' piece, before covering the polls in neighbouring

Guatemala. They were then scheduled to drop in on Nicaragua where Bianca Jagger was actively helping the new regime with its aid programme, and then back to El Salvador to cover the final days of the election. Jon Snow was again the natural choice, and Don Warren's experience, plus his ability to speak Spanish, made him an obvious candidate as sound-man. This time, however, the cameraman was Alan Downes who, in his twenty-three years as an ITN camerman, had covered just about everything. Everything, that is, except the situation he found in El Salvador. 'It seemed that a Press card gave you total diplomatic immunity,' he said. 'I've covered wars all over the world but it's the only place where pressmen have been able to drive through the government lines to the guerilla positions a few hundred yards away, and later allowed back to join the federal troops.'

While Downes, Warren, and Snow managed to get away with it regularly, such action was not designed to appease the government. They finally ran out of patience with members of a Dutch left-wing television crew who, after several heavy warnings, persisted in filming and interviewing FMLN rebels and a death squad was called in. The official government explanation that the Dutch had been accidentally caught in crossfire during a skirmish with rebel troops seemed spectacularly transparent; in such a case, it is more likely that they would have been injured rather than killed outright, and each body would not have contained half a dozen bullets from an automatic rifle. It is hardly surprising that the murders had a most depressing effect on the rest of the Press contingent, and the television crews knew that it could have happened to any one of them if they too had repeatedly ignored government warnings.

The ITN crew had been filming several miles away, and heard of the killings when they called the ABC office on their two-way radio, and rushed back to piece together the tragic story. The dead men had been brought back to the mortuary in San Salvador and Snow, Downes, and Warren had the distasteful job of filming their dead colleagues before the bodies were flown home for burial in Holland.

They knew where the murder had taken place and, the following morning, the crew, together with Marcello Zannini of UPITN and two stills photographers, headed for the area where the Dutch crew had liaised with the rebels. They turned off the main road and bounced down the dusty track, hoping for some sign which would indicate the exact spot where the Dutchmen had died, but found nothing. They even enquired at a nearby peasant's farm cottage but the occupant had either seen nothing, or was too frightened to talk.

They climbed back into the car and were debating whether to walk across the fields or drive to a nearby village to solicit the assistance of the commander of the local militia group, when an old truck suddenly appeared along the track and pulled up sharply alongside them, kicking up a cloud of dust. Downes remembers that it resembled an old greengrocer's vehicle of the 1950s, with open wooden slats along the sides. He remembers too, that it contained a dozen of the most evil-looking armed civilians he had ever seen, and as they leapt from the truck and surrounded the car, he realised he was face to face with a death squad.

Inside the car, everybody froze, certain that death was only seconds away as the leader of the group walked menacingly towards them. He looked like the archetypal thug – short, squat, with dark glasses and sawn-off shotgun. Zannini, the UPITN man, started to explain that they were looking for the local village and had stopped to consult a map. The leader listened, but seemed unimpressed. Then he nodded towards the house. 'Have you been there?' he demanded and Zannini, doing his best to look puzzled by the question, gave an emphatic 'no'. Fortunately, they did not check his denial, and slowly the small Press group felt their hearts resume a more normal pace as Zannini explained that they had an appointment with the local militia leader in the village. All the time, Downes had his eye on a teenager aged about thirteen who carried a loaded rifle and appeared to be particularly twitchy.

Eventually, they were allowed to proceed towards the village wondering whether they had just encountered the murderers of the Dutch crew, and knowing that they themselves had narrowly escaped execution. They reached the village to find that the militia leader was out and then had the heart-stopping experience of seeing the greengrocer's truck drive into the village a few minutes behind them, presumably to check their story.

During their spell in El Salvador, ITN had only one crew operating, while the major American networks had as many as five. Downes could not understand why he rarely saw them in the field until he discovered that several US stations were actually using ITN material. 'Many of the American crews were fairly green and had been warned off by the government heavies,' said Downes. 'After the Dutch crew had been killed, we found that some of them were pulling out and were so jittery that they contacted the US embassy and insisted on an armed escort to the airport.'

The marauding death squads continued their activities during the final days of political campaigning, which prompted many observers to suggest that the election would prove to be little more than a farce, with only a small percentage turnout. They could not have been more wrong. The poll was massive with the people so keen to vote that they even broke down the door of one polling station before it opened. Duarte's ruling Christian Democrat party failed to win an overall majority and, after much political juggling and haranguing, it was decided to appoint Dr Alvara Mangana, Commander-in-Chief of the Armed Forces, as interim President for the ensuing eighteen months, leading a coalition claiming to be 'a moderate and independent party of national unity'.

For the ITN men it had been a tough assignment with a demanding schedule, and they were later to hear that their polling-day coverage embracing footage of an abortive guerilla raid, during which the army slaughtered a dozen men and a woman in a San Salvador suburb, won a major award from the Royal Television Society.

They remained in El Salvador for a couple of days after the election to tie up the loose ends. It had been a hectic five weeks; the men were tired and Downes had cracked a rib into the bargain. The trip home, and a few days rest, beckoned invitingly. Back in Wells Street, however, the assignments desk had other ideas. The Falklands affair was looming and, instead of finding themselves homeward bound, the three men were instead diverted to southern Chile, where they remained for a further two months. 'It was a real Red Alert job – sparks were

flying and our feet hardly touched the ground,' said Downes.
By the time they eventually landed in London, their five week
assignment had stretched to thirteen and a half weeks.

LEBANON

❦❦❦❦❦❦❦❦❦❦❦❦❦❦❦❦❦❦❦❦❦❦❦❦❦❦❦❦❦❦❦

Kidnapped!

The summer of 1982 was the season of the Foreign Desk as
overseas war news commanded most of the available time and
space in the media. British forces were dispatched to the South
Atlantic to do sterling service in what politicians and his-
torians alike will for ever term the 'Falklands Conflict' while,
nearly halfway around the world, the uneasy peace in the
Lebanon was again breaking down.

It was late spring when ripples in the eastern Mediterranean
suggested that the Israelis again had Beirut in their sights. The
small town of Khalde had been bombed 'as a retaliatory
measure' and cameraman Sebastian Rich, soundman Mike
Parkin, and reporter Brent Sadler were dispatched to Beirut
with all haste. This time, however, it was a false start; the
Israelis were merely flexing their muscles in readiness for the
invasion of the Lebanon two months later. After two weeks it
was apparent that nothing was imminent and, with news crews
being dispatched to vantage points throughout South America
as well as with the Falklands task force, the crew was recalled to
London.

The tension lasted for five weeks before it finally exploded
in June and Rich, already familiar with Middle East trouble-
spots, was again assigned to the job. This time, he would be
with his regular sound recordist Nigel Thomson, reporter
Desmond Hamill, and VTR editor Peter Read. It was almost the
last job for all of them.

Reaching the Lebanon was a major problem in itself. The

men were already at Heathrow when news filtered through
that Beirut airport had been closed that morning, and hopes
of flying to Damascus and driving into the Lebanon had been
thwarted by an obstructive official at Heathrow who would
not allow journalists to leave without a Syrian visa. It soon
became clear that the only viable route would be a flight to
Cyprus, followed by a boat trip to the Lebanese port of
Jounieh. This, however, presented problems. There was no
regular ferry service to the Lebanese coast, and the Cypriots
were reluctant to make their boats available for charter. Eventually, some hard-nosed bargaining clinched the deal with the
skipper of a battered tramp steamer, normally used for
delivering drums of oil to Mediterranean fishing ports, but the
ITN men found the £1,800 price tag prohibitive. They had
ascertained that the skipper was prepared to take a maximum
of twelve passengers, and the complement was made up by
Dutch and German camera crews, a couple of European
businessmen, and a French military attaché, each of whom
paid a share of the exorbitant 'inconvenience fee'.

The crews humped their equipment on board and settled
on their open air 'bunks', which were nothing more than
rough planks simply placed over the open hatches. They cast
off at 2.30 pm, and settled down to make the most of a very
spartan and bizarre Mediterranean cruise. They had come
well victualled, and a surfeit of Cyprus wine ensured that they
slept beneath the stars as soundly as if they had been on
feather beds. The first hint of aggression in the peaceful
eastern Mediterranean came at dawn, when they were hailed
by an Israeli gunboat, demanding identification of both crew
and passengers. Against the orders of the Israelis, the
cameramen were able to shoot a few feet before the vessel was
allowed to continue towards the Lebanese coast.

Jounieh, the least energetic of all Mediterranean ports,
exceeded even its own high standards of inertia that morning
when, despite docking at 6.30 am, the crews had to wait until
almost ten o'clock before a part-time customs official eventually emerged to give them permission to disembark. They
arrived at the Commodore Hotel in Beirut, the traditional
haunt of pressmen in the Lebanon – and while Read set up his
VTR editing equipment, Hamill, Rich, and Thomson rushed

out to get the all important first story in time for 'News at Ten' that night.They grabbed the first available taxi and Rich assumed the role of liaison man with special responsibilities for directing the Lebanese driver. Showing him the camera to make it clear that they were newsmen, he explained in the simplest way that they were looking for bombing action. 'Boom-boom, boom-boom!' he said, painting an imaginary explosion in the air with his hands.

The three men and the taxi driver were scouring the horizon for the tell-tale pillars of smoke which would pinpoint the latest Israeli target, and eventually found the small town which had been strafed by Israeli Phantoms just fifteen minutes earlier. Rich shot some impressive footage of the aftermath of the raid, and the three men rushed back to the Commodore where Read was waiting to edit and dispatch the story to London via the Beirut satellite station. The television newsman's maxim – always hit the ground running – had proved successful, and they had every reason to feel pleased with their first dispatch, particularly since they had been in Beirut for barely a couple of hours. Now they had time to relax over lunch and plan their strategy for the afternoon, when they hoped to put together a more in-depth report of the deteriorating situation in the Lebanon and, with any luck, get some action of the Israeli air raids.

They were fortunate in obtaining the services of a young and enthusiastic driver, the nineteen year old brother of Hassan, the local taxi 'fixer' who acted rather like an agent, negotiating terms with camera crews and other newsmen requiring transport to cover the action. The youngest of a family of immigrant Kurds, he had been polite and efficient as he guided the ITN men around the stricken city in his gleaming new VW Scirocco. He knew the areas which had suffered most, and was able to help them capture the emotive scenes of bombed buildings, burning tanks and corpses, which provided a tragic requiem for this once proud and beautiful city.

While at the hotel, they heard that the town of Khalde was under air attack about ten miles away, and immediately ordered their young driver to head for the action. A fast and furious drive brought them to within a mile of the town, giving

them a clear view of the Israeli Phantoms as they dived low to
deliver their lethal rocket attacks. It would have been folly to
go any closer; Rich and Thomson were able to record the
action from the middle of the road, and Hamill's 'into-
camera' report was dramatized by the scene of the blazing
town in the background.

They decided to hang on until the raid finished, and then
drive into the centre of Khalde to film the effects of the bombing. For fifteen minutes they sat and watched as the Phantoms
circled overhead, before swooping to unleash their cargo of
destruction into the heart of the tiny town. Eventually, the raid
subsided, leaving buildings either aflame, or belching thick
black smoke as a legacy of the air attack. Self-preservation
warned them to wait another ten minutes before deciding it
was safe to proceed into the centre of the shattered town. It was
to prove the worst decision any of them would ever make.

The young Kurd drove slowly, carefully threading his car
between the craters and unrecognizable chunks of assorted
masonry which littered the road. When the crew spotted a
handful of PLO soldiers standing by a trench thirty yards away,
they told the driver to stop. If one of them spoke English, they
thought, it would be a chance to get some first-hand reaction
and accounts of the raid.

Rich and Thomson grabbed their camera and recording
gear, while Hamill walked towards the PLO men, a few paces
ahead of them. Their driver, still sitting at the wheel, leaned
across and closed the door. In broken English, he called after
them: 'If you want me, I'll be here.' They were the last words
he uttered.

Suddenly, the PLO soldiers were shouting 'Ishi, Ishi' (They're
coming, they're coming!), and started to dive into the trench as
four Phantoms screamed down towards them. Hamill, closely
followed by Thomson and Rich, hurled themselves on top of
the PLO men, and had barely ducked below ground level when
it seemed that the entire world was rocked by a tremendous
explosion. The car in which the ITN crew had been sitting a few
seconds beforehand had received a direct hit barely thirty
yards away, and its young owner, who had taken just two paces
in his frenzied bid to reach the safety of the trenches, had been
blown into fragments.

Rich described the following fifteen minutes as the most terrifying of his life as shells exploded all around them, suggesting that the tiny slit trench was the sole target for this second phase of the Israeli attack. 'Many of the PLO fighters were crying with fright' he said. 'They were mostly young students of eighteen or twenty. We were huddled together at the bottom of this tiny trench and, although it started only three feet deep, it was probably nearer five feet by the time we'd tried furiously to bury ourselves deeper.' At the other end of the trench, they were more calm, realizing they could do little about their situation. '*Inshallah*,' they shrugged, meaning that their lives were in the hands of fate. Hamill, standing in the midst of them, tended to agree.

As the bombs seemed to fall nearer – according to Hamill, the closest was no more than twenty yards from the trench – the mud walls of their refuge would vibrate and Rich, with his head in Thomson's lap, was not alone in thinking that death was imminent. 'If I die now,' he told himself, 'I won't feel a thing.' Never a religious man, he was convinced that the next few minutes would prove whether his theories on 'life after death' had been right or wrong. It was Thomson, the youngest of the three, who appeared the most calm as he started to dispense ice-cold logic : 'The chances of a bomb landing in this trench,' he would say, 'are almost impossible.' And then the walls would vibrate fiercely as another shell exploded rather closer than the last. To Hamill, this was a sharp contrast to his past three years as a crime and court reporter. He had seen action as a captain with the King's African Rifles in Kenya and, in his fifteen years with ITN , he had covered front-line action in Rhodesia, the Middle East, and Northern Ireland, but this was the first time he had been bombed.

It was Thomson's idea that they should do an 'into-camera' piece to take their minds off the action. 'Just talk – say anything,' he told Hamill, 'we can sort it out later.' Hamill remembered being impressed by Thomson's control of the situation. 'He was immensely cool and efficient,' he said. 'It was as though he had lived in a trench all his life.' In spite of the cramped conditions and the minimal natural light available in their subterranean studio, they succeeded in putting together a passable 'mood' piece, although it was punctuated by a series of ad-libbed expletives on the 'Christ – here they come again' theme.

When he had finished filming, Rich froze in fright as he felt his left leg. His fingers touched wet, warm liquid, and momentarily his brain was numbed as he braced himself for the worst. Surely, he must have shrapnel in his leg? He could not feel a thing, and swallowed hard as he looked down, expecting to see the crimson signal of a severed artery. He was overjoyed with the evidence. 'I was delighted,' he said later. 'It seems that I had become a victim of a well-known physical phenomenon, and had literally pissed myself with fright.'

Although action appeared to be escalating and life in the trench seemed to have only short-term prospects, the PLO students then made what Thomson could only describe later as a 'suicidal bid for safety', dashing across the road to one of the few high-rise buildings still largely intact. Hamill, Rich, and Thomson dashed across the road with them. The building had already received several direct hits and within seconds the three men realized that there was a very real danger of being buried alive. 'In the circumstances, it wasn't the wisest of moves,' said Rich. 'There were about thirty young PLO men running around like headless chickens – they were so phased they didn't know where they were, or what to do. It was obvious we had to get out.'

The Israelis, meanwhile, had turned their attention to another target further down the road, but there was a very real possibility that they would return. The men ran out of the building towards the Beirut road, passing the limbless corpses of young men whose lives, once so full of hope, had come to a meaningless end. Their names would live on, but only as statistics of death. Rich, meanwhile, had discovered that he really was bleeding, this time from a head wound caused by a small piece of shrapnel, and Hamill carried the camera gear as they jogged back towards the sand dunes adjacent to the road. A devastatingly fit man, he had completed the London marathon a few weeks beforehand in the highly creditable time of three hours, thirty-five minutes.

All three were still in a state of shock, but remember being shot at from a passing vehicle before they had covered a mile. Hamill recalled seeing an open truck coming towards them, presumably on its way to evacuate some of the wounded troops from Khalde. Ten minutes later it passed them again, this time heading towards Beirut, and some PLO soldiers unleashed a few rounds which came dangerously close to the three ITN men. Thomson saw it more as an action of high spirits, with a couple of shots fired into the air, while Rich, who was suffering from mild concussion, is convinced that the vehicle was an ambulance, and clearly recalled the tail-gate dropping followed by a short burst from a light machine gun. Whatever the facts, the three men dived headlong into the sand, reflecting on the irony of being attacked by both the Israelis and the Palestinians within thirty minutes.

When they came across a mobile anti-aircraft unit further along the road, the ITN men explained to the officer in charge that they had lost their driver during the air raids. Two men were immediately dispatched to Khalde in the futile hope of finding him, while the unit medic attended to Rich's head wound. Later, the crew was driven back to Beirut by car. The Phantoms were still prowling around the sky and the enthusiastic, if ineffective action by the gunners on a passing ack-ack trailer, did nothing to ease Rich's headache.

By the time they reached the hotel, the three men were still in a high state of shock, and their condition was not eased later that night, when Tom Aspell, Chief of Bureau for the American Broadcasting Corporation, informed them that members of their dead driver's family had been asking for them, and that they were all armed. Taking Aspell's advice to 'stay in the hotel and keep a low profile', they sought solace in a bottle of whisky as they sat together, each reflecting on the day's events, but not wanting to talk about them. They later heard that the young PLO students, with whom they had shared a trench and the most terrifying experience of their lives, had been killed that afternoon.

By comparison, the following day was uneventful. Hamill had visited the offices of UPI (with whom ITN have close links) and asked them to contact the family of the dead driver, offering to pay whatever cost or compensation might be deemed necessary. The crew, meanwhile, had other things on its mind. The first temporary cease-fire was due to start at noon, and they were anxious to get their story in the can while there was still some action. Taxis, however, were a problem. They were considered to be a high risk, and none of the drivers was prepared to take them. Eventually, they 'borrowed' a taxi from the Dutch journalist they had met on the boat, with the stipulation that they must return within the hour.

They were able to hire the same driver for the third day. He had been helpful and since they had run into no danger he seemed happy to take their money and comply with their simple request to follow the action. He knew he had made a mistake when, within yards of pulling away from the hotel, a car swung in front of them, forcing them to the side of the road. Two armed men leapt out and, waving their AK-47 Kalashnikovs menacingly, leapt into the taxi. Rich, sitting in the front with his camera, suddenly had the cumbersome weight of an armed rebel on his lap, holding a gun at his stomach. In the back, Thomson and Read found they were jointly supporting a teenage gunman who went to great pains to show that the safety catch of his rifle was off as he held the barrel two inches from the back of Rich's head. For Read, who had decided to accompany the crew for the day's shooting, it was instant action. Perhaps a little too instant, he reflected.

The rest of the crew, however, were not unduly worried. Factions of the PLO and other organizations were hijacking cars and taxis every day and, providing that nobody tried to act the hero, it meant nothing more than short-term discomfort while the gunmen grabbed a joyride to their destination. 'A bit like the Keystone Cops,' thought Rich to himself although the slightest movement of the Kalashnikov aimed at his head would send a bullet crashing through his brain. If Hamill was perturbed about Rich's safety, what he saw when he turned to look out of the back window turned his stomach to lead. Following them in the car which had barred their way shortly after leaving the hotel was Hassan, the taxi 'fixer' and brother of their dead driver.

The law of the Lebanon is based very much on the maxim 'an eye for an eye' and Hamill suddenly saw the situation with startling clarity. He knew that the crew had not simply been hijacked – they were being driven to a quiet out-of-town location where they would be shot. Thomson, too, had recognized the driver of the car behind and shared Hamill's fears that they were about to become the victims of a revenge killing. Read, on the other hand, had no way of knowing and, deciding that the best method of defence was to attack, sharpened his best Oxford accent: 'I do wish you chaps would tell us what's going on,' he said, before Thomson and Hamill simultaneously elbowed him in the ribs to signal that question time was over.

At the orders of the man in front, the car then swung off the road and seemed to be heading for a small underground car park which, to Hamill, spelt certain death for all of them. His relief at not driving through the underground tunnel was short-lived, and when the car turned into a deserted courtyard and stopped, he was still certain that they were about to be shot. Hamill's fears were given some credibility when Hassan drove into the courtyard and came to a standstill just a few yards away, and the armed Kurds climbed out still training their rifles on the ITN men. When the driver was ordered out, leaving only the crew inside the car, it was an even more ominous sign.

Thomson too, saw no reason to feel anything but pessimistic: 'I thought that we were probably all going to be shot inside the car,' he said. 'There seemed no point in making a run for it at that stage.' Only if they were lined up against a wall and the other three had already been shot, would he think of making a dash. 'They weren't trained soldiers, and their weapons weren't serviced regularly,' he said. 'It might have worked, but I'm glad I didn't have to put the theory to the test.'

As the crew sat in the car, they remained remarkably cool. 'We were just like little ice cubes loooking for a means of escape, ' Hamill said later, 'all wondering how many seconds we were from certain death.' Then, a fourth man appeared and started arguing with Hassan, who had made it clear that he wanted to kill them on the spot as retribution for the death of his brother. The new arrival seemed to be telling him that they would make money by holding the men to ransom. Uncertain who had won the argument, they were taken into a nearby house and marched upstairs where they were interrogated by an English-speaking representative from a little-known splinter faction, calling itself the Democratic

Party for the Liberation of Kurds in Palestine

They were shown a picture of their dead driver. 'Where was he? What had happened? Had they killed him?' Sebastian Rich then became the centre of attention for Hassan, who seemed convinced he was an Israeli spy. Then it was the reporter's turn: 'Hamill – that's not a British name?' Throughout the interrogation, the crew stuck faithfully to the true story, still aware that their lives were very much in the balance. 'It was a very frightening experience,' said Thomson. 'It's not easy to communicate with people who want to kill you.'

Hamill was then escorted to a butcher's shop next door to make a telephone call either to London, or UPITN, to explain the situation. He could not make contact with either, and his growing hope that they might escape with their lives was severely dented by the driver, who had also been detained by the Kurds. 'They still think you killed the boy,' he said, 'and they will kill you, too, if they don't find him.' Knowing that there was little of the boy left to find, Hamill returned his attentions to the frustrations of the Beirut telephone exchange finding it preferable to the mournful predictions of a distressed taxi driver.

By now, their captors seemed uncertain of their next move, and it was decided to take the ITN men from the house to a spartan, but official-looking, office which appeared to be the headquarters of the Kurd faction. Here they were again interrogated and Hamill was ordered to write a lengthy report about the circumstances under which their young driver met his death. Suddenly, he remembered that the PLO men by the trench had been filmed as the action had escalated. 'We have proof,' he said. 'We can show you the film.'

Under guard, Read was allowed to return to the hotel to collect the evidence and a monitor screen, and grabbed the chance to let the ABC bureau know that they had been kidnapped. The reaction was one of numbed disbelief as the Press contingent watched Read walk out of the hotel with his video equipment, step into a car and be driven away at gunpoint. Back at the Kurd headquarters, the recording of the action seemed to pacify their captors, although Hassan made it clear that he was most reluctant to exonerate the crew from his brother's death.

The arrival of BBC freelance reporter Chris Drake helped to calm the situation. He had spent many years running the Middle-East News Agency, and was well versed on the rival political factions in Beirut. 'He was invaluable in negotiating our freedom,' said Rich afterwards. 'He actually remained with us until he knew that we would be unharmed.'

By now, the men had a fair idea that they were being held to ransom, but they did not learn of the 40,000 dollar price tag until later. Meanwhile, the Kurds' attitude had changed dramatically since Drake's arrival, and the captives were plied with cigarettes, coffee, and food; they were told repeatedly, 'Don't worry – we are not going to kill you.' Hamill smiled graciously, and thanked them with a civilized sarcasm. Read, on the other hand, was reaching boiling point as the English-speaking Kurd officer insisted on recalling some of the finer restaurants in the Knightsbridge area, suggesting them as possible venues for a reunion 'when he was next in London'.

Eventually, the required financial assurances were received after Drake had succeeded in getting messages through to London via the British Embassy, and the ITN men were told they were free to go. The surly Hassan, who had engineered their kidnapping, and still appeared to want to kill them, offered them a lift back to their hotel. They declined. By the time they returned to the Commodore, they had been held for almost five hours. They had been in Beirut for only three days and, already, they had been bombed, hijacked at gunpoint, almost murdered and, finally, held to ransom. Their toast in the bar that night was simple, but sincere: 'Here's to living.'

On the advice of pressmen experienced in the vagaries and vendettas of the Lebanon, the crew moved out of the Commodore and took a small hotel in East Beirut. In spite of a suggestion from the ITN Foreign Desk that they should fly home, they remained to cover the Israeli advance on Beirut, filming a column of Hemel tanks in Baabda, and some dramatic footage of the shelling of mountain villages and PLO camps around the Lebanese capital.

They also returned to Khalde, filming the Israelis as they passed through the town which had almost claimed the lives of the three men. They found it an emotional experience as

they stood beside the remains of the trench which had saved
their lives. The area around was littered with the dead and the
stench of decomposing bodies became more putrid each time
the wind changed. Fifty yards away, in the rubble of the building under which they had briefly sheltered, was a gleaming
piece of metal, barely recognizable as the radiator grille of a vw
Scirocco. At this stage, the war was so fluid that, while their
drive into Khalde had been unimpeded, an Israeli roadblock
had been erected behind them, and they were apprehended
on their way back into Beirut. They had no official Israeli
papers and were given a very uncomfortable hour before
being allowed to proceed.

Their voluntary exile from west of the town also presented
them with an exclusive interview with General Sharon in the
streets of East Beirut, which was given full emergency treatment to ensure that it reached London in time for transmission on 'News at Ten' the same night. It was a strong note on
which to leave Beirut. Wherever they go, and whatever jobs
they may cover, Hamill, Rich and Thomson will not forget the
first three days of their Beirut assignment. 'It formed a very
close bond between us, which is still there,' said Hamill. 'We
had been so close to death that we were better able to adjust
and compensate for each other's weaknesses, and to make use
of our strengths.'

The barber of Beirut

When Rich, Thomson and Hamill were recalled to London, it
seemed both unlikely and unwise that any of them should be
expected to return within the forseeable future. In the
Lebanon, emotions and promises tend to be as changeable as
the Mediterranean breeze, and Hassan's permanent presence in West Beirut suggested that, at the best, their lives
would be uncomfortable.

By early September, the Palestinians had started to
withdraw from Beirut and the ITN crews were called back from
the Lebanon. Then, on 14 September news of the assassina-

tion of President Bachir Gemayel shook the world, triggering off an orgy of hatred and killings which culminated in one of the most barbaric acts of mass murder since World War Two.

It was 9 pm on 16 September when the ITN Foreign Desk decided to rush a crew out to Beirut at first light the following morning. Normally, by early evening, most major news stories of the day have been covered, and a late duty crew stands by for emergencies until 'News at Ten' comes off the air. The assignment desk knew that the stand-by crew that night should have been Sebastian Rich and Nigel Thomson who, in the light of their recent experiences, were the worst possible pair to send to the Lebanon.

Rich, however, had already arranged to swap duties with fellow cameraman Tony Walsh. His wife had been unwell and, with a young family, he thought it preferable to work during the day and spend the evening at home. For Walsh, a short-notice trip to the Lebanon seemed an attractive proposition. He had not been to Beirut since covering the civil war in 1976 and the job would provide a welcome respite from the daily round of diary assignments which account for at least seventy-five per cent of any cameraman's working life.

It was Thomson who posed the problem for the assignments desk. Although fully aware of his terrifying experiences during his last job in the Lebanon, and the dangers that a subsequent visit would hold, they had little choice. He was the only sound recordist on duty, and it was imperative that someone should be briefed immediately to assemble his gear ready for a dawn departure the following morning. The assignments people never issue orders – it is normally a request to a camera crew: 'Would you like to . . . ', or 'Do you fancy doing . . . ', or 'Here's a nice one for you . . . '. This time there was no pressure; the situation was explained in some detail to Thomson and the final decision was his alone. After a pause which, to Thomson, seemed to last an eternity, the duty assignments manager quietly asked: 'How do you feel about it?'

Television news had always played a major role in Thomson's life. Although still in his twenties, he had already completed almost five years as a sound recordist, his father had spent nearly twenty years in the business, and he had recently

married ITN reporter-newscaster Carol Barnes. He knew the
risks but, accepting that they are all part of the job, he agreed
to go. 'I felt the trip shouldn't provide too many problems,' he
said.'Apart from that, I knew my way around rather better
than Tony, who hadn't been there for six years.' With the
camera and sound gear safely packed, Walsh and Thomson
took Carol for a 'last supper' to break the news that the following morning they would be departing for Beirut. By normal
Walsh-Thomson-Barnes standards, it was a quiet meal.

The reporter assigned to the job was Brent Sadler who had
earlier accompanied Sebastian Rich to Beirut when it seemed
that an Israeli invasion was imminent in late spring. He was
fairly conversant with the town and his local knowledge,
together with Thomson's experience, would be of considerable benefit to cameraman Walsh.

Early the next morning, the three boarded a British Airways
flight from Heathrow to Cyprus and, following the same route
that Thomson, Rich, and Hamill had pioneered earlier in the
summer, they successfully negotiated a passage on a cargo
boat leaving for Jounieh the following day. For Thomson, the
new level of commercialism adopted by the Cypriot boatmen
was a revelation. On his first trip, it had taken some very
persuasive talking to charter the battered old craft; but they
were now virtually advertising the service in their enthusiasm
to make some big money. The cost per head was still extor-
tionately high, however, and a young Cypriot was showing
signs of his potential by charging as much as thirty dollars for a
coffee and a cheese roll during the voyage.

This cargo vessel was considerably larger and faster than the
tiny tramp steamer in which Thomson and the team had previously sailed to Beirut, and the night crossing took only ten
hours, instead of twenty. For the passengers, however, there
was little sign of additional comfort, the only concession being
a large canvas awning transformed into a makeshift wind-
break. Otherwise, it was the same spartan 'steerage only' class,
with planks again providing makeshift bunks over the hold.
There were no fixed lights on board, and the ITN men passed
the night playing poker by torchlight for seven hours. To keep
the game within the bounds of sanity, they carved up a
reporter's notebook into one-dollar vouchers, but the session

came to a premature end when, just two hours out of Jounieh, a gust of wind blew the entire treasury and the accounts into the Mediterranean.

Shortly before reaching port, they were approached by an Israeli gunboat, demanding identification of all passengers. Walsh and the other cameramen on board tried to film the action but were stopped abruptly by the hysterical cries from the captain of the cargo boat. He feared that the cameras would upset the Israelis and result in the possible searching of his boat, which could delay his departure by two days. Eventually, the vessel nosed its way into Jounieh and the passsengers disembarked. Thomson disappeared swiftly in the hope of finding his old ally Charlie, a helpful taxi driver who had proved invaluable during his recent exile with Rich and Hamill, in East Beirut.

Charlie was located almost immediately, and after paying the standard gratuity demanded by the Jounieh customs as 'insurance' against having their camera gear impounded, they headed towards West Beirut and the familiar sight of the Commodore Hotel .They had already discussed a plan of action after hearing BBC World Service reports, initially unconfirmed, of massacres by the Christian Phalange militia in Lebanese refugee camps. As soon as they unpacked their gear and set up the editing equipment in their hotel, they would investigate the reports and head out towards the scene of the alleged mass murders. When they were eventually allowed close to the camps, three days later, it was under circumstances that none of them had ever contemplated.

Charlie pulled up outside the Commodore and helped the crew unload the equipment. Thomson picked up the editing monitor screen and walked towards the hotel foyer. As he walked through the large glass doors, he was confronted by an unwelcome but perhaps inevitable sight. There, just a few feet in front of him, was Hassan, the villain who had desperately wanted the lives of the ITN team, but had instead reluctantly settled for a ransom demand. It took a few seconds for him to realize that, while he had seen his would-be killer, Hassan at this stage probably had not seen him. Turning his back, he caught Walsh's eye and whispered 'That's him', jerking his thumb over his shoulder. Walsh looked towards Hassan who was negotiating terms with a prospective punter, and reflected that the basic philosophy of sod's law was as sound at that moment as it had ever been.

Deciding to adopt the lowest of profiles, Thomson crept off towards the darkest corner of the bar where a couple of stiff drinks helped his pulse to return to a more normal rate. Here, he felt, he would at least be out of the sight of Hassan. With any luck, he mused, the bastard might get shot tomorrow. It was a forlorn and short-lived hope, shattered by the sudden appearance of Hassan in the bar. He walked slowly and deliberately towards Thomson and looked at him long and hard from one side. Then, walking slowly around him, he stared pointedly from the other side as though giving himself a second opinion. Then, perhaps realizing that his presence had the desired effect on the ITN man, he sauntered away smiling smugly to himself.

When the sinister exercise was repeated a few minutes later – this time by Hassan's younger gunman who had hijacked the crew – Thomson was beginning to feel that he may have made an error of judgement in accepting the assignment, fearing that Hassan's reaction to his presence might jeopardize the crew's operation. Clearly, the low profile he had adopted was far too high; now it was time to become virtually invisible and, with the rest of the crew, Thomson moved back to the sanctuary of the Alexander Hotel in East Beirut for one night, to re-assess the situation.

The following morning, Walsh and Sadler moved back to the Commodore in West Beirut, which was after all the heart of the Press operation. Thomson, still fearing that his presence might evoke some hostile reaction from Hassan, remained in the East of the city, thus minimizing the chance of a second meeting which might endanger the entire crew. Thomson remained confined to his hotel for long periods, and only joined the crew on location when they considered it was necessary for him to do so.

The problems of operating with Thomson in a separate hotel manifested themselves under pressure, and matters came to a head on 22 September. The crew had to cover the inauguration of the new Lebanese president, Amin Gemayel, successor to his assassinated brother; and they had gained

Israeli permission to film the results of the horrendous massacre in the refugee camps at Sabra and Chatila where Christian Phalangists had murdered more than eight hundred Palestinian refugees. It was not known, at that point, that the highest Israeli military authorities had been aware of the massacre, and had made no move to prevent or stop it. This ignorance of their superiors' connivance probably accounts for the Israeli guards' co-operation in letting television news crews film the tragic and macabre scene. The Lebanese army, however, refused to allow television crews into the camps, and the more inventive newsmen saw it as a challenge to use their wits and imagination. They shot some highly emotive footage of the wretched scene, and decided to call it a day after watching one four-man crew become the target for some fairly heavy threats from Lebanese troops.

By now, rumours were rife that the Phalange were poised to return and stage another massacre. To Walsh, it seemed that neither the Lebanese nor the Moslems would be able to cope with the situation, and widespread panic seemed inevitable. It was imperative that he had an operational soundman close at hand, so he telephoned Thomson in East Beirut, and arranged to meet him at the Alexander Hotel to discuss the problem.

Walsh organized a taxi to take him from the Commodore, across the green line, and into East Beirut. He did not expect to enjoy the next hour, but he knew that Thomson had a thoroughly professional attitude to the job, and that he would understand it was impossible for the others to operate without a trained and experienced sound recordist. 'In certain circumstances,' Walsh said later, 'you *can* just get away with it; but not in Beirut in wartime.'

Thomson, meanwhile, had contemplated the problem at length. He knew for certain that his presence would jeopardize the safety of Walsh and Sadler, and he now realized that he must either contact London and ask them to send a replacement, or disguise himself to such an extent that the dreaded Hassan would not recognize him. He enjoyed his work; it had been his own decision to come back to Beirut; as long as he was there, he would do his job. He opted for the disguise.

When the taxi dropped Walsh at the Alexander Hotel in the early evening, he was approached by the familiar figure of Charlie. 'Your friend will be back in ten minutes,' he said. 'He has gone for a haircut.' Walsh wandered off, returning ten minutes later to find Charlie still at the hotel entrance. Walsh acknowledged him as he passed, but stopped in mid-stride as Charlie checked him: 'He's not in there.'

'Then where the hell is he?' asked Walsh impatiently. He wanted to get the delicate discussion over as swiftly as possible, so that he and Thomson could then relax over a friendly drink or two.

Charlie did not answer, but pointed instead to the grinning bald-headed figure standing next to him. Walsh stared in disbelief. 'He was like a junior Kojak, without the suntan and minus the lollipop,' he said. 'It took me fully five seconds to convince myself it was really Nigel.'

Thomson's motive was laudable enough. He did not want to let the crew down, and he wanted to vindicate his own judgement by remaining in the Lebanon for the duration of the job. Unfortunately, instead of making him anonymous, his Beirut barber had ensured that he would be instantly spotted wherever he went. 'He would have been less recognizable striding around like Groucho Marx with a cigar and a stick-on moustache,' Walsh reflected later. 'His head was an incredible sight – all white and shiny!'

Feeling confident enough to test the 'disguise', Thomson moved back into West Beirut but, in the interests of safety, stayed at the Cavalier Hotel, some five hundred yards away from the Commodore. The new hotel did not have telephones however, and the problems created by the lack of immediate communications were such that after two days Thomson himself contacted ITN in London and, explaining that his presence was hampering the crew's operational ability, asked to be replaced. Two days later, Walsh and Sadler were joined by Jon Hunt, a vastly experienced sound recordist, who remained with the crew until they were recalled two weeks later. By the time they got back, Thomson had lost his Kojak image; but he now looked more like a convict.

NORTHERN IRELAND AND . . .

❦❦❦❦❦❦❦❦❦❦❦❦❦❦❦❦❦❦❦❦❦❦❦❦❦❦❦❦❦❦❦❦❦❦

All in a day's work

The sad history of Northern Ireland during the 1970s meant that ITN maintained a constant presence for nearly a decade and that camera crews came to accept that a tour of duty in Belfast was as inevitable as an assignment in Westminster, Whitehall, or a bout of doorstepping in Downing Street. There is hardly a television crew in the UK which did not fly across the Irish Sea at least a couple of dozen times, and many of them collected bruises, broken bones, and even scars for their trouble. On the whole, television newsmen were accepted as a part of the everyday scene and given a relatively free rein. Their cars were hijacked regularly, but most of the time their camera and sound equipment was returned intact, even if their hired vehicles were not. 'We were always given new cars,' said Peter Wilkinson, 'they never seemed to last long enough to become old.'

Wilkinson has probably spent more time in Northern Ireland than any other news cameraman. Certainly, he has made more sorties than any of his ITN colleagues and he estimates that between 1970 and 1975 he spent a total of three years covering civil unrest in the troubled province. He has seen the results of a tar-and-feather reprisal, he has watched booby-trapped bodies explode, he has been shot at (but hasn't everybody?), his car has been hijacked twice, he has witnessed two bomb-disposal officers killed while trying to defuse explosives, and he has seen a suicide victim left hanging by a rope for a whole day while the Army deliberated at length on the chances of it being linked to a detonator. He has, in fact,

seen most of the horrors that contributed to the unhappy state
of Northern Ireland in the seventies. There is, however, one
date that looms larger in his memory than any other over the
years. It is 13 January 1972. Bloody Sunday.

It was the time of internment in Londonderry and barely a
night passed without a riot on the streets, mostly at a spot
labelled by newsmen (with their penchant for explicit brevity)
as 'Aggro Corner'. The Bloody Sunday riots started as a Civil
March in the Bogside area in protest at the policy of internment and resulted in a head-on clash between the Catholics
and the British Army. It was to become one of the most tragic
chapters in the history of Northern Ireland and the deaths of
the thirteen victims are still widely mourned. 'It was a complete overkill situation ' said Wilkinson. 'The Paras were told
to go in hard, and they did. Young kids were shot running
away and some were even shot lying down. You could see
where the bullets had gone in through their backside and out
through their shoulder.'

During the early 1970s, evidence of the internal justice meted
out by the IRA to transgressors within their own camp was
commonplace: the dreadful practice of 'kneecapping' offen-
ders was seen to serve as an effective deterrent to others and,
even for young girls, there was always the fear of being shaved,
tarred, and feathered if they were seen to fraternize, or even to
liaise, with the opposition. Such retribution was the price paid
by one teenage boy after his efforts to emulate his senior IRA
idols quite literally misfired.

Cameraman Derek Seymour and his soundman Tom
Phillips were driving through the Turf Lodge area of Belfast
when they were waved down at a large roundabout by four
armed teenagers. A BBC crew whom they had acknowledged
only seconds before was flagged down behind them and both
crews assumed that their cars were about to be 'borrowed'
either for a joyride or some more furtive reason. Instead the
apprentice 'heavies' ushered them to the back of a nearby
block of flats and lined them up against the wall.

The ringleader, who was no more than seventeen, bran-
dished a modern .45 pistol while the others carried a sub-

machine gun, a .303 Lee Enfield and an old revolver. He stood no more than six feet away from the two news crews and scowled with his automatic levelled at Seymour's stomach. He nodded towards the far corner of the wall and started to say 'move over there'. As he waved the gun to emphasize the point, the morning peace was shattered by a single shot and Seymour felt a sudden hot blast on the side of his face. Instinctively, he dived to the ground while the others looked on in horror, believing him to have been shot. Suddenly, out of the woodwork, emerged half a dozen senior IRA men aged between twenty and thirty and the young thug, so menacing with the aid of a loaded weapon, now looked a very frightened youth. Seymour was helped to his feet, still marvelling at his luck. The gun, originally aimed at his stomach, had traversed his chest and his shoulder before the sudden movement had tripped the hair trigger, sending a .45 bullet crashing deep into the wall less than six inches from his head.

Both crews were hustled into a nearby flat where they were offered drinks amid the repeated requests, 'Are you all right?' 'Are you sure?' To both crews, and Seymour in particular, the top priority was to get out of the building and back to their hotel, and eventually they were allowed to leave, with the profuse apologies of the IRA men still ringing in their ears. 'It's an unforgivable breach of discipline' they were told. 'We'll punish him in our own way,' adding that, if Seymour wanted a souvenir of his narrow escape, he could buy the offending weapon for ten pounds. He declined the offer. The following morning, both crews knew that the IRA had meted out more of their own justice, when the seventeen-year-old boy was found in the Turf Lodge area, shot through both knees.

Paul Carleton spent much of his time commuting between Heathrow and Belfast Airport during the early and mid seventies when anti-British feeling was running at its peak. Apart from the standard beating-up which has become an anticipated feature of the job, he has come within an ace of being murdered by IRA thugs who mistook him for a British Army officer, and has been sucked out of a helicopter with only a single strap preventing a fatal fall to earth.

Most beatings inflicted on camera crews have been at the hands of the Protestant, rather than the Catholic, extremists in or around the Shankhill Road area. At the time, the popular pastime seemed to be hijacking buses and other large vehicles to create a road block, and then setting fire to them. Carleton, then working with sound recordist Mike Doyle, was filming the action with a 16mm Auricon ('the oldest in the company') when both men were attacked from behind. Carleton was felled by a fierce blow to the back of the neck, while Doyle was savagely thrown to the ground.

'We were thumped around a bit and I was kicked in the head several times,' remembered Doyle. Both men have vivid recollections of the camera being hurled to the ground and smashed into a dozen pieces, before someone decided to jump on the shattered remains for good measure. Even through the pain of the kicks and punches that rained down upon them, Carleton remembered thinking that the days of that particular old Auricon were indisputably over. Both men later recovered after hospital treatment, although Carleton continued to suffer from concussion, but he was horrified to hear the following morning that a Shankhill samaritan had carefully gathered all the pieces of the smashed camera into a plastic carrier bag and wanted to return it to the ITN men. The technical department at Wells Street rose to the challenge and was able to rebuild it, much to Carleton's disgust.

The first law of covering civil disturbances in Northern Ireland is that a cameraman never ventures out alone. It has become accepted that while his left eye is closed and his right eye is glued to the view finder, the soundman acts as his 'eyes' and helps him to dodge bricks, bombs, and any other missiles. It was a rule that Carleton chose to ignore one afternoon when he was on a routine assignment in the Catholic-dominated Falls Road area of Belfast. He had heard that a fire had been started in a ghetto in Leison Street, and decided to investigate with the reasonable expectation of obtaining some decent footage for transmission that same night. He approached the area cautiously and showed his Press card to a couple of IRA heavies on the corner of the street. They allowed him to proceed but he had not covered more than ten yards before he was brutally thrown to the ground with somebody sitting

astride him with a knee in his mouth. 'Suddenly, I was surrounded by young yobs and when one of them pulled a gun,
cocked it, and held it at my head, I was certain that it was cur-
tains,' he said. He also remembers with alarming clarity the
brusque order: 'Shoot the fucker now,' and closed his eyes
waiting for the end. With a knee in his mouth he was given
little chance to protest that he was a bona-fide television news
cameraman. A Sandhurst accent, coupled with the fact that he
was alone and not accompanied by a soundman, had aroused
the suspicion of the IRA men. 'It seems they were under the
impression that I was a plain clothes Army officer masquerading as a cameraman,' he said later.

The bang did not come; instead, he was yanked to his feet
and searched at gunpoint in the doorway still, by his own
admission,'bloody petrified'. Then they took him inside the
house and made his life very unpleasant while they meticulously
checked his papers and his diaries. Eventually, after a brief
apology for their mistake, they let him go.

A couple of years later, he nearly died laughing. Together
with sound recordist Jon Hunt and John Holland, then a
lighting man, he was assigned to a feature on Army helicopter
deliveries in Crossmaglen, in South Armagh, an area then
considered to be too dangerous for normal truck deliveries.

The three men wore safety straps and Carleton was perched
on the floor with his legs and the camera out of the helicopter.
They were flying low and fast and one of them – probably
Holland – delivered a bon mot. 'We started to giggle and soon
I was helpless. I could feel myself being sucked out of the
helicopter by the slipstream, and the further I went, the funnier
it seemed to be,' said Carleton. 'The last thing I remember
was disappearing out of the door with the other two waving to
me and blowing kisses.'

Then it ceased to be funny. His safety strap jerked up
towards his head and, still clutching the camera, he had the
terrifying experience of being dragged along at a hundred
miles an hour by his neck in the slipstream of a helicopter.
'They eventually stopped and hauled me in,' he said later, 'but
although it might have been vastly amusing at the time, it was
a bit hairy. I could have easily slipped through the strap.'

It has long been something of an enigma to people living outside Northern Ireland, how a Catholic can tell a Protestant (or vice versa) simply by sight, yet there seems to be a sixth sense which clearly labels them as antagonists. Chris Squires, who has made many sorties to the Province both as a soundman and more recently as a cameraman, is probably as accurate as anyone with his simple observation: 'Belfast is a village. Everyone knows everyone else, and they even know who we are.'

The fact that the camera crews are known, however, is no guarantee of safe passage. Squires was beaten up twice in two days while covering Loyalist rallies, and the second assault came after he had received assurances from a UDA Commander that it would be safe to film on the streets. 'They suddenly turned on us, chased us, and cornered us in an alley,' he said, confirming that it was the most frightening experience of his life until the day when he was 'fancied' by a homosexual police sergeant after being apprehended in Iran at the time of the fall of the Peacock throne.

Squires had been in the thick of it all, standing shoulder-to-shoulder with hooded IRA men as they had launched assaults on the British Army with bricks, and petrol bombs, but maintained that, like all news cameramen in a similar situation, he is merely doing his job. He still fumes about the time when he was falsely accused by a newspaper of 'staging' a shot, when a young boy was being shown how to throw a petrol bomb at an army vehicle. Squires merely happened to be on hand (as, incidentally, the BBC also were) and the result was a strong piece of film which told its own story. 'It's a fact that the Catholics are easier to film because they are after publicity for their cause, but we take great care not to distort or create a news situation,' he said.

He cites with particular distaste an incident when the world's Press was gathered in Belfast at the time when it was fashionable for Catholic extremists to starve themselves to death in support of their cause. A French crew was seen to pay two young children to throw a petrol bomb, purely for the benefit of their own camera. 'The rest of the Press was livid,' said Squires. 'That sort of behaviour is not tolerated and they were left in no doubt about that, by an American producer who felt particularly strongly about the incident.'

Ups and downs

Occasionally, even in television news, the best-laid plans produce no footage at all but instead give birth to a tale which outlives any news item. It was 1978; the Shah had fled Iran and there was open talk of him surfacing somewhere in Mexico. ITN wanted a crew in the vicinity, but it seemed to be an expensive gamble unless they could be gainfully employed covering something else at the same time.

Earlier in the year, an ITN crew had linked with Anglia Television for a story about Tim Earl, a young man from the Luton area who had won a national competition mounted by Smirnoff, the Vodka manufacturers. In tandem with their advertising campaign, the theme of the competition was 'Make your dream come true . . . ' and the first prize was the realization of the dream. Earl's dream was to become the first Englishman to make the famous 'Acapulco dive' – a plunge of 130 feet from the cliff tops, made all the more perilous by the critical timing necessary to ensure that there is sufficient water beneath. The 'human interest' angle was magnified considerably by the fact that Earl had not even dived from the top board at his local baths.

An expert from Acapulco was flown in and, having satisfied himself that the young man was probably capable of making the plunge, a party from the sponsors together with an entourage of fascinated media men, later boarded a flight for Mexico, providing the ITN crew – cameraman Tony Walsh and sound recordist John McFarlane – with a strong story and the perfect perch from which to await the anticipated arrival of the Shah.

For over a week, Earl's training went according to plan, with Fleet Street and television following his progress from ten feet to twenty feet and eventually up to a hundred feet. The stage was set, it seemed, for the ultimate plunge the following day.

During the build-up period, Walsh and McFarlane had come to know Earl fairly well and, on the morning before the dive, they welcomed the suggestion that the three men, together with a young lady whom Earl had met in Mexico, should have breakfast together. McFarlane and Earl took the hired ITN

Land Rover to collect the girl, leaving Walsh to deliberate over camera positions and angles to ensure the best results. It would have to be right first time – for this one, there was no chance of a re-take.

When he got back to the hotel, Walsh was mildly surprised to receive a telephone call. When he heard it was the hospital, his surprise turned to anxiety; there had been an accident, he was told, and his colleague and the passenger had been injured. Could he come to the hospital straight away? 'It was like an abattoir,'said Walsh. 'John was in the operating theatre with his bone sticking out of one elbow, and had hurt the other arm. Tim had one leg supported by a weight and both arms were in plaster.' It was later established that they had been forced to swerve violently to avoid a dog, and the open vehicle had turned over on top of them.

The dive was off, and the Press scurried away to pursue the angle they had least expected, leaving disappointed Smirnoff executives to reflect on the ease with which a dream promotion in one of the world's glamour spots can easily become a nightmare. For the ITN men, it was not only painful and newsless, it was also frustrating. The Shah did not show up either.